CUSTOMER SERVICE: UTILITY STYLE

CUSTOMER SERVICE: UTILITY STYLE

Proven Strategies For Improving Customer Service and Reducing Customer Care Costs

Penni McLean-Conner

Disclaimer

The recommendations, advice, descriptions, and the methods in this book are presented solely for educational purposes. The author and publisher assume no liability whatsoever for any loss or damage that results from the use of any of the material in this book. Use of the material in this book is solely at the risk of the user.

Copyright © 2006 by
PennWell Corporation
1421 South Sheridan Road
Tulsa, Oklahoma 74112-6600 USA

800.752.9764
+1.918.831.9421
sales@pennwell.com
www.pennwellbooks.com
www.pennwell.com

Director: Mary McGee
Managing Editor: Steve Hill
Production / Operations Manager: Traci Huntsman
Assistant Editor: Amethyst Hensley
Production Assistant: Amanda Seiders
Cover Designer: Mike Reeder
Book Designer: Brigitte Pumford-Coffman

Library of Congress Cataloging-in-Publication Data Available on Request

McLean-Conner, Penni
Customer Service: Utility Style
ISBN 1-59370-053-9

1 2 3 4 5   10 09 08 07 06

To my husband Nick and my son McLean

CONTENTS

PART II REDUCE BUSINESS COSTS

PART III MAXIMIZE TECHNOLOGY, PROCESSES, AND EFFICIENCY

FOREWORD

Confronted with demands from increasingly informed customers, the utility industry's emphasis on customer care has grown in importance over the last decade. After J.D. Power and Associates came out with its first survey of customer care in the utility industry in the late 1990s, utilities began to focus on customer care like never before. The old saying, "Whatever gets measured, gets done," applies here. There is now a report card in our industry, and utilities want to make a high score.

Improving customer care matters—and utilities only comparing themselves to one another is no longer enough. Today utilities have to match their customers' experiences within other industries. New technologies and practices experienced elsewhere are expected in the utility industry as well. The Web, IVR, CTI, electronic payments, and speech-enabled systems have all emerged, enabling utilities to communicate effectively with their customers in more and different ways. Besides new technologies, other common customer expectations, such as extended hours and bilingual or multilingual customer service representatives, are increasing.

As the importance placed on customer care continues to increase, it is more important than ever as utilities prepare for the future. Rate cases, environmental concerns, reliability issues—the list goes on, and these and other issues that arise will require the customer's good will, which can only come from having a customer base with high satisfaction with the utility.

Effectively addressing the issue of improving customer care is critical to the long-term well-being of the utility. It requires a person with technical knowledge, commonsense decision making, years of experience, and outstanding communication skills. Penni McLean-Conner has refined these skills, but what sets her apart is her passion for customer care, her passion for knowledge, and her passion for people. She wants to know the latest technologies, and she wants to know the people and story behind those technologies. Her passion is contagious, and that is what makes this book engaging.

Penni's background as an engineer gives her the ability to understand, but more importantly, to explain the many new technologies that are impacting customer care. She provides a comprehensive list of the many new technologies and shows how they impact a utility's customer care operations. She makes it clear that technology is only tool and not an end in itself.

Penni's perspective is important. It is a viewpoint formed not only from experience within one utility but with three large utilities in different parts of the country. She is uniquely able to provide an insider's view of customer care from several different perspectives. She offers the reader stories about her experiences that show how customer care and employee situations should be handled. She is not afraid to relate both the good and the bad if it makes her case for how customer care should be managed. Many of the issues facing customer care professionals, such as outsourcing and credit and collections, require commonsense approaches. Penni has a commonsense approach to issues that only someone who has actually done it can provide. She demonstrates how to combine new techniques and procedures with the tried-and-true practical methods to make the best decisions.

We are fortunate that Penni has taken this opportunity to share her wisdom. She combines the attention to detail and focus of an engineer with the vision of a customer care professional with broad and varied experiences. This comprehensive look at how to improve the people, processes, and technologies that make up customer care provides a foundation that can benefit all of us in the utility industry.

Philip Dunklin

Chartwell

PREFACE

What is customer service, utility style? Is utility customer service different from customer service in the hospitality, retail, banking, or other industry? My response is yes, it is different. It is different because in a utility, we serve all customers. It is different because we deliver a product that is a necessity for customers. It is different because utility customer service leaders most often have responsibilities for the meter-to-cash operations in addition to customer contact. It is different because it is highly regulated with rules unique to the utility business.

Utility customer service has transformed over the years. Utilities are recognizing that serving their customers well is not just a cost but a real value. Utilities have evolved over the years from referring to customers as meters, then rate payers, and now more commonly as customers. The most progressive utilities listen, understand, and respond to their diverse customer base. These utilities deliver segmented products and services through a variety of channels to meet a variety of customers needs.

The wonderful news is that many utilities are delivering excellent customer service. The very best have a customer-focused culture and are taking costs out of the business and maximizing technology, processes, and efficiency.

Utilities with a customer-focused culture have a trained team that understands its role and the importance of this role in delivering great service. A customer-focused culture is one where the customer's voice is heard and acted upon. A utility with a customer-focused culture understands customer segmentation and offers a variety of products and services to meet various customer needs.

The very best utilities deliver excellent customer service while reducing customer service costs. These utilities understand the meter-to-cash cycle and as such continue to improve delivery of this cycle. Utilities are lowering their cost per customer served by selectively partnering with other service providers, migrating customers to lower cost channels, and proactively aiding credit-challenged customers.

The very best utilities have a customer-focused culture, are taking costs out of the business, and are maximizing technology, processes, and efficiency. These utilities have mapped their customer service processes and measure the process performance against other companies. The very best have a strategy for their CIS units to ensure they continue to support the meter-to-cash cycle and serve customers. The very best are applying technology to enhance service delivery, improve productivity, and reduce costs.

This book is designed to serve as a primer for utility customer service leaders at all levels. Readers can expect to gain ideas and best practices that will aid them to create a customer-focused culture and take costs out of the business, as well as maximizing technology, processes, and efficiency. I wish you success as you continue to enhance customer service in your organization.

ACKNOWLEDGMENTS

I owe my sincere thanks to many individuals who were instrumental in making this book a reality. A very special group of folks volunteered early on to serve as my advisory board: Philip Dunklin, Dave Tomlinson, Jim Linn, Bill Mayer, Lewis Walton, and Carol Collins. I want to thank each of you for your insight, advice, and consultation throughout the development of this manuscript.

Many of my friends and colleagues in the industry quickly stepped up to aid in the development of this manuscript. I give my thanks to Dave Steele, Bob Hall, Bob LaLima, Bill Zdep, Al Destribats, Todd Arnold, Glenn Kiser, Sharon Decker, Carl Blevins, Pat Carney, Sharon Bueno Washington, Marie McLam, Angi Clinton, Rod Litke, Vicky Westra, Jim Josie, Wayne Norris, Sam Turner, Rose Minton, Joe Gentile, Brad Kates, Giro Iuliano, Meg Matt, Diane Simpson, Susan Gilbert, Joel Gilbert, John McAleenan, Greg Sawyers, Arthur Webb, Jerry Oppenheim, Harvey Michaels, Bill Parrish, Ariel Nelson, Jeff Elliott, and Fred Bishop, and Tom Converse.

Many industry leaders volunteered their time and insights to be interviewed for this manuscript. I want to thank all of those who provided me with ideas, input and ultimately quotes for this book, including: Denise Cooper, Commissioner Robert Keating, Michael O'Shea, Richard Taglienti, LeRoy Nosbaum, Jon Brock, George Pollard, Greg Galluzzi, Charles Vincent, Robert Camp, Wanda Campbell, Elaine Weinstein, Bruce Gay, Terry Casey, Brian Hurst, Jeff Banks, and Jim Watson.

I want to also thank Joe Nolan and the many other leaders at NSTAR for their contributions, advice, and support during this project. This great team provided ideas, feedback, and quotes for this manuscript. I thank Gene Zimon, Kurt Belken, Jack Griffin, Bill Van Dam, Margarita Postoli, Vicki Marchart, Tony Simas, Sheila Whitaker, Jim Connelly, Chris Carmody, George Popovici, and Linda Barone. NSTAR is an excellent case study of a company committed to serving customers well. I am fortunate to be a part of this fantastic team.

Thanks also to Steve Hill and the PennWell team for their confidence in me in writing this manuscript.

Let me close by expressing my gratitude to my family. My husband Nick not only provided me with ongoing encouragement and support, but served as my sounding board for ideas and concepts. I owe my sincere thanks to my mom, Cathy, and my sister, Judy, for their ongoing encouragement and optimism as I encountered challenging points during the project. And I thank my son McLean who helped make sure that I kept my life in perspective while working on this manuscript. I am blessed to have such a wonderful, loving, and supportive family.

PART I

Create A Customer-Focused Culture

1 BUILD A HIGH-PERFORMANCE TEAM

I was asked to provide advice to a utility on ideas to improve its call center. My first visit was to the call center on a Monday morning. As I scanned the floor, I saw many customer service representatives walking around and chatting. Two employees were busy decorating the call center with streamers from the ceiling. One of them was standing on a chair to hang the streamers. The chair, by the way, was on rollers. And as I paused to look at the reader board, I noticed that more than 35 customers were in queue on the phone waiting for service. I did notice that one supervisor was aware that there was a customer queue. This supervisor was pointing and yelling to a customer service representative (CSR) on the other side of the room to "get back on the phone."

I met the manager of the call center in a private office away from the bustle of the call center floor. The manager boasted of the great work environment on the call center floor and remarked that celebration was one of the hallmarks of the team. I could not help but notice a panoramic photo of what appeared to be every CSR and supervisor in the call center. The manager confirmed that this was the case. The picture was to recognize the team for great teamwork. I remarked that it must have cost a bit in overtime to have the employees come in early to take the picture. I should not have been surprised, based on my recent observation of the call center floor, when the manager replied, "Oh, it didn't cost any overtime. I just had the phone system provide an auto message to the customer." This message indicated that due to an emergency, they were unable to take the customer's phone call.

This utility was wise to be looking for advice and consultation on improving its call center. The manager and supervisor did not display effective leadership skills or good business judgment. The manager was distanced from the daily operations and did not seem to have a sense of urgency in serving customers. The CSRs modeled the leadership behaviors and focused on celebration rather than customer service. While the supervisor had a sense of urgency, the method of communicating with and reprimanding the CSRs was public and demeaning. Several key elements of a high-performance team were missing, including effective leadership, clarity around mission and goals, and engaged employees.

Sears, Roebuck and Company has a business model that tracked "success from management behavior through employee attitudes to customer satisfaction and financial performance."[1] The Sears model shows that "a 5 point improvement in employee attitudes will drive a 1.3 point improvement in customer satisfaction, which in turn will drive a 0.5% improvement in revenue growth."[2] The Sears experience highlights that customer satisfaction increases when the company has an engaged, aligned employee team, or in other words, a high-performance team.

Nick Conner, president of Teambuilders, describes a high-performance team as one that "consistently achieves business results from a customer, employee, and financial perspective." In his work with Fortune 20 companies across the nation, Conner finds the most common barriers to a high-performance team are "lack of clarity on mission, low levels of trust among employees, and poor communications."[3]

This chapter will review key strategies that build a high-performance team, including:

- Effective leadership

- Common mission

- Communications

- Union partnership

From personal experience, I have found these strategies to be successful. During my four years leading customer service at Tampa Electric, the satisfaction of customers with the level of customer service, which is one component of the annual J.D. Power utility customer satisfaction survey, moved from number 20 to a tie for number 1 in the nation.[4] At NSTAR, similar business results have been achieved. Call center service levels have improved by 23%, while bad debt write-off has been reduced by 25%. Customer satisfaction, as based on the J.D. Power survey, has achieved noticeable improvement from very last to just shy of average in two years.[5] At the same time, NSTAR's internal employee opinion survey revealed that trust and respect of immediate management improved from 51% to 72% in two years.[6]

EFFECTIVE LEADERSHIP

Sharon Decker was the first female vice president at Duke Power Company in 1989. Her job as vice president of customer service was to transform Duke's culture to one that excelled in serving the customer. Duke Power recognized that the transformation was going to be a difficult challenge. Sharon tells the story of the chief executive officer (CEO) communicating her assignment to management. He told Duke's leaders that the creation of a customer service center and culture was the single most important initiative Duke Power had taken on since the construction of its first nuclear plant.[7]

Sharon did indeed encounter many challenges on her mission to transform the customer service organization. Her efforts resulted in Duke Power re-engineering its customer service processes to support telephony-based customer service. In the early 1990s, Duke Power was one of the first utilities in the nation to provide customer service 24 hours a day, 7 days a week.

Sharon believes the key to the success was having the right leaders. She looked for "leaders that were willing to take risks and who would pay as much attention to relationships with peers, employees and customers as they did to being technically proficient."[8]

Effective leadership is a cornerstone to creating a high-performance team. One study found that 50% of work satisfaction is determined by the relationship a worker has with his or her immediate boss.[9] The right leadership can create a positive working environment based on trust and respect. The Corporate Leadership Council reports that hourly employees reporting to the highest rated managers outperform their less-well-managed peers by as much as 26%.[10] The challenge is to develop or put in place the right leaders who can create positive relationship with employees. This is particularly important with frontline leaders. Employees will trust their immediate supervisors more than they will trust management above the supervisors.

This means that first-line leadership needs to be extremely effective in working with employee teams. The irony is that the most inexperienced leaders are often in first-line leadership. Developing frontline leaders is one of the most effective methods to impact levels of trust and respect.

I personally spend a great deal of time developing the leadership on my team. I believe my efforts in this area are a key to the improved business results that I achieved at Tampa Electric and at NSTAR. Some basics that I have personally found to be highly effective in creating an aligned team include setting clear expectations for leaders and developing and coaching leaders by providing learning experiences and feedback.

To set clear expectations and to provide coaching, one should consider communicating key attributes needed in a leader. For the past 10 years, I have been using a consistent set of expectations with leaders that I have found to be effective. A leader should:

- Model the behavior expected from his team

- Provide performance feedback

- Understand his role and its linkage to the success of the organization

- Embrace diversity

- Be customer focused

- Be a change agent

- Plan safety into the work

I meet with every leader on my team to review these leadership expectations, from first-line supervisor to director to project manager. New leaders joining my customer care team meet with me within their first month in their new role.

Model behavior expected from one's team

As a leader, whether one works in customer care at a utility or for any other organization, one is always being watched and copied. I tell leaders that it is a great compliment when employees copy their approach to meetings, their dress, and their mannerisms. However, it is also an albatross. The reason is that leaders are always on stage, from the moment they drive onto the property until they leave, and even when they are not at work. This was drilled home to me when I worked in Tampa. At the time, I came into work very early, around 5:30 AM, in order to go first to the gym and then to the office. The parking garage was across the street from our office. The fastest way from the garage to the office was straight across the street, versus going up to the traffic light and crossing at the crosswalk. Now as an effort to emphasize safety, the safety team had even put footprints along the sidewalk to encourage employees to go to the light.

Faithfully during the normal working hours, I modeled the appropriate safe behavior and crossed at the light. But at 5:30 AM, when there was no traffic or people to see me, I cut straight across. One morning, a CSR came by my office. This CSR also happened to be the safety coordinator for customer service. She commented that she had observed me cutting across the street, versus crossing at the light. I was caught. She was right, and I apologized on the spot. This CSR probably did not realize at the time what an impact she made on me. But since then, I have used this story to emphasize the importance of modeling the behavior one expects from one's team, all the time.

At NSTAR, the leadership team has embraced this expectation. One aspect of the employee opinion survey asks the employees to rate the statement, "My immediate manager inspires high performance through his/her personal leadership." This response has increased from 49% to 66% in two years.

Provide performance feedback

Of all developmental activities, those with the highest impact provide employees with clarity around job expectations and feedback on their performance.[11] Research by the Corporate Leadership Council found that a 25%–30% performance improvement could be achieved through manager-led activities that ensure job clarity and provide performance feedback to the employees. An effective leader of frontline hourly employees consistently provides answers to two simple questions: "What is my job?" and "How am I doing?"[12]

A leader must provide feedback to employees so that they understand how they are doing in their jobs. A combination of real-time feedback that recognizes and rewards outstanding behavior or addresses poor performance, along with regular performance plan updates, is an effective approach. Feedback given in real time is the most meaningful. This ensures that the experience is fresh with the employee.

Recognition can be public and can combine real-time positive reinforcement and more formal recognition of efforts above and beyond the normal. Successful recognition is meaningful to the individual employee. Successful leaders know each team member personally and can provide recognition that resonates with the employee.

Performance issues are best addressed in private. Coaching in public, as the supervisor did when pointing across the room and directing the employee to get back on the phones, is not effective in building trust and respect. Coaching in private facilitates a learning discussion with the employee, allowing a review of the specific area for improvement, the importance of the behavior, and ideas on how to improve. It is difficult to address performance issues, but it can also be rewarding as a leader. When I reflect on some of the top highlights of my career, a couple of those occurred when I worked with challenged employees and watched them blossom into excellent performers.

An effective leader should actively use performance plans to identify development opportunities. Great leaders are great coaches. They provide quality performance feedback. Effective performance discussions are identified by good conversations between supervisor and employee on the performance and the impact of performance on goals and objectives.

Understand the leader's role and its linkage to the success of the organization

Employees who can answer the question, "What is my job?" are demonstrating an understanding of their role to the success of the organization. Leaders need to help employees achieve a line of sight whereby employees understand and connect their work and the goals of the organization.

I challenge leaders to be able to articulate the linkage between their role, the department's plan, and the company's plan. I ask them to imagine they just got onto the elevator with the CEO. They have a two-minute ride to the offices on the top. Their goal is to explain to the CEO in two minutes why their role is critical to the success of the company. If they can do that with the CEO, then they can also do that with employees on their teams.

Vicki Marchant is a long-term employee at NSTAR and is currently an account executive handling some of our top accounts. In a one-on-one visit with Vicki, she shared this example of how important it is to create a linkage between an employee's job and company success. A customer had mailed in a payment to Vicki's attention, but used an incorrect internal mail address. This payment was associated with a new construction job that was on a tight time frame. It was critical that the payment be processed promptly so that construction work could begin.

Vicki went down to the mailroom to begin her search for this check. She asked the mailroom clerk what happens to mail that is incorrectly addressed and the response was, "I don't know, could be anywhere." At this point, Vicki was ready to give up, but she decided to create linkage for this employee. She explained to the mailroom clerk why this piece of mail was important from not only a customer's perspective, but from an NSTAR perspective, and linked this to NSTAR's stated mission of serving customers well. The clerk's attitude completely changed. The mailroom clerk identified the department where the payment was routed, and Vicki thanked her and went over to that department to continue the search.

What made this linkage complete and memorable was the telephone call Vicki received the next morning from the mailroom clerk. She was calling to find out if Vicki had in fact located the payment! The mailroom clerk was ready to continue her role in serving the customer well. What Vicki accomplished by providing that linkage was to remind the employee that her role was important. It made that piece of mail, and now other pieces of mail, more important to that employee and provided a link with serving customers well.

Embrace diversity

It is important to recognize and value diverse personal and professional backgrounds, along with unique perspectives and skills. Diversity creates a stronger, more dynamic team. It is especially important that a utility customer care team embrace diversity, as this is the team that is serving a very diverse customer base.

I encouraged my leaders to embrace diversity by staffing project teams with employees representing diverse perspectives and to ensure a diverse candidate pool when hiring for a position. If the candidate pool is not diverse, the leader should challenge the recruitment staff to provide a more diverse pool. As leaders, it is important to demonstrate a passion to create diversity. I believe it is imperative for customer care leaders to have this passion so that they can better serve their customers.

Be customer focused

A leader must understand internal and external customer expectations and look for ways to meet these expectations. For both internal and external customers, surveys and focus groups are excellent tools for gaining an understanding of expectations. Surveys also provide a way to measure the success of initiatives targeted at improving satisfaction.

There are a variety of ways to listen to the voice of the customer, including reviewing complaint data, meeting with customers, and organizing focus groups to explore particular customer issues. It is not enough to elicit feedback. More importantly, a leader should identify actions from the feedback and follow through. I believe one of the quickest ways to lose trust and respect with an employee is for a leader to listen to an idea, tell the employee that it will be researched, and then never respond. Leaders need to listen and follow up with employees with answers to their questions.

Be a change agent

Leaders adapt and respond to change. Successful change in an organization requires alignment from all the leaders on one's team. I encourage leaders to read the book *Managing at the Speed of Change* by Daryl R. Conner.[13] Conner uses the analogy of people's ability to absorb change being similar to a sponge. If one keeps adding water to a sponge, at some point it becomes saturated and unable to absorb any more fluid. The sponge becomes dysfunctional.

Leaders need to be aware of the amount of change they are requiring of their team. They also need to be considerate and understand that employees may be dealing with other personal challenges or changes in addition to whatever business changes are occurring. Leaders need to be on the watch for people who are struggling with the business changes and then personally work with them to help them better adjust to the change. I also ask leaders to raise the flag if they feel that there is too much change coming on too rapidly. I believe one gets better business results if one is effective at managing change, including recognizing when to slow down business change in order to effectively assimilate the change into the organization.

During my career, I have observed both effective and ineffective leaders with respect to implementing change. The difference was in communications with employees. I have observed ineffective leaders communicating change with phrases like, "They have re-engineered the process," or "They believe the changes will create savings." The subtle message was that if this leader had made the decision, it would have been different. The result was that employees would not fully embrace the change because they did not believe their leader embraced the change.

I encourage my leaders to have a full understanding of the reasons behind business changes in order to communicate the changes effectively. I remind leaders that decisions are made based on the best information available at the time, including feedback from leaders and employees. I reassure leaders that I know that at times the business changes they are communicating may not be the decisions they personally would have made. I ask leaders to support decisions that have been made when communicating to others.

Plan safety into the work

A leader should plan safety into the work processes. The leader should review, understand, and be actively engaged in the safety initiatives. Safety must be encouraged with employees in an office environment just as in a field environment.

I have found that some utilities do have a tremendous focus on safety, and it has become an integral part of what they do every day. In one utility call center, a safety review of near misses exposed a trend of repeated slips on the stairs. Further examination of the near misses revealed that the slips occurred on the landings at the top or bottom of the stairs, where the carpeted stairs transitioned to a hard surface. The team decided to add in rugs at the landings and monitor to see if this change had the desired effect of reducing slips. They were successful with this strategy. But more important to the result was the culture they had successfully created in their call center, where employees felt comfortable and accountable for sharing near-miss situations.

In addition to setting expectations with leaders, it is important to develop and coach leaders. I expect each leader to have developmental goals and plans. I review these personally with each customer service leader. I find this helps me to match various developmental opportunities, like special projects, with individual leaders. Chapter 2 will explore developmental strategies, including training, mentoring, and job experience.

In addition to coaching on an individual level, it is important to coach on a team level. Individuals must work together in a highly productive manner to achieve high performance. At both Tampa Electric and NSTAR, I used planned team-building experiences to accelerate the growth and development of my team. There are several firms that specialize in team development. These organizations specialize in creating unique facilitated experiences that create learning moments for a team.

At Tampa Electric, we hired Teambuilders™ to design a one and one-half day program to reinforce the concepts of process-based organizations and the interdependence of each customer care area on the other. This program was not only a lot of fun, it created experiences that my team referenced throughout my tenure at Tampa Electric.

One of the core benefits from team building for my team was the common language and experiences that could be referenced in a nonthreatening way to discuss or review mishandled situations. For example, one of the experiential exercises had the goal of *good throws* and *good catches*. As the activity progressed, we as a team lost focus on good throws and catches and moved into a production mode that concentrated on throughput, rather than quality. The result was a lot of dropped balls. As we debriefed this exercise, we as a team discussed situations at work where we give each other bad throws that are difficult, if not impossible, to catch. We identified action items as a team that we adopted to minimize these.

These phrases became a part of our vernacular. In fact, a few months after the team-building exercise, I failed to update a manager on a conversation that I had had with one of his employees. He was caught blindsided when the employee referenced this conversation. The manager stopped by my office. He told me that I gave him a bad throw and further detailed the experience. I knew he was right. We discussed how this might be prevented in the future.

This was a great reminder for me that I need to ensure that communications to the team include the entire team. More importantly to me, because of our shared experiences and common vernacular, this manager felt comfortable enough to tell me, as his boss, that I had messed up. This was a great barometer that our team-building exercises had had an impact.

COMMON MISSION

A basic building block for developing an aligned, motivated team is defining the team's mission. A mission statement is an enduring statement of purpose for an organization that identifies the scope of its operations in product and market terms and reflects its values and priorities.

Perhaps even more important than the actual words in the mission statement is the process by which it is developed. It is an excellent opportunity to reflect and reframe the customer care organization. Developing a mission statement for customer care was on my list of things to do in my first 100 days at NSTAR. My team did not agonize over this exercise. Rather, we developed it in a single afternoon that also included a bit of fun with a quick round of candlestick bowling. (Because I was new to Boston, my team felt it important that I experience their unique bowling using smaller balls and pins.) Our finished statement was, "We are the eyes, ears, and voices for NSTAR's customers. By leveraging our people, process, and technology, we educate consumers on energy management, provide service, value, and solutions, and ensure customer data integrity."

This statement has continued to guide our team here at NSTAR. It was the time spent as a team reflecting on who we are and what we do that was most important. The final words should reflect that passion. A leader who has not developed a mission statement for the team should take an afternoon to do this. Some considerations when developing a mission statement include:

- **Content.** This should include what the team is, what they do, why they do it, and what they stand for.

- **Input.** The leader should involve all members of the team.

- **"Snicker" test.** The leader should try out this statement with key stakeholders and gain their feedback.

- **Length.** This should typically be three or four sentences; however, some are as long as a page.

- **Tone.** The tone should be simple, honest, and frank.

- **Review.** The leader should assess the team's statement regularly.

- **Effectiveness.** The leader should ensure that team members can rephrase the statement in their own words.

The mission statement identifies who the team is and what they do. Defining a business plan to support the mission statement provides clarity to the team on key objectives, goals, and initiatives that will support the organization in fulfilling its mission.

I am fond of saying, "Hope is not a plan." I find tremendous value in spending thoughtful time as a team reflecting on the current performance, brainstorming on future goals, and then designing a plan to achieve that future state. Each year, I have an advance with my team with the expected outcome being a very good draft of our business plan for the upcoming year. Our agenda for the advance remains constant and includes:

- Review of our company's business and strategic plan

- Review of the current state of our company and our team

- Discussion on the future state of our team given the strategic direction of our company

- SWOT analysis—strengths, weaknesses, opportunities, and threats

- Gap analysis—of our future state versus our current state

- Brainstorm on key initiatives to bridge gaps

- Sort and prioritize key initiatives, which become the foundation of the plan

This agenda has been consistently successful in driving out a business plan in a relatively short amount of time. Usually this can be done in less than one day. To document the plan, a leader should use the company's business plan framework. My observation is that while the framework may look a bit different from company to company, business plans have some common elements, as shown in figure 1–1.

STRATEGIC FOCUS: CUSTOMER

OBJECTIVES

- Improve overall customer satisfaction ratings for all customer segments

- Expand self service as well as energy efficiency program offerings and maintain consistent promotion

Measures	Target
Contact center performance	
• Service level	% calls answered 30 seconds or less
• Percent calls answered	% calls answered
Meter reading	% meters read
	% read on cycle
Customer satisfaction	Annual customer survey
	Transactional survey

INITIATIVES

	Initiative	Owner	Date
1	Develop & implement a comprehensive Customer Care web strategy to promote self-service	Directors	March 2004
2	Promote energy management services for all customer segments by: 1. Creating & implementing education programs for residential EE programs, and 2. Developing targeted marketing to promote all C&I programs to achieve cost-effective spending.	Directors	December 2004

Fig. 1–1. Format for operating plan

COMMUNICATIONS

A good plan is nothing unless executed. Successful execution occurs when the entire team is aligned and motivated to achieve the plan. Effective communication is a key to successfully executing plans and strategies.

Last year I surveyed a group of 14 diverse utilities on best practices. The group included representatives from large, small, investor-owned, cooperatives, and municipalities in gas, electric, water, and wastewater utilities from around the country. I found that the best practices grouped into three categories: people, process, and technology. Interestingly, the top best practices referenced in the people area were around communicating and engaging the employee team.

There are some important best practices that continue to be referenced by utilities. These include:

- Regular team meetings

- Team talks

- State of the team meetings

Regular team meetings

Regular team meetings are meetings between an intact employee team and its immediate supervisor. The agenda consists of updates on policies, procedures, and other issues affecting the individual team. Team meetings may also include refreshers on safety and developmental items. Team meetings are good opportunities to recognize employees for serving customers well and for highlighting employee personal accomplishments.

Recently I observed a team meeting of CSRs serving commercial and industrial customers. The agenda started with recognition by an employee of another employee for exceptional customer service efforts. The supervisor provided a brief update on procedural changes for misapplied payments. An employee provided a safety tip for the team on office safety. A visiting representative from the strategic accounts gave an update on recent customer developments. The meeting closed with a 10-minute video reinforcing the importance of quality in customer service. The entire meeting took only 30 minutes, due to good planning by the supervisor. This was a great team meeting. It combined employee, customer, and business updates along with a developmental aspect.

I personally will sit in on two or more team meetings each month so that I can observe the dynamics. Observing the meetings is a great developmental tool for supervisors. Well-planned and executed meetings stand out from others. Additionally, I can tell from the interaction with the team any areas in which a supervisor can improve on communications with the team.

Team talks

Team talks are skip level meetings that I personally host as vice president of customer care. These meetings with frontline employees allow me to hear about employee issues or questions they may have about our department or company. Team talks provide me with a firsthand understanding of issues important to the team. To ensure that every team member has the opportunity to meet with me, I complete two team talks per month.

I schedule these meetings to best fit the needs of the team. For example, when I meet with meter readers, I usually meet first thing in the morning so that they may get out early to complete their routes. I poll leaders prior to the team meetings to learn of potential hot topics so that I am prepared to respond.

Success with team talks also means following up on issues that surface in the meeting. In a typical meeting, a leader will hear some great ideas on improving service and also learn about systemic issues that are pervasive from location to location.

In one of my team talks on Martha's Vineyard, the team updated me that our payment agent on the island had recently closed, and a new one had not been established. This meant that a customer who needed a payment processed immediately had to ferry to the mainland to the nearest payment agent. They also mentioned that they found that many of these customers spoke Spanish or Portuguese. They indicated that these customers would come directly to the operations center looking for information on payment options.

The result was that in two weeks, we had a new payment agent and had posted signage in English, Spanish, and Portuguese at the operations center directing customers to the agent. Additionally, our billing team has put in a process to more expeditiously follow up when a payment agent closes. Most of the time, the loss of a payment agent does not have such a dramatic impact on the customer. It took the excellent team on Martha's Vineyard to remind us of the uniqueness of their situation and have us look at this problem through the customer's perspective.

State of the team meetings

The state of the team meetings are a forum to update every customer service employee on progress to date against company goals. I copied this concept from Sharon Decker. Sharon had a flair for mixing in a little fun and creativity. Two times a year, the state of the team meetings were conducted. The meat of the meeting was an update on our key performance indicators. The fun of the meeting would be the format, which might include some team building, skits, or funny videos. A combined employee and management team was in place to design each state of the team meeting. Attendees could be guaranteed that not only would they learn about how customer service was doing, but also that they would have fun in the process.

Some cultures may not support the more creative and fun aspect of state of the team meetings. It is important to be considerate of what works best in each situation and with the multiple employee teams that are in customer care, from call center to billing to field personnel. At NSTAR, our state of the team meetings are much more focused on communicating the key business results to date, having plenty of time for questions and answers, and having highly visible leadership at each meeting. In summary, some key elements to a good state of the team meeting are:

- Visible management

- Update on progress toward key goals

- Question and answer time

UNION PARTNERSHIP

When I moved to Tampa Electric Company, I got my introduction to leading a union-represented team. While I had gained experience at Duke with unions, my experience was more as an observer. At Tampa, I was faced with a customer care team of meter reading, field services, billing, call center, and credit employees, all represented by the Office and Professional Employees International Union (OPEIU), Local 46. Carl Blevins was president of this local.

Carl epitomizes what I consider to be a great union leader. He is an advocate for employees but is very clear that when the company succeeds, employees succeed. He takes seriously the importance of mutual gains bargaining. And I have found since moving to NSTAR that well-run unions have leaders like Carl Blevins.

Having a union is not counterproductive to having a high-performing team. A high-performance team can be achieved in a union environment by adopting some key strategies that create a strong partnership with union leaders.

In interviews with union leaders, some common strategies emerge that support a high-performance team, including mutual gains bargaining, adherence to the contract, and regular meetings of union and company management. *Mutual gains bargaining* is the process by which a contract is jointly developed between company management and the union, with a focus on common goals. Carl Blevins states that "Tampa Electric does it right. Management at Tampa Electric makes the union feel a part of the entire organization. The union employees are not just working for management and making management look good; management ensures we look good too. We are a part of the team."[14]

Patrick Carney, retired president of the Utility Workers Union of America (UWUA) local 369, echoes Carl's strategies. Both Patrick and Carl are articulate, visionary, and very effective leaders. Patrick and the current leadership of the union are consistent in their belief and understanding that success of the company yields success for its employees. Patrick emphasizes that management needs to own and adhere to the contact. Carney states, "It is not the union's contract. It is a management and union contract. It is a contract that was negotiated in good faith by both parties." Carney points out that when the contract is not adhered to, grievances are more likely.[15]

Carl is an advocate for joint council meetings, which are regular meetings between management and union leadership along with labor relationship personnel. The meetings are forums to discuss proposed changes and to plan for effective implementation.

At NSTAR, for example, the joint council meetings were used to plan out the implementation of automated meter reading (AMR). The installation of more than 200,000 AMR units impacted employees and work processes. The union and management jointly developed communications plans to discuss the project with all employees and to talk frankly about the impacts of the change. Company and union leadership hosted the actual communications meetings jointly.

High-performance teams can be built. These teams start with effective leadership that creates a positive work environment based on trust and respect. High-performing teams are clear about their mission and goals and work together to achieve these goals. Members of high-performing teams are good communicators and change agents. Implementing proven strategies will ensure that a leader's team becomes a high-performing team.

REFERENCES

1 Rucci, Anthony J., Steven P. Kirn, and Richard T. Quinn. "The Employee-Customer-Profit Chain at Sears." *Harvard Business Review,* January–February 1998, pp. 82–90.

2 Ibid.

3 Conner, Nicholas. President, TeamBuilders; Interview, October 9, 2004.

4 J.D. Power Annual Customer Satisfaction Survey, 1998 to 2001.

5 J.D. Power Annual Customer Satisfaction Survey, 2002 to 2004.

6 NSTAR EOS, 2002 and 2004.

7 Decker, Sharon. The Tapestry Group, LLC; Interview, August 11, 2004.

8 Ibid.

9 "Study of the Emerging Workforce." Saratoga Institute, Interim Services, Inc., Santa Clara, CA, 1997.

10 "The Hourly Manager, Strategies for Increasing Frontline Managers' People Development Effectiveness." Corporate Leadership Council, 2004.

11 "Corporate Executive Board." publication of The Hourly Manager, March 2004.

12 Ibid.

13 Conner, Daryl R. *Managing at the Speed of Change*, O.D. Resources Inc., Villard Books, 1992.

14 Blevins, Carl. Interview, August 4, 2004.

15 Carney, Patrick. Utility Workers Union of America, Local 369 (retired); Interview, August 5, 2004.

2 HIRE, TRAIN, AND RETAIN THE BEST CUSTOMER SERVICE PROFESSIONALS

Customer care is the face of the utility to its customers. Having a team of talented, trained customer service professionals can have a major impact on customer satisfaction with a utility. Sears, Roebuck and Company has proven this relationship in the retail world with a business model that links employee attitudes to customer satisfaction and then to financial performance. As explained in chapter 1, the Sears model shows a definite link between improved employee attitudes and improvements in customer satisfaction, which result, in turn, in additional revenue growth.[1]

Customer service leaders are challenged to maintain a talented team in light of turnover both internally to other areas of the company and externally. Turnover based on voluntary separation in the utility and energy industry averages 6.7%.[2] Customer service organizations in utilities often trend higher than the average. A 2003 Watson Wyatt survey found that 40% of companies experience higher-than-average turnover rates within their customer service departments. Thus it is critical for customer care leaders to have a clear strategy to hire, train, and retain the best customer service professionals. This chapter will explore the strategies around hiring, training, and retaining the best customer service professionals.

HIRING STRATEGIES

I was at a call center conference among more than 1,000 call center professionals from around the world, specifically looking for best practices for hiring customer service professionals. As I was talking to a call center manager in the hospitality industry, I asked him about screening techniques he used in his company. He replied that his company uses the *fog the mirror* test. I told him I had not heard of this test before. He chuckled and said, "That's our internal code for, if they are breathing, they are qualified." I probed further concerning why his company was not doing screening and learned that they were in a crisis mode trying to rapidly respond to a high increase in turnover. They simply needed bodies answering the phone, and the quality of the candidate was not important.

Hiring for the right candidate has a huge impact on ongoing resource costs in training and ongoing performance management. Wanda Campbell, director of employee testing for Edison Electric Institute, states that "hiring for the right candidate significantly reduces the training, learning curve cycle time, and supervisory coaching time required to develop the employee." Key strategies in hiring include diversifying the workforce, employing creative sourcing strategies, screening, and competitive offers.

Diversify the workforce

Utilities have very diverse customer bases, making it even more important that the customer care team also be diverse in order to best understand and meet the unique needs of the customer base. Sharon Bueno Washington, a diversity and organizational consultant, suggests that an ideal future state to strive for is "a workforce that is demographically representative of the communities that you serve. But in light of the fact that this ideal state is unattainable for most organizations, what is really important is to have an understanding of the various cultures of the communities that you service."[3] Sharon recommends parallel initiatives of hiring for diversity and educating existing employees on the diversity aspects within the communities served. While this type of long-term goal may seem unachievable, it does help to identify the most significant gaps when one compares the demographics of the current workforce to the demographics of the service territory.

So what are some techniques to use to diversify specific segments of a customer service team?

Ensure a diverse candidate pool. If the candidate pool is not diverse, then the hiring selection will obviously not increase the diversity of the team. Creating a diverse candidate pool can be a challenge in and of itself.

My team had an opening for a graduate engineer. Our internal posting did not yield any candidates, so we moved to the external recruitment process. The manager and I reviewed the candidate pool, which was homogenous. When I expressed concern, the manager responded that he also was surprised, but that since the team in which the vacancy had occurred was diverse, human resources did not do a second posting.

This response did not satisfy me, as I knew from a bigger picture that our company was trying to fill the pipeline with a diverse, technically talented team. As such, I felt strongly that our opportunity in customer care to bring in a talented graduate engineer should start with a diverse candidate pool.

The manager did ask for a second external search in an effort to diversify the candidate pool. The manager also provided input to human resources on external diversity candidates that had applied for other similar positions, but not on this posting. Human resources posted a second time and reviewed prior applications for engineering positions. They communicated the opening to candidates who had applied for other similar positions at the company. The end result was a diverse candidate pool. From this pool, we were able to select the best candidate who also happened to be a diversity candidate.

Achieving a diverse candidate pool requires passion by the hiring organization for a diverse candidate pool, along with a good relationship with human resources. The business and human resources teams need to work together and brainstorm on posting options that will yield a diverse candidate pool. For some jobs, the normal human resource posting process may not be adequate to ensure a diverse candidate pool.

Create management accountability for diversity. It is important for leaders to create an expectation and accountability on management to build diverse teams. This includes not only intact work teams, but also teams put together to address special projects. Accountability can be achieved by training management on the business case for diversity and incorporating a diversity initiative into performance plans.

One utility went as far as implementing a candidate review form that was signed by the manager. On the form, the manager would indicate whether the candidate pool was diverse, and if not, provide an explanation as to why an exception should be made. This is a great tool that increases attention and accountability on line management for ensuring that a diverse candidate pool is considered.

Employ creative sourcing strategies

A successful recruitment process provides timely, sufficient, screened, and qualified employees. In today's economy, creative sourcing strategies are needed to find and attract diverse candidate pools. For external hires, effective strategies include campus-focused activities and internships. These are the most effective methods of sourcing when seeking diversity candidates. The least effective are print advertising.[4] Utilities are also finding value in networking with organizations in the community and participating in associations that support diversity initiatives.

Interns or co-op students are another excellent recruitment method. Many companies are leveraging this recruitment method as evidenced by the placement annually of more than 250,000 U.S. students.[5] Cooperative education enables students to apply their technical knowledge, gain an understanding of professional and ethical responsibility, and practice effective communication. Research on cooperative education indicates that co-op students make more informed career decisions, have higher grade point averages, and are more successful in early socialization and adjustment to a company.[6]

I am a personal example of the benefits of a co-op program. Duke Power has had a long tradition of using co-op engineering students. I was one of those students who had the opportunity to work in the generation services area of Duke Power, completing work-sampling studies on craft workers. For me, it was an opportunity to apply my industrial engineering skills and to develop and present recommendations to management. Additionally, I experienced the culture of Duke Power Company. At the end of my co-op experience, I had not only learned a great deal, but also found that Duke Power was the type of company that I wanted to work for after graduating. And they also decided that they wanted me to work for them on a permanent basis. Two weeks after graduation, my career in utilities was launched officially into Duke Power's distribution engineering department.

Screen for the best candidates

To effectively screen candidates, many companies are turning to validated testing tools. Testing tools are often cost-effective solutions for volume hiring situations, like for call center representatives. Wanda Campbell, director of employee testing at Edison Electric Institute (EEI), indicates that it is not unusual for companies using the EEI customer service test to report that training is reduced by one-third.[7] Anecdotal feedback from trainers highlights the reduced turnover in the training classes after implementing a CSR screening test and a reduced cycle time to achieve productivity expectations when on the floor. Additionally, screening tools may enable companies to expand the candidate pools to nontraditional candidates, such as candidates who do not have customer service experience. This is because the tool tests for aptitude for customer service skills.

Screening tools are effective in screening external and internal candidates. I had to chuckle as I listened to one call center manager lament about a struggle they were having with a transferred internal employee.

This employee was a former line technician who could no longer climb. He was relocated to the call center with his pay intact. It was soon apparent that he did not like being tethered, as he called it, to the workstation.

Supervisory feedback and coaching went unheeded. He had no solutions for reducing his long call handle time nor was he interested in taking a typing class. The typing class had been highly recommended due to his one-finger approach to typing. Call monitoring revealed customers waiting patiently while this line technician attempted to record their order. Often these customers were rewarded with disparaging remarks about the company or the company's ability to respond to their issue.

But perhaps the most discouraging issue was that he shared his unhappiness and discontent with the employees around him. He talked openly about how hard the job was, and how underpaid the employees were. He made no secret of his higher pay. The situation deteriorated quickly. In this case, the call center manager eventually was able to relocate the employee back to a field operations center in a position more to his liking, but not before much damage had been done from an employee and customer perspective.

As I talk to others in the industry, I find that this situation is not unique. There is the perception that anyone can answer the phone. The result is that employees who need to be relocated often find themselves in a call center.

Sometimes this situation can be for the best. The call center can gain an employee with other utility experience who loves the new job. Too often, though, the transition from a self-managed, highly independent field position to a more contained, monitored office environment is too difficult. In the worst cases, the relocated employee not only does a poor job with customers, but also breeds discontent with the surrounding employees.

A screening tool should be used consistently with all applicants. It is a fantastic way to tease out the good internal candidates who will bring some diversity, experience, and maturity to a call center from the ones who will find that the call center environment is too much of a stretch. There are a variety of commercially available screening tools that simulate the work environment.

An effective testing tool to screen candidates will provide a realistic job preview. This means that while the test is not exactly like the job, it is close enough that the applicant gets an understanding of the requirements of the role. This enables candidates to self-screen. Some may find based on the realistic job preview that the job is not for them.

A testing tool assesses an applicant's ability to learn, understand instructions, record information accurately, and interface with a keyboard. The tool simulates screens and forms that might be found on the actual job. The tests are typically timed and offer detailed instructions and practice prior to the applicant actually completing the test. The screens include pull down tabs for reference information.

If one does choose to use a testing tool, it is imperative that the tool be validated for the specific employee base. If one's company did not participate in the original validation of the test tool, then it is necessary to complete some form of job analysis. The job analysis will establish that the jobs in one's organization are sufficiently similar to those in the validation that the results from the validity testing can be expected to transport to one's organization.

The vendor of the test tool should be able to provide technical reports documenting the job analysis and validation completed originally on the tool for review by a professional of one's choosing. Some utilities have experts on staff, and others will hire a professional industrial psychologist to review the tool.

It is important to investigate the type of customer support for the testing tool that the vendor has in place. With use, questions may arise with respect to how the tool is performing or as to the results, thus one should ensure that the tool has appropriate, qualified support. It is also helpful to understand the nature and cost of legal defense support provided by the vendor. Most providers of testing tools will share in the expense associated with a plaintiff challenge on the hiring process.

A great way to fast-forward the identification of a testing tool for an organization is for a leader to talk to peers. It is helpful to learn from them about tools they may be using and the success they have had with these tools.

Interviews are perhaps the most common screening strategy. A best practice is to use behavioral-based interviews to predict a candidate's performance based on responses to situations. Behavioral-based interviewing has identified up front the key competencies needed for the position and their relative weights. The actual interview or interviews include behavioral-based questions that are worded to probe into each of the key competencies. For example, if customer focus is a key competency, then a behavioral-based question might ask the employee to describe a situation in which they experienced poor customer service and what they did about it. The responses to a series of behavioral-based questions start to paint a picture of how the candidate will perform with respect to each of the competencies.

Develop competitive offers

The final step in recruiting is having a competitive offer from a salary and benefits perspective. For union-represented work forces, salary and benefits are negotiated at the time of the contract. Generally compensation studies are completed in order to negotiate a package that attracts new talent and retains current employees. Nonrepresented positions may be annually reviewed for competitiveness on compensation. In the end, the candidate will make a final decision based on the combination of job, workplace culture, and compensation package.

Provide onboard process

Onboarding is the process by which new hires are oriented to the company in a way that makes them feel competent and confident. It is more than a one-day orientation; rather, it is a process that ensures a new employee knows what is expected, understands how he can add value to the company, and learns how to successfully navigate the culture. Onboarding includes prestart engagement activities, along with assimilation activities once joining the company.

Elaine Weinstein, senior vice president of human resources and chief diversity officer for Keyspan, has implemented an onboarding program in which new hires are matched with ambassadors. The ambassadors are carefully selected with strong interpersonal communication skills and knowledge of the organization. The onboarding process serves as a developmental tool for both the new hire and the ambassador. Weinstein notes that the feedback from new hires is extremely positive. "New hires can more quickly assimilate and contribute to Keyspan having participated in this process."[8]

Human resource experts note that for some key positions, the competition for talented diversity candidates is intense. Talented diversity candidates may be considering multiple offers concurrently. In situations like this, an onboarding process can be perceived as a benefit of joining the new organization.

TRAINING STRATEGIES

Training refers to a broad range of activities that develop employees' skills. This section will explore a variety of training and coaching strategies being used by utilities to develop their customer service employees at all levels.

Systems training

When I meet with other utility customer service leaders and talk about training, most think first of the high-volume training associated with the customer information system (CIS). In fact, with one utility with which I worked, training for a new CSR was 12 weeks. With re-engineering, this systems training was reduced by 50%. How did they achieve such a dramatic reduction? The techniques used are now common in utility customer service and include some basic review of the actual training material, delivery of the training, and measurement of training effectiveness.

Review training topics and time allotted. One should spend time on the important and frequent types of calls to ensure that the CSRs have the basics and are confident when they are live with a customer. One should review the training syllabus with a critical eye for the amount of time spent on each subject. It is also important to consider if one is devoting appropriate time to the very common types of calls and less time to more obscure calls. For example, while energy theft is a fascinating topic, it does not represent a large volume of calls. In fact, it is such a rare call that it is more important that the CSRs are trained where to look for reference information as opposed to hoping they will recall the theft training on the one-in-a-million chance of a theft call. One utility was spending more than four hours in initial CSR training on how to respond to energy theft calls. Their review of the training syllabus refocused time on using the online reference tool. The online reference tool provided procedures and instruction for this and other rare types of calls.

Training delivery. Modular delivery is being rapidly adopted by utilities customer service organizations, because it gets CSRs onto the floor more quickly. In modular delivery, CSRs are trained on one or two call types and then placed on the floor handling only those types of calls. After the CSRs demonstrate proficiency at those calls, they are returned to the classroom for training on additional types of calls. Skill-based routing on the telephony systems is a key support mechanism for a modular training approach.

Once employees are on the call center floor, they need additional support on customer calls. *Nesting* is a term commonly used in the call center industry to refer to the process of successfully bringing newly trained employees onto the call center floor. There are variations in how companies accomplish nesting. These range from maintaining the new training class as an intact team, and providing them with extra support from a senior representative and supervisory perspective, to pairing new trainees with an ambassador or experienced CSR. Regardless of the approach, newly trained CSRs will have questions when calls come along that vary from the norm until they gain more experience. Some form of nesting to ensure they have timely support when needed will expedite their learning curve cycle time.

Measure training for effectiveness. Training should not be measured just by the review at the end of the session. A more rigorous measure is on learning curve cycle time. For example, how long after completing training does it take a CSR to reach productivity levels of a proficient CSR? Some training organizations measure by using a survey of both the trainee and the supervisor some time after the training, i.e., several months. The survey will ask the supervisor to assess how the new employee is performing with respect to call handling. This feedback is then used to revise training approaches.

Targeted training

Augmenting systems training with targeted training is an excellent way to address specific gaps in skill sets. Some common training modules include call quality training, diversity, and safety and stress management.

There are a variety of firms that can provide training to refresh customer and phone quality skills. An annual call quality refresher program with the CSRs is an excellent strategy to maintain or improve customer satisfaction transactional results. While the information is not new, having a fresh reminder of some fundamentals in providing great service via the phone is welcomed by the CSRs.

Diversity training and education is particularly helpful to sensitize customer care employees on the unique cultures and needs of the customers they serve. This increased awareness of diversity in one's team can help surface ideas and suggestions to better serve a diverse customer base. Content to consider in diversity training includes a demographic overview of one's specific customer base along with some insights on each group's unique preferences.

Behavioral-based stress management and safety training are also good investments. One utility had a wake-up call when a review of mental health claims revealed that 20% of the claims came from 5% of the employees, all from the call center. The utility responded with behavioral-based stress management training for all call center employees. The objective of the training was to provide tools to employees that put wellness clearly in their control. The result was reduced absenteeism and mental health claims.

Like the stress management training, the behavioral-based safe driving training is also a great tool. This type of training has been proven more effective in reducing the number of accidents or injuries than traditional safety training. NSTAR noted a 10% reduction in responsible motor vehicle accidents in 2004 as compared to 2003 after the implementation of behavioral-based training.

Specialized training for call center supervisors that orients them to some of the common issues, challenges, technologies, and staffing strategies is well worth the investment. There are seminars on incoming call center management. This type of orientation for call center leaders helps them appreciate and understand why availability and adherence to schedule are so important to achieving service levels.

Computer-based training

Utilities are rapidly moving to computer-based or e-learning training as more cost-effective ways to delivery training. Apogee's Susan Gilbert is a leader in developing utility-specific computer-based training. Susan indicates that the growth in the medium has been steadily increasing.

Flexibility, availability, and cost savings are key reasons utilities are migrating to computer-based training. Tools such as e-learning provide flexibility to the user in that they can create their own training schedules and learn at their own pace. For the training organization, e-learning supports easy and rapid update of lesson material. The computer-based training facilitates dynamic training development. This flexibility is particularly useful when training development is happening concurrently with system development. There are many advantages to e-learning. It enables the user to learn anywhere and at any time, as it is available 24/7.

Cost savings are significant, and trainers are not needed to facilitate the sessions. Learners do not require travel time or overtime for the sessions.

NSTAR introduced e-learning with desktop applications like Word, Excel, and Powerpoint. Chris Carmody, director of training and staffing, indicates that NSTAR reduced costs to deliver desktop applications training by 80% with e-learning.[9]

Utilities are expanding e-learning tools for legacy systems training due to the same benefits of flexibility, availability, and cost savings. At NSTAR training via e-learning is now available for several legacy systems, including some portions of the CIS training. More than 2,900 employees have used the NSTAR e-learning tools, netting a 70% reduction in training time.[10] Elaine Weinstein, Keyspan, has seen similar benefits from computer-based training for new customer service representatives on the CIS system. Keyspan augments the online training with classroom training and role-play activities. The computer-based training includes tests for the user to measure comprehension of the material. This combination has been very effective for Keyspan.

Opportunities with e-learning are expanding with innovative new training programs, including diversity, quality, and new employee orientation training. In the area of diversity, an online tool provides utility field employees with an overview of the many cultures served by the utility. Quality training is also moving to computer-based offerings, where customer service representatives can actually handle simulated calls and learn from the training how to improve their call effectiveness.

Performance feedback

Of all developmental activities, those with the highest impact provide employees with clarity concerning job expectations and also provide feedback on their performance.[11] Research by the Corporate Leadership Council found that a 25%–30% performance improvement could be achieved through manager-led activities that ensure job clarity and provide performance feedback. An effective leader of frontline hourly employees consistently provides answers to two simple questions: "What is my job?" and "How am I doing?"[12]

Many utilities today have created clear linkages between company goals, business plans, key measures, and individual performance. The opportunity exists to help first-line supervisors complete the many tasks they are challenged with, including leading a large team, servicing the customer, and developing their employees. Almost one-half of these leaders, 44%, spend insufficient time on developing their employees.[13]

Real-time feedback is one of the best methods to coaching improved performance. Real-time performance feedback is also available in all areas of customer care, including meter reading, field credit and billing, and of course, the call center. The challenge faced by supervisors is how to manage the large volume of performance information available. This is particularly true for call center operations, where real-time statistical information is available in abundance.

Some utilities are providing this real-time information directly to the frontline employees for their own review and action. Supervisors augment this real-time individual information with regular one-on-one meetings to review key successes and areas for improvement.

Linking daily performance with departmental goals and objectives is typically done in a more formal performance appraisal. Too often formal performance reviews are viewed as a burden by frontline supervisors due to the time involved in gathering the appropriate information. One way to help these key frontline supervisors is to put performance management tools in place that ease the administrative burden often associated with performance reviews.

If a performance review package is more than one page in length, there are opportunities to reduce this administrative burden while still ensuring a quality discussion between the frontline employee and the supervisors. Providing a simple evaluation tool and automating the data collection will allow the supervisor to spend the quality time talking to the employee about performance, rather than stressing over completing a performance review.

It takes time to create a simple evaluation tool. A cross-functional team of frontline leaders and human resource experts can identify the key performance attributes and provide a simple-to-complete form.

Performance-based compensation places a few more challenges on crafting a simple tool, but this can be successfully done with a focus on making performance data retrieval simple. This may involve some investment in information technology programming, but it can be tremendously helpful to the supervisor who may have a team of 20 CSRs to review. Figure 2–1 illustrates the combination of a simple performance-based form that is linked to key systems.

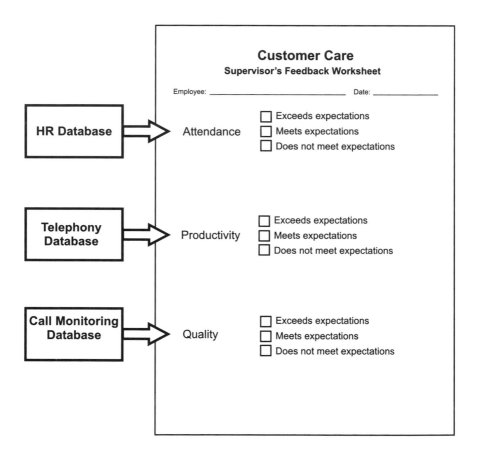

Fig. 2–1. Performance management tool linked to databases

One should ensure that training and coaching is provided to supervisors on how to give performance feedback. If the performance management tools are to remove the administrative burden of preparing the performance review, then the supervisor can focus on having a quality discussion with the employee. One great coaching tool allows practice of the upcoming performance discussion via role-playing. I use this technique myself to prepare for potentially difficult performance discussions. This practice allows me to ensure that the delivery of my message is clear and that I am fully prepared to answer questions that may come up in the session.

It takes a foundation of aligned performance metrics in order to prepare leaders to answer frontline employees' questions concerning "What is my job?" and "How am I doing?" With this foundation, one can enhance the process by simplifying the performance management tool and providing training on how to give performance feedback.

RETENTION STRATEGIES

Retention of diverse, talented, trained employees may be an area of opportunity for utilities. Retention experts agree that replacing key talent will cost a company two times the employee's annual salary.[14] Additionally, there is the intangible cost of lost knowledge and skill that may not be successfully transferred to replacement employees. Common retention strategies include attention to workplace environment, mentoring, rewards and recognition, and career pathing.

Workplace environment

Workplace environment strategies are designed to support a customer-focused culture and provide a workplace that is safe and conducive to productivity. It should be clear to employees working in the area what the mission of the team is and how well they are performing. Strategies include a comprehensive ergonomic program, providing appropriate tools and equipment, and support for work/home-life balance.

Comprehensive ergonomic program. Ergonomics is a discipline that involves arranging the work environment to fit the person in it. When ergonomics is applied correctly, visual and musculoskeletal discomfort and fatigue are reduced significantly. The U.S. Bureau of Labor and Statistics indicates that work-related musculoskeletal disorders represent one-third of total nonfatal injuries and illnesses. A best practice to reduce these types of injuries is to have a complete ergonomics program in place.

An ergonomics program will generally be a part of the company's overall safety program. It is a systematic method for preventing, evaluating, and managing work-related musculoskeletal disorders. Elements to include in an ergonomics program are worksite analysis, workstation design, and training.

Worksite analysis identifies jobs and workstations that may contain musculoskeletal hazards, the risk factors, and the causes of the risk factors. Outputs of the analysis will include recommendations to eliminate or minimize hazards by changing the jobs, workstations, tools, or environment to fit the worker.

This type of analysis may include individual consulting for employees with unique physical challenges. During my pregnancy, for example, George Popovici, senior safety engineer at NSTAR, personally checked and adjusted my workstation three times to accommodate my physical changes. George calls this his "desk-side service," and it has proved invaluable in addressing specific, unique employee needs in customer care.

It is important to ensure that adequate budget is allotted for fully adjustable workstations and ergonomic chairs. To ensure effective use of limited budget dollars, one should consider gaining advice from either internal safety professionals or external resources on the Internet or from facilities designers. Popovici indicates, "NSTAR has seen a return on investment in approximately a three-year period based on productivity and medical claims."[15]

Ergonomics awareness training can be particularly helpful to raise awareness of each employee concerning the importance of appropriate workstation positioning. Additionally, the training will provide the employees with steps they can take themselves to ensure their workstations are appropriately positioned, or exercises they can complete to mitigate fatigue. The comprehensive approach is successful. At NSTAR, for example, a 60% reduction of repetitive motion injuries was realized following ergonomic intervention and basic awareness training.

Providing appropriate tools and equipment. For customer care field employees, it is important to focus on proper attire, tools, and vehicles.

Uniforms that clearly identify employees as utility workers are helpful for customers to quickly and easily identify utility workers. Appropriate tools and equipment ensure that the employee can complete assignments safely and productively.

I find that the best ideas for tools, attire, and vehicles come from employees who use these every day. At NSTAR, employee teams are involved in decisions on attributes for new vehicles. Supervisors are constantly asking for employee feedback and ideas on tools that make their jobs easier.

A group of meter readers in Cape Cod pointed out that having a sign on the rear of their trucks notifying others that the vehicle makes frequent stops would be helpful, particularly during tourist season, where tempers can be short. Meter readers in the Boston area recommended gloves that covered the fingertips with a removable, mitten like top. This glove gave them freedom with their fingers to key in specific readings but provided needed warmth when walking between homes.

Support for work/home-life balance. Besides the physical workspace, it is important to consider the amenities that enhance a work area. Public Service of New Hampshire found home-life initiatives to be very successful. Their program, called *lickety split*, was a huge success as measured by the employee opinion survey. Over a five-year period, scores on work environment improved by 15 points. Marie McLam, call center manager at Public Service of New Hampshire, says that lickety split provides services that "help take the home-life pressure off." They offer on-site dry cleaning, movie rental, and greeting cards. Other workplace amenities to consider are on-site fitness centers, lactation centers, and relaxation rooms. Offering these types of services reinforces the utility's commitment to its employees.[16]

Mentoring

Mentoring is an excellent retention tool for key talent. People with mentors are twice as likely to stay.[17] Mentoring is a professional relationship in which an experienced person assists another less-experienced person in developing specific skills or knowledge that will enhance professional and personal growth. Mentoring supports knowledge sharing across functions and organizations and increases employee loyalty to the company.

I find that I learn at least as much from the employees I mentor as they do from me. I particularly enjoy mentoring employees who are not in my organization, as it ensures that I am objective as I listen to their leadership challenges, but it also educates me on the culture of other teams.

A good mentoring program will have clear objectives in place that are linked to the company's strategic goals. Human resources will often serve as a matchmaker, bringing the right people together. The mentoring engagement will start with an orientation of the mentor and protégé to discuss the program and developmental needs, and to finalize objectives. Subsequent meetings between the mentor and protégé will support knowledge transfer. The mentor is a role model and will be encouraging, teaching, and nurturing the protégé. Some mentoring programs include evaluation stages where both the protégé and mentor review the status, success, and knowledge gained from the engagement. A mentoring engagement will have an end date, but often a strong relationship continues between the mentor and protégé.

When I mentor, I ask the protégé to come to the session with a situation he felt he did not handle as effectively as possible. The key to these sessions is listening, asking probing questions, and then providing observations. I am currently mentoring a first-line supervisor in gas operations. She told me, "You cannot gain this learning from reading a book. It is not possible. What I am learning from the mentoring program is unmatched by other techniques."

Offering flexible schedules can be very attractive to today's workforce, which is trying to balance the demands of work and family. Flexibility can be achieved by offering a variety of work schedules, or in offering flexibility in vacation and flexible holidays. Call center scheduling packages available today can craft a variety of work schedules that ensure meeting service levels and offer variety and flexibility to CSRs. Duke Power offers more than 30 different schedules in its call center. Angi Clinton, vice president of residential and commercial customers, states that "offering a variety of schedules allows us to attract and retain a diverse employee team."[18]

Rewards and recognition

How employees are rewarded and recognized becomes part of the workplace culture that is being created. Sharon Allred Decker, former vice president of Duke Power's customer service, highlighted celebrating milestones as one of the five key elements in creating the customer-focused culture at Duke. Sharon's objective was to create that connection of people to their work. A personal connection drives performance. A tour of Duke Power's customer service center reveals its Hall of Fame, which displays pictures of outstanding customer service representatives. Sharon was one of the very first leaders to implement team-based incentives in 1990 at Duke Power. The culture that was created balanced performance with the celebration of milestones.

Some of the most motivating incentives require little or no cost to implement. Recognition can range from a simple word of praise to a bonus. Recognition needs to match the employee's needs and wants. Some employees relish being recognized in public, and others would prefer a word of thanks in private.

Public recognition and written notes are both great tools. But this feedback needs to be specific, relevant, and meaningful. It must be more than saying "great job" at the end of a presentation. This was brought home to me by a group of employees who were remarking on how much my comment meant to them on their project. I replied that I heard several other leaders sharing praise. They explained to me that the difference was that my feedback and praise was specific to them about an aspect of their presentation. The others just closed the meeting with "great job."

Sharon said it best when she stated, "How you treat your employees is how they will treat your customers. If you show your employees you care and praise them for their efforts, then they in turn will care for your customers."[19]

Consider including some fun into the workplace environment. Anchorage Water-Wastewater Utility has Wacky Wednesdays, which has a different theme each month. The employees create the lineup of themes for the Wacky Wednesdays, which have included such memorable ones as crazy tie day, crazy hair day, and cowboy day. John McAleenan, customer service manager in Anchorage, says, "Wacky Wednesday has been a hit with employees and customers. It has helped with morale and productivity and best of all, it does not cost anything to do."[20]

Tampa Electric's call center manager, Gina Zahran, has Manic Mondays during the summer. Call volume on a Monday is always high, particularly during the busy summer months where more customers are being impacted by storms. So on Mondays, Gina goes through the call center with a pushcart filled with various small snacks. Carl Blevins, union president at Tampa Electric, says, "Seeing Gina on Manic Mondays lets the CSRs know that management understands that the call center can at times be a tough job. And it is always great to see leadership on the floor."[21]

A recognition and reward team is one way to generate ideas for unique, meaningful recognition for one's team. Additionally, this is a great opportunity to build teamwork and engagement.

Career path development and compensation

Providing the opportunity for professional growth, development, and advancement is attractive for recruiting and retaining employees. This takes a combination of an organizational design that supports upward progression, along with workforce planning that identifies and develops key talent.

Typically utility customer care organizations are designed to support upward progression. It is not uncommon in a utility's customer care organization to have talented leaders like Betty Ferguson, manager of customer care for Baltimore Gas and Electric (BG&E). Ferguson started at BG&E as an office aide delivering mail. She worked her way up the organization through a variety of roles in the contact center, finally progressing to a supervisory role. Her success continued as she was given opportunities to enhance her skills in still more challenging roles, leading to her current assignment. She believes she is credible in her role and says, "Once a rep, always a rep."[22]

To encourage success stories like Ferguson's, it is important to review the organizational design with a critical eye towards whether it supports continued growth and development. Some utility call centers are revising their pay structures to support job progression. For example, a new representative may master billing and outage calls and be paid correspondingly for handling those calls. Over time, the representative may gain skills to handle new construction or business calls and progress in grade level and pay.

Career advancement can take other forms like lateral movement, enrichment, or exploration. Lateral promotion refers to moving across or horizontally. It is an excellent way to broaden the skills of customer service leaders. An example of a lateral promotion might be a call center supervisor who bids for the position of meter reading supervisor. Enrichment involves growing in place. Examples might be a supervisor serving on a union negotiation team or leading a special project. Exploration involves a temporary move. All of these develop employees and make them more marketable for future higher level positions, while broadening their skills.

Recently one of our supervisors went out on disability for eight weeks. An account executive that had identified a supervisory role in his developmental plan volunteered to lead the team during the absence. In this situation, the manager was able to observe and provide real-time feedback to the account executive on his leadership style and skills. The team had continuity and leadership support. Most importantly, the account executive gained valuable leadership experience that will help in future assignments.

Denise Cooper, vice president of human resources for Peoples Energy, sums up a common problem for utilities in that "retaining the best performers is not the problem, but rather identifying who the best are."[23] Workforce planning is one of the tools being used to analyze the current work force and future needs. This process identifies key positions and skills that will be needed in the upcoming 5 to 10 years, along with turnover analysis. Many utilities are coupling talent reviews and workforce planning in an attempt to identify the best performers.

Once the best performers are identified, specific developmental opportunities can be designed to prepare them for future higher level positions. One very effective strategy is to use key talent in special projects, which solves business needs, enhances their personal development, and allows their leader to observe them in action.

Our strategy at NSTAR is to fill every opening with a mindset towards bringing in talent that can move beyond this entry-level position. Margarita Postoli is one of many examples of the success we have had at NSTAR with this strategy. Margarita hails originally from Albania and has a bachelor's degree in economics, specialized in finance. She started at NSTAR in 1998 as a billing representative. She then moved to the role of customer service representative and in 2001 became a billing supervisor. Most recently, she is a strategic account executive.

Margarita is a great example of hiring, training, and retaining the best customer service professionals. She is providing great service now to our largest customers. More importantly, Margarita loves her job.[24]

It is very important for the customer care employee team to consist of talented, trained, engaged professionals. Effective hiring strategies ensure a pipeline of talented, diverse employees. Training provides the employees with the skills to provide quality customer service. Retaining these employees by offering developmental growth opportunities will assist a leader's team in providing the best customer service.

REFERENCES

[1] Rucci, Anthony J., Steven P. Kirn, and Richard T. Quinn. "The Employee-Customer-Profit Chain at Sears." *Harvard Business Review.* January–February 1998, pp. 82–90.

[2] Watson Wyatt Workforce Efficiency Survey, 2003/3004.

[3] Bueno, Sharon. 2004. Interview with author. August 25. Washington.

[4] "Recruiting Roundtable Diversity." Recruiting Benchmark Survey 2004. Recruiting Roundtable Research.

[5] Pettit, D.E. "1998 Census of Cooperative Education Executive Summary." Maryland: The Clearinghouse for Cooperative Education, 1998.

[6] Brows, S. "The Relationship of Cooperative Education to Organizational Socialization and Sense of Power in First Job after College." Doctoral dissertation, Boston College, 1985.; Edison, K. "Cooperative Education and Career Development at Central State and Wilberforce Universities." Doctoral dissertation, Harvard University, 1981.; Gardner, Philip, and Steve W.J. Koslowski. "Learning the Ropes: Coop Students Do It Faster." *Journal of Cooperative Education.* 28 (3), 1998, pp. 30–41.; Gardner, Philip D., David C. Nison, and Garth Motschenbacker. "Starting Salary Outcomes of Cooperative Education Graduates." *Journal of Cooperative Education.* 27 (3), 1992, pp. 16–26.; Gillin, L., R. Davie, and K. Beissel. "Evaluating the Career Progress of Australian Engineering Graduates." *Journal of Cooperative Education.* 23 (3), 1984, pp. 53–70.; Mann, R. and D. Schlueter. "The Relationship Between Realistic Expectations about Work and the Cooperative Education Work Experience." Boston: Northeastern University, Cooperative Education Research Center, 1985.; Patterson, Valerie. "The Employers Guide:

Successful Inter/Co-op Programs." NACE's *Journal of Career Planning & Employment*, 57 (2), Winter 1997. Retrieved June 10, 2004, from http://www.naceweb.org/pubs/journal/wi97/patterson.htm.; Pittenger, K. "The Role of Cooperative Education in the Career Growth of Engineering Students." *Journal of Cooperative Education.* 28 (3), 1993, pp. 21–29.; Pettit, D.E. "1998 Census of Cooperative Education Executive Summary." Maryland; The Clearinghouse for Cooperative Education, 1998.; Van Gyn, G., J. Cutt, M. Loken, and F. Ricks. "Investigating the Education Benefits of Cooperative Education: A Longitudinal Study." *Journal of Cooperative Education.* 32 (2), 1997, pp. 70–85.; Wessels, W. and G. Pumphrey. "The Effects of Cooperative Education on Job Search, Quality of Job Placement, and Advancement." *Journal of Cooperative Education.* 31(1), 1995, pp. 42–52.

[7] Campbell, Wanda. Interview, August 13, 2004.

[8] Weinstein, Elaine. Senior vice president of human resources, chief diversity officer, Keyspan; Interview, August 26, 2004.

[9] Carmody, Chris. Director of staffing and training, NSTAR; Interview, September 25, 2004.

[10] Ibid.

[11] "Corporate Executive Board," publication of The Hourly Manager, March 2004.

[12] Ibid.

[13] Corporate Leadership Council Research. Winter 2004. The Hourly Manager.

[14] Kaye, Beverly, and Sharon Jordan-Evans. *Love'em or Lose'em.* Berrett-Koehler Publishers, Inc., San Francisco, CA, 2002.

[15] Popovici, George. Senior safety engineer, NSTAR; Interview, September 23, 2004.

[16] McLam, Marie. Call center manager, Public Service of New Hampshire; Interview, March 2004.

[17] Kaye, Beverly, and Sharon Jordan-Evans. 117.

[18] Clinton, Angi. Vice president of residential and commercial customers, Duke Power Company; Interview, August 2004.

[19] Decker, Sharon. The Tapestry Group, LLC, August 11, 2004.

[20] "Best Practices Survey." CIS Conference, Miami, May 2004.

[21] Blevins, Carl. President, OPEIU, Local 46; Interview, August 4, 2004.

[22] "How BGE Turned Service Around." *Fortnightly's Energy Customer Management.* September/October 2002. pp. 20–26.

[23] Cooper, Denise. Peoples Energy; Interview, August 24, 2004.

[24] Postoli, Margarita. Interview, October 2004.

3   DISCOVER THE MAGIC OF
CUSTOMER COMPLAINTS

Customer complaints are the magic in improving customer service. Bill Lee, former CEO of Duke Power Company, believed this so much that he personally championed the team that established the complaint management process at Duke Power. I was honored to lead that team.

Mr. Lee was responding to an internal Baldridge assessment finding that Duke Power did not have a systematic complaint process. He further clearly recognized that effective complaint management results in increased customer satisfaction, improved customer service processes, and the identification of new products and services. This chapter will outline the elements needed for an effective complaint management process. Such a process will not only ensure that when a customer complains, the customer is handled effectively, but also that the complaints are tracked to identify trends and improvement opportunities.

Six months from the inception of Mr. Lee's complaint management team, Duke Power implemented a new way to handle complaints when they occurred and to capture the complaints for analysis. The results were dramatic. Transactional survey data revealed a significant difference in the satisfaction levels of customers who had a problem and complained versus those who did not complain. In fact, more than 70% of customers who experienced a problem and complained overall felt satisfied or very satisfied with the experience, versus only 28% of those who did not complain.[1]

I used my findings from Duke to implement similar complaint management processes at TECO and NSTAR with similar results. I found that a successful complaint management process includes key elements, and it is important to:

- Create a culture where complaints are gifts

- Establish a complaint resolution process

- Track, trend, and measure complaint data

- Improve processes based on the data

CREATE A CULTURE WHERE COMPLAINTS ARE GIFTS

Creating a culture where complaints are considered gifts starts with leadership. To create the culture change, leadership must be supportive and engaged. Janelle Barlow and Claus Moller, authors of *A Complaint Is a Gift*, state, "Company leaders have to provide the direction, the monetary support, and the motivational juice to inspire all this activity."[2] This may be a difficult transition for leadership. Many leaders have been hurt in the past by openly revealing complaints.

This was reinforced to me at a conference where I gave a presentation on effective complaint management. A utility business office manager told me his story about honestly sharing complaint data. Being recently promoted, he was attending one of his first meetings with other office managers. The meeting was supposed to be a forum for sharing ideas and best practices. One of the standing agenda items was for each office to review its complaints. Each manager self-reported on his office, as there was not a complaint tracking system in place at this utility. Many offices, like the office this manager took over, kept a hand-written log.

The manager proceeded to share the actual results from the log. He said the other managers looked at him in amazement. They expressed surprise at how much the complaints had increased since the last report by the previous manager. Further, this office manager was reprimanded for poor management. What did he do the next time? He reported data that the others expected to hear. He was congratulated then for the improvement. His question to me was, "How do I know that they (management) really want to hear the truth?"

To create the culture change, one should start by providing leadership with the business case for change and define the complaint management process. A commonly cited statistic to share in this business case is that dissatisfied customers will tell 8–10 people about bad service they receive. Furthermore, 1 in 5 will tell 20 people.[3] It is additionally important to provide leadership with a definition of a complaint along with a process to address, capture, and use complaints for process improvement. The book *A Complaint is a Gift* defines a complaint as "a statement about expectations that have not been met."[4]

The process of establishing a culture that valued complaints was accelerated at Duke Power because of the personal passion and support from the CEO, Bill Lee. Our team met with leaders from all areas of Duke, communicating the value of complaints and the new process that had been implemented to address, capture, and use complaint data. At each of these sessions, Bill Lee was present either in person or on video, sharing his personal passion for effective complaint management. We reinforced these sessions with articles and e-mails on our progress in implementing a new complaint management process.

Once the communication of the goals and the education of leadership are complete, it is time to train all employees on the new process. This training will include many of the components from the leadership communication, but it should also provide specifics on exactly how to address and record complaints.

ESTABLISH A COMPLAINT RESOLUTION PROCESS

A quick way to improve customer satisfaction is to review and refine the complaint resolution process. Frontline employees are great resources for a quick hit team on effectively responding to complaints. As the complaint resolution process is re-engineered, one should consider the following elements:

- Training

- Responding to letter and e-mail complaints

- Escalating complaints

Training

Establishing a culture where complaints are considered gifts will go a long way toward ensuring that customer service representatives recognize complaints. Additionally, it is very helpful to provide training to customer service representatives on how to effectively handle a customer complaint via phone or in person. There are many vendors who have training available to improve customer service representatives' abilities to handle complaints. Some key elements in handling complaints include:

Thank the customer. The representative should thank the customer for sharing the feedback or complaint. This helps turn the conversation to a more positive perspective.

Apologize. The representative should apologize for the situation happening. It helps to reassure customer service representatives that apologizing does not indicate that they or the company did something wrong. Rather, they are recognizing that the situation caused the customer to be angry and unhappy and are stating that they are sorry that this occurred.

Ask for specific information. It is important for a representative to ask and listen carefully to the information the customer is providing on the complaint. This will help the customer service representative identify the root cause of the problem.

Develop an action plan. It is important to create a plan to address the customer's complaint and review this with the customer. Many times the customer service representative can fix the problem on the spot, or within a short period of time. But some complaints, like those involving the potential of a switched meter, require research or field investigation. In cases like this, the representative should provide the customer with information on who will be researching the matter, the time frame for the research, and how the result will be communicated.

Resolve the complaint. A complaint management system is helpful to track complaints and ensure resolution. Too many times, without a tracking system, complaints get lost. One utility was analyzing repeat calls and identified that many were associated with customers asking for the meter to be reread. Meter reread requests are actually complaints. The customer requests a reread when the bill is higher or lower than they expected. In this case, the utility realized that the meter rereads were being completed promptly. The problem occurred in the feedback loop to the customer in order to communicate the results of the reread. The customers kept calling to find out the resolution. The utility significantly reduced the repeat calls by providing field personnel with door hangers detailing the results of the meter reread.

Prepare for the call. Sometimes angry customers can impact a customer service representative's ability to handle the next customer with appropriate care and quality. Providing customer service representatives with the ability to log out for a few minutes and walk around can do wonders for their effectiveness for the remainder of the day. It is important to reassure customer service representatives that the complaints by customers are not directed at them personally. They are gifts (though not well wrapped) that can lead to process improvements.

Responding to letter and e-mail complaints

It takes time to compose a letter outlining a complaint. Generally, if the customer has resorted to writing, he is quite upset or frustrated by the repeated lack of response he has received when trying to resolve the issue via easier mediums, like the phone.

Some of the most challenging complaints for a utility come in letter format. These are challenging for a couple of reasons. One is that typically in customer service, employees are hired in part for their abilities to communicate effectively verbally versus written communication skills. By the time the customer is irate enough to write a letter, the issue is probably thorny, since it could not be resolved via phone. Consequently, many organizations struggle to respond professionally, appropriately, and timely to written complaints.

Successfully responding to written complaints can have a big impact on customer satisfaction. In research completed by Technical Assistance Research Programs (TARP), 90% of the people who write complaint letters will remain customers if they receive a satisfactory reply in two weeks or less.[5] Some suggestions to improve the response to letters and e-mails are to recruit and provide specialized training for the team responding to written complaints. Another effective technique is to respond immediately to a customer with a letter or phone call indicating: a) the complaint was received; b) it is being investigated; and c) when the customer can expect a resolution. Generally customers are reasonable. They understand that sometimes these situations require a bit of research. They just want to have a confidence level that there is ownership to resolve the issue.

Escalating complaints

Hopefully well-trained customer service representatives can resolve complaints with the original call. But some customers require, or even demand, special handling. In extreme cases, customer service representatives may be faced with what I refer to as a *terrorist customer,* or one who is angry, volatile, and perhaps even abusive. It is helpful to train one's customer service representatives in a procedure to effectively deal with very aggravated customers via the phone and in person.

One solution that customer service representatives can offer is to escalate the call to their supervisor. In talking to utility customer service leaders, I find this is the most common approach. Another approach is to create a specialized team of trained customer service representatives to deal with the more challenging situations, or a *hotline team.*

A hotline team is a group of folks handling the most escalated customer complaints originating via phone or letter. This team needs to be well trained on dealing with very highly irate customers. Often the issues handled by this team require some research and assistance from various other departments, including the legal department, field operations, and claims, etc. It is important for this team to have reliable contacts in each area and commitments to expedite research of hotline complaints.

I give credit for the hotline team concept to Duke Power Company. I have replicated this concept at both Tampa Electric and NSTAR with great results. In Tampa, for example, prior to the hotline team, executive complaints were treated like hot potatoes that nobody wanted. These letters would spend days in internal mail being routed from one department to another. Meanwhile, the customer was getting increasingly frustrated by the lack of timely response.

The organizational change of the hotline team was not only welcomed by the Tampa customers, who saw much quicker and more thorough responses to their complaints, but also by the internal staff. They were thrilled that they could pass the customer to a team that could be relied upon to handle the customer appropriately. Because the responses were centralized, many standard letters were crafted and used as starting points for responses. All in all, it became not only a more effective process, but also more efficient.

The hotline team is a natural for handling not only the highly escalated phone complaints, but also the letter-based complaints. This smaller team can be provided with customized training on handling highly escalated types of complaints. The team also provides a consistent area to capture complaints as an input for improvement opportunities.

An escalation process can be enhanced through technology tools that track the points of escalation and the response time at each stage. There are technology tools available today that are helpful in ensuring that complaints are responded to promptly as they escalate up the ladder. Additionally, these tools ensure ownership and accountability for follow-through with customer complaints. Without some type of tracking tool, one runs the risk of not following through with follow-up commitments.

I had this experience at NSTAR. In almost every customer letter the customer would say, "I was promised a call back by a supervisor, but I never got one." My initial approach to this problem was to meet one-on-one with each call center supervisor and manager to stress the importance of customer callbacks. Additionally, as letters came in, I would have them reviewed by the call center leadership team. My team was committed to calling these customers back, and this approach worked. The references to lack of callbacks were now the exception rather than the rule. However, it was not error proof. We still had situations in which customers understood a supervisor would call them back, but they never received a call.

I was proud of my call center supervisory team. As they debriefed the results of the process, they recognized that a more rigorous system was needed to ensure complaints were resolved. We implemented a new system, which was developed in-house. The online system allows customer service representatives to document and escalate a complaint to a supervisor. If the supervisor fails to respond in a timely fashion, the tracking system sends an e-mail prompt to the supervisor and manager. The combination of passion by the call center leadership team and technology support will ensure that we do follow through with customer callbacks.

TRACK, TREND, AND MEASURE COMPLAINT DATA

An important element to discovering the magic of customer complaints is to establish an objective system to capture complaint data. This can be done in a variety of ways. Most utility CIS units have the capability to record a customer call type. This is often needed for external reporting. Sometimes it is fairly easy to enhance this feature to also note whether it was a complaint (*yes* or *no*). More advanced CIS units come equipped with graphical user interface (GUI) front ends that not only prompt for call type but will attach telephony data, such as call handle time, to each call. This type of data can be very helpful to quantify the benefits of reducing complaints on work volume.

To assist in tracking, it is helpful to start with a review of the call type categories. I have found that many companies will categorize calls as *other* or *multiple*, neither of which is a helpful category for complaint analysis. A suggestion is to eliminate categories such as these and encourage one's customer service representatives to note the closest match when faced with an odd situation or multiple complaints.

In an age of increasing Internet usage, this same functionality can be provided directly to customers on the Web and enable them to self-report complaints or feedback. This type of Internet or intranet functionality is also helpful for other utility employees outside of customer care to report complaints they may hear at social or community events.

In addition to adding the feature to capture the complaint, reports need to be created to review the complaints by parameters such as type or area. Ideally this information is stored in an easily accessible database where it can be mapped to other data. At a minimum, reports listing complaints by type and repeat complaints are a great way to start.

Measurement of the complaint data can often be challenging and threatening to an organization. The key is to identify measures that are customer centric and then set achievable goals. One common measure used in relation to complaints is the number of complaints per 1,000 customers. This can be a useful measure in aggregate to evaluate overall progress and to compare against other entities. Public service commissions commonly use this as they compare utilities. I do urge caution around adopting this as a measure, as it can lead to the behavior of hiding complaints. Some measures I find more appealing are centered on response time, customer satisfaction with the complaint process, and reduction in specific complaints where intervention has occurred. Here are some suggested measures:

- Percent of complaints resolved within 24 hours

- Percent of complaints resolved within seven days

- Percent of customers satisfied or very satisfied with complaint process

- Number of repeat customers with complaints

- Number of complaints by type

Setting goals around measures will help provide focus on the importance of the complaint management process. The measures based on the complaint resolution time frame are good measures for shared scorecards with other departments, particularly departments that are integral to resolving specific complaints.

We have reviewed how to create a culture that celebrates complaints. We have discussed methods to improve the process of responding to complaints. And we have reviewed techniques to track, trend, and measure the complaint data. Now we are ready for our final step of using the data to improve the process.

IMPROVE THE PROCESS BASED ON THE DATA

When I talk to other utility leaders, I find that all capture customer complaints at some level. Some utilities only review the most escalated customer complaints that go to executives or the public service commission. The interesting phenomenon is that few utilities have a process in place to review the complaint data for trends that can be used to make improvements. To improve the customer experience, it is necessary to organize and analyze complaint data, establish ownership for the complaint process, and implement improvement results.

Organize and analyze complaint data

Utility customer care organizations respond to a wide variety of customer complaints. Besides the typical customer complaints of high bills and outages, utilities also must handle complaints around employee conduct, switched meters, and missed appointments. The challenge for a utility is to determine which of these complaint opportunities are avoidable and can be re-engineered to prevent future customers from experiencing the process breakdown. The utility must also determine which complaints are unavoidable and need a service recovery and customer education process in place.

One concept that may be helpful in analyzing complaints is to sort them by avoidable and unavoidable, as is sometimes done in safety programs. The benefit here is that avoidable complaints are candidates for process re-engineering, with the goal of preventing the product or service breakdown. With avoidable complaints, the focus is on designing a service recovery process for an organization that educates the customer and provides a good overall customer experience. The caution on using this approach is that the tendency may be to categorize complaints as unavoidable, when in fact with enough resources, technology, and creativity, the complaint could be avoided. The definition of unavoidable and avoidable will be utility specific. One utility's unavoidable complaint is another utility's avoidable complaint (Table 3–1).

Avoidable	Unavoidable
Missed customer appointment	Missed appointment because field representative could not get in.
Meter reading error	High bill, accurate read
Switched meter	Customer provided information is incorrect

Table 3–1. Examples of avoidable and unavoidable customer complaints

Avoidable. In utilities, complaints will arise from service breakdowns, like a missed service appointment for connection of service. In analyzing avoidable complaints, some can be easily solved and are quick hits. Others will require more detailed process review and may require improvement from other departments beyond customer care.

Soon after implementing the complaint management process at Duke Power, a billing manager noticed a series of complaints concerning the amount of time for payments to post. He researched the complaints and found that these customers were all from the same service location. Looking further, he discovered that the return envelope reflected an address of a business office that had been relocated. This resulted in the payment being routed internally a few extra days before being posted. The billing manager fixed the envelope, but also went a step beyond to ensure that with future business office changes, a step would be added to check all addresses and phone numbers.

In this example, the investigation was short and the resolution was fairly easy to implement. Other complaints may require more creativity to investigate and resolve. A great example of this was what I call the "mystery of the drop box payment." A utility was experiencing a series of customer complaints around drop box payments. When the complaints first appeared, business office managers personally inspected the drop boxes and found nothing amiss. But the complaints continued. The utility decided to call the complaining customers to learn more. They discovered a common denominator in that all payments were made at night.

The business office managers again inspected the drop boxes, but this time at night. What they found was eye-opening. When the office managers visited their drop boxes at night, they experienced what the customers experienced, which included poor lighting, overgrown bushes, and poor signage, among other issues.

The office managers were quick to resolve these issues. The result was the elimination of complaints on drop boxes.

Complaints like these are avoidable. With research, the root cause of the complaint was discovered and an action plan was put into place to resolve the problem. Other complaints may not be avoidable.

Unavoidable. Many utilities would classify a high-bill complaint, where the bill is accurate, as unavoidable. With complaints such as this, the process of reading the meter and delivering a bill worked to design. The challenge with high-bill complaints, and others like these, is to design an appropriate service recovery that is cost-effective. Obviously, handling a high-bill complaint via phone is more cost-effective than a personal visit. Preventing the phone call from coming in by proactively educating customers during the high-bill season can be even more effective.

Some utilities have become very adept at designing service recovery solutions for unavoidable complaints. With high-bill complaints, for example, some innovative utilities are mining their CIS databases to identify customers with a propensity to call concerning a high bill. Once identified, utilities are using a variety of tools to educate these customers on usage, including proactive mailings during high-bill season.

I believe the biggest challenge with unavoidable complaints is determining if they are truly unavoidable. In fact most, if not all, unavoidable complaints could be prevented. The cost to prevent the complaints is more of the issue. As a leader in customer care, I reluctantly classify complaints as unavoidable but will do so if the cost to prevent them is too high or unachievable.

For example, recently a retiree, Frank, called me personally concerning the experience he had when his account was closed at NSTAR. The problem was that he was not moving out. With research we learned that another customer in the same apartment complex had called to initiate service but had referenced the wrong apartment number. They referenced Frank's apartment. Frank discovered this when he received a final bill from NSTAR.

His complaint was not that the situation had occurred, but rather his treatment when he called us about the problem. Our customer service representative made him feel like it was his error. To add insult to injury, when we reinitiated his account, he got a new account number. This was problematic, as he was a fuel assistance customer and had to update the information at the fuel assistance agency.

Frank was right to raise this issue. Indeed this was a complaint that had been raised by other customers. NSTAR launched a small team to review the process. Their recommendation was to improve our response to this situation. The rationale behind this approach was that this problem occurred very rarely, and prevention efforts would be costly. Additionally, they indicated that the option to reuse the original account number was not an option in our CIS. One of the control features on our CIS is the fact that account numbers do not get recycled.

They recommended that when a customer does get *finaled*, or receives a final bill to close out the account, incorrectly, that we do the following: a) apologize for the inconvenience; b) offer the customer our service guarantee credit on their account; and c) identify any organizations that may need the customer's account information and then update these organizations with the change in account number. This was a good, cost-effective service recovery solution.

Complaint data ownership

To have magic, it takes a magician. With customer complaints, the magician is the owner of the complaint data. The owner's responsibility is to review complaint data for trends and recommendations. The best candidates for this role are subject matter experts within one's organization. Ideally, complaint data owners are empowered to solve quick-hit issues.

In addition to identifying a complaint data owner, one should create an outlet for the owner to share and communicate findings and actions. One simple approach is to have the complaint data owner update the customer service leadership team at a regular staff meeting. Another approach is to establish a customer listening post. Chapter 5 will explore integrating complaint data with other forms of customer feedback via this concept. The listening post includes not only the complaint data owner, but also other key individuals in the organization who are in contact with customer issues.

At NSTAR, I implemented the concept of having complaints reviewed at our regular customer care staff meeting. David Matthews is our operations manager, and his team performs the back office work associated with customer care. As part of that, his team responds to all escalated and written complaints. David has taken on the role of complaint data owner. Each month, he brings a complaint to my staff to review. This serves a couple of purposes. It is an opportunity for us to hear the voice of the customer, and it raises awareness of key problems. David also looks for trends and recommends appropriate actions, including forming teams to address the problems.

David recently reviewed complaints with my staff. One complaint came from an elderly customer concerned that her meter was being replaced with a new AMR meter. David admitted that when the complaint was escalated to him, he expected to hear concerns about the bill being higher due to the new meter.

In this case, though, the customer was calling to request that NSTAR give her the meter. It turns out that the customer's husband had died, and one of the ways that she kept his memory was to keep special mementos in a box. For 22 years, she and her husband faithfully read this meter each month and called the reading into the same customer service representative. This meter brought her special memories of her husband.

The field representative who removed the meter had indicated to the customer that he could not give her the meter, but he did give her the numbers to call. Once David got the call, he worked with meter operations to track down the meter. The meter was returned to her for her memory box. NSTAR also sent a meter lamp as a special gift.

It is important to discover the magic of customer complaints in one's organization. The keys to the magic are establishing a culture where complaints are gifts, developing a complaint resolution process, tracking trends and measuring complaint data, and improving the processes based on the data. Savvy utilities have discovered the magic of complaints and have used the magic to increase customer satisfaction, improve customer service processes, and identify new products and services.

REFERENCES

1   Duke Power, a Duke Energy Company, transactional research, October 30, 1998.

2   Barlow, Janelle, and Claus Moller. *A Complaint Is a Gift*. Berrett-Koehler Publishers, Inc., 1996, p. 192.

3   Summarized in Alan R. Andreasen, "Consumer Complaints and Redress: What We Know and What We Don't Know." *The Frontier of Research in the Consumer Interest*, ed. E. Scott Maynes, et al.; Columbia, MO: American Council on Consumer Interests, 1988, p. 708.

4   Barlow and Moller, p. 11.

5   TARP (Technical Assistance Research Programs). *Consumer Complaint Handling in America, An Update Study*. Washington, D.C.: U.S. Office of Consumer Affairs, 1986, p. 81.

4 LISTEN AND RESPOND TO
THE VOICE OF THE CUSTOMER

Some companies make taking care of their customers look simple, and others struggle tremendously. What leads to the difference? *Customer experience* can be defined as the sum of feelings evoked as a result of any interaction at any touch point in an organization. It is based on the customer's perception of the value delivered, tangible or intangible. Customer satisfaction is the culmination of all of a customer's experiences with that organization. Those companies with a culture focused on creating value for their customers seem to be the ones who make it look effortless.

JoAnna Brandi (JoAnna Brandi & Company, Inc.) and Steve Simpson (Keystone Management Services) collaborated in 2003 on a worldwide survey about corporate cultures. One of the questions asked respondents to complete the statement, "Around here, customers are..." The results showed that only 60% had something positive to say about their customers. Companies that do not think positively about their customers must have a difficult time consistently creating a positive experience.

The research by Brandi & Simpson seems to hold true for utilities. Research by Dennis Smith, director of editorial and research for Chartwell Inc., indicates that there is a correlation between top performing utilities in the J.D. Power annual utility survey and their focus on customer satisfaction. Smith analyzed top and bottom utility performers from the 2004 J.D. Power survey. He then reviewed their respective annual reports. He found that 88% of top performing utilities referenced customer satisfaction in their annual reports to shareholders as opposed to 27% of the low performers.[1]

A successful customer-focused culture is one that actively listens to the voice of the customer. Listening to the voice of the customer means that the company actively seeks input from customers from multiple touch points and has a systematic process in place to aggregate the customer feedback to use for improvement. There are multiple methods to gather feedback from the customer ranging from formal, comprehensive customer surveys to informal customer conversations that utility staff members may have. To fully understand the meaning behind the research, it is necessary to gather the feedback from multiple listening points, integrate the feedback, and act on trends.

This chapter will outline various methods to gather customer feedback and will review common pitfalls to avoid. The chapter closes with a discussion on the customer listening post as a framework to integrate the various feedback mechanisms to ensure effective listening and response to the customer.

METHODS TO GATHER CUSTOMER FEEDBACK

There are multiple ways to gather customer feedback. Generally a combination of several tools provides the best insight to the voice of the customers. Each tool has a specific purpose. A market research expert can provide consulting and insight on the best tool to use based on the desired outcomes of the research.

Broad-based customer satisfaction tracking studies

Most utilities complete broad-based customer satisfaction tracking studies to monitor customer perceptions and measure progress in meeting customers' expectations. Broad-based surveys are often completed quarterly with a statistically valid, randomly selected group of customers. While most are telephone based, these can also be completed in written form. Attributes of a good broad-based survey include:

Format. A customer satisfaction tracking survey runs no more than 15 minutes in length. One of the first questions in a typical survey involves a customer's overall customer satisfaction rating. Further questions explore the customer's perceptions of the various attributes driving overall satisfaction, including the importance the customer places on these various attributes. The final part of the survey can often include questions that determine the customer's frame of reference, like exposure to ads or news articles and demographics.

Participants. This tool uses a statistically valid sample of randomly selected customers who demographically represent the utility's service territory. These customers may or may not have had an interaction with the utility.

Results. Key trends and findings are summarized by attribute. More rigorous analysis will detail the findings by customer segment and by an analysis of dissatisfied customers. Sometimes the results will include recommendations based on the research and attribute importance.

Utilities may augment their own broad customer satisfaction research by participating in various national surveys in order to benchmark their own performance against others in their industry. Organizations like J.D. Power and Associates, RKS, and the American Customer Satisfaction Index meet this need. Many of these offer instruments that give the utility the option of over sampling in their specific service territory to provide statistically valid data for the utility.

Some industry organizations also complete market research for the broad industry perspective. Edison Electric Institute (EEI) offers the National Monitor, which is a semiannual telephone survey that has been in place since 1997. This research tracks public perception on key issues facing the electric utility industry, provides benchmarks on customer attributes around utility issues, and explores current topics of interest. This research is used to support EEI public policy development and outreach and serves as a point of reference for member utilities. This instrument has been valuable in understanding the impact of deregulation, Enron, blackouts, and other events on the perception of customers as a whole with the utility industry. The value for utilities in the EEI instrument and others like it is that experts in market research produce them, and the attributes and importance are statistically valid. So if one's company has not updated its attributes or confirmed attribute importance recently, these tools can provide some direction, at least from a national perspective.

Transactional surveys

A transactional survey is a survey of customers who have recently contacted their utility. These surveys are completed usually within a very short window of the actual customer transaction, generally no longer than one week. These surveys are short in nature, running around 15 minutes or less.

Utilities partner with external firms to complete their transactional surveys by sending files containing customer transaction and contact information to the research firm. It is important that the customers are carefully screened to ensure that they are the actual customers who had the transaction. These surveys will start with a question to gauge the overall satisfaction with the service received. Then a battery of more detailed questions will explore the satisfaction with accessing information, the accuracy of the information, and their satisfaction with the service they received.

Real-time surveys

Real-time surveys are completed at the end of the transaction. These can be automated surveys using interactive voice response (IVR) technology to randomly select customers to ask a brief series of questions. These real-time surveys can be an effective tool to gain feedback on recent process changes. Caution needs to be exercised in using automated real-time surveys, because many customers have a negative perception of IVR automation. Asking these customers to complete a survey may have a negative impact on their perception of the utility.

Some companies have had success with automated real-time surveys. For example, one company changed its voice-response unit options and information. Once a customer completed his transaction using the IVR options, he was given the opportunity to provide feedback on the new IVR format and information. Utilities also use real-time Internet surveys to gain feedback on various changes to their customer Web sites.

Focus groups

Focus groups are great for delving into a particular subject or issue to gain a more thorough understanding and a dose of reality. The challenge of educating customers on green power was brought home to one utility in a focus group. The customers struggled to comprehend that green power would be available without building new power lines to their homes, and that the actual electrons they received were not necessarily produced from a renewable energy source.

Other uses for focus groups are to test communication messages. One utility used a series of focus groups to refine its outage notification messaging on its IVR system. In the first focus group, respondents were asked to listen to the prompts provided by the IVR in an outage situation. After hearing the recorded messages, the respondents said that it appeared the utility did not care or have a sense of urgency about responding to the outage. The facilitator probed concerning what words or phrases would give them comfort about urgency and care, and these words were included in the subsequent focus groups. By the last focus group, the customer feedback on the messaging was extremely positive, and the utility was able to feel comfortable that it conveyed the message that it was working diligently to respond to the outage.

Customer meetings

Utilities meet with customers in a variety of settings ranging from very personalized individual meetings with a customer to group settings in communities, various trade organizations, and town halls. Customer feedback from these various venues can be valuable in understanding and appreciating the passion customers may have on certain issues.

Account management and community affairs teams often take the lead in meeting with customers either in a reactive mode to respond to an issue, or in a proactive mode to provide key updates on utility initiatives. Often, however, feedback from these meetings is not communicated to others at the utility who may gain ideas from the feedback. It is not pulled out and combined with other feedback in order to learn about trends.

A simple way to gain this feedback is to add it as an agenda item for regular team or staff meetings of account executives or community relations personnel. Another method is to have a quick feedback session once or twice a year with a cross-representative group of folks to find out what they are hearing from customers.

Additionally, some companies have created a customer knowledge database, which allows for quick and easy input of customer intelligence. Information in this database can be queried for trends or used for education on customer concerns or issues.

Commissioner Robert Keating of the Massachusetts Department of Telecommunications and Energy encourages utilities to be "more proactive in communicating the achievements in improving reliability and customer service." He recommends "town meetings as an excellent tool to understand the unique, diverse community needs." He adds, "I find these are sometimes underutilized by utilities." Keating recommends that utilities have a systematic plan to meet with communities on a regular basis to proactively communicate about the progress made by the utilities with respect to reliability and customer service and to understand key issues in that community.[2]

In an effort to learn about customer concerns, one utility added the voice of the customer as an agenda item in the account management department staff meetings. At the first meeting with this agenda item, an account executive told about a customer meeting in which the customer expressed a desire to understand the company's system reliability efforts. Interestingly, more than 50% of the account executives had heard this comment, but until they were sharing this feedback in a room, they did not realize how pervasive the interest was from customers. Their response was to add this information into their quarterly newsletter to customers, in the form of a grid highlighting projects by area in the service territory.

Employee meetings

Employee review and input on the customer satisfaction results will often provide a more thorough understanding of the customer issue. Perhaps more importantly, it reinforces that the company is customer focused and engages employees in working to improve customer satisfaction at every opportunity.

Frontline employees know more about the customers' needs than anyone in the company. Teasing the information out of them becomes the challenge. One should consider conducting frontline employee focus groups to gather information about what customers are saying about the company. Often these focus groups will reveal common trends or bring issues to management that might not have been received from other methods. In creating this type of forum, one also increases the employees' connection with the importance of their role in customer satisfaction. This can be a win-win-win situation for the company, customers, and employees.

Complaint data

The last chapter revealed the magic in effective complaint management. Complaint data can be very revealing with respect to key concerns of customers and serves as a leading indicator. The opportunity with complaint data is to create an environment where complaints are considered gifts, and to capture the complaint data so that trends can be identified.

COMMON PITFALLS TO AVOID

As I interviewed customer research experts on utility usage of customer data, they all concurred that many, if not most utilities, do not gain the full value of customer research. Some, in fact, are just checking the box that says that they have conducted research. One utility went so far as to confirm that indeed they were still required to provide customer satisfaction results to their public service commission before renewing their contract with their research organization. Unfortunately, for some utilities, talking to and interviewing customers is more of a ritual than a practice used to help make positive changes in the customer relationship. This is an example of one of the common pitfalls (fig. 4–1).

1 Old survey questions

2 Lack of understanding of importance of various attributes on customer satisfaction

3 No review of data at senior levels

4 General rather than specific

5 No review of dis-satisfied customers

6 Survey results used for public relations

7 Lack of expertise in utility to anlyze results

8 Lack of integration with other feedback mechanisms

9 Lack of communication of results to all employees

10 Customer research used for evaluation versus strategy

Fig. 4–1. Pitfalls in customer research

Old survey questions

It is important that the customer satisfaction survey questions be reviewed annually. During this review, one should consider new and emerging products and services that may benefit from customer feedback. One should also discuss the survey with the survey administrators. Many times utilities have a third-party administer the surveys. These companies are experts in customer research and can provide rich feedback on areas to improve the survey instrument. Additionally, they can identify where the wording in the questions is causing some misleading results. One should also critically evaluate the survey for areas where questions can be deleted.

Sometimes utilities maintain the same question. They have years, literally, of history on this particular topic. For example, one utility has asked its customers about their knowledge of the energy crisis for almost two decades! Of course, there has not been an energy crisis for all of that time. The topic is no longer of any relevance to the utility. A key test in a survey review is to ask the question, "What are we going to do with the information once we get it?" If tangible changes cannot be made based on the answer, then perhaps it could be replaced with a more useful question. And most critically, one must recalibrate the questions with respect to attributes of satisfaction that are important to the customer.

Lack of understanding of importance of various attributes on customer satisfaction

Research on attributes can be out of date or it might never have been completed to validate which attributes are important in driving customer satisfaction. Attributes are sometimes developed based on internal utility review and perception, rather than via validation from customers. So how does a utility recalibrate importance? One way is to conduct focus groups and add some quantitative questions to its next satisfaction survey that get at importance.

Research experts concur that customer satisfaction is most affected by price, reliability, and response to inquiries. Other attributes that impact satisfaction include billing and payment options and communications. For each utility, customers inherently perceive the weighting of these attributes differently. Understanding these differences is important to ensure that a utility spends its resources fixing the problems that customers consider most important. This enables sound decision making and prioritization around initiatives directed at improving customer satisfaction. If a utility understands the relationship between importance and satisfaction, then plotting various improvement opportunities on a chart similar to figure 4–2 will enable a utility to successfully prioritize opportunities. Using such a chart aids in clearly identifying attributes highly important to customers where satisfaction is low.

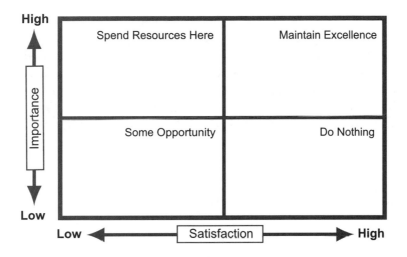

Fig. 4–2. Customer satisfaction prioritization tool

Duke Power's customer research department was excellent at evaluating the impact of initiatives on customer satisfaction. In one example, the research department was able to predict using survey data the impact of offering Saturday connection service to customers.

Analysis of survey and complaint data revealed that customers were frustrated with the delays associated in connecting service. When customers were moving into a new residence, they had no power until they had applied for service and a connect order had been completed in the field. While customers were encouraged to contact Duke Power early about moves, many would wait until the last minute to call for service. Often this was on Friday as they completed their plans for moving over the weekend. Due to resource constraints, many requests that came in on a Friday had to be scheduled for Monday. As one might imagine, this brought with it distressed customers and repeat phone calls.

Duke's customer research department analyzed the lift in customer satisfaction if Saturday service was offered. The data was compelling, and Duke implemented this offering. The results from subsequent transactional customer satisfaction surveys validated that customer satisfaction with the turn on/off process increased with the implementation of the new Saturday service.

Lack of review of data at senior levels

When the survey results are completed, who reviews the data within one's utility? Some companies simply route the final survey summary results around to key leaders and check the box as complete. To create a customer-focused culture, a utility's leaders need to model their expectations of employees to listen to customers and address their needs. A great way to do this is by reviewing the key learnings from the customer research and communicating with employees on the actions the company is taking to address the opportunities.

General rather than specific

The survey results are frequently generalized. Companies laud the fact that 75% of customers are satisfied or very satisfied with their experience. These companies sometimes miss the opportunity to look more specifically at what is driving the satisfaction scores.

This data analysis is available. For example, the EEI National Monitor provides an analysis on service reliability and overall satisfaction. This detailed analysis reveals that "overall customer satisfaction drops sharply for those who report having three or more outages in the past year."[3]

At NSTAR, for example, more detailed customer research on the impact of first call resolution proved valuable in the business case to fund a customer relationship management package to augment our CIS. The analysis on repeat callers confirmed that there was a significant drop in overall satisfaction when customers had to call again on a request. The satisfaction dropped from 91% satisfied and very satisfied to 62% satisfied and very satisfied.[4]

No review of dissatisfied customers

Another view of customer research is from the perspective of a dissatisfied customer. Too often utilities are quick to celebrate an increase in score from

70% to 73%, without understanding the reasons behind the increase or focusing on the 27% who were not satisfied.

Matching dissatisfied customer research to complaint data can be very helpful to identify key problem areas. If the complaint data is sorted, it can be a very quick exercise to gain more specific details on what is driving the negative responses. Another method is to take problem areas and complete focus groups with frontline employees. Our employees talk to and listen to our customers every day. They often are well aware of issues that are driving the results.

One small gas utility found tremendous benefits from analyzing dissatisfied customers. A more detailed analysis of the drivers of dissatisfied customer scores on transactional surveys revealed a trend. It seemed a common denominator for dissatisfaction occurred among customers on home-heating coverage packages.

This utility sought feedback from a cross-functional team that included representatives from the various operating and support areas to explore why customers were dissatisfied. It also had a mix of frontline and management personnel. Call center representatives noted that customers were complaining about service charges. A field technician in the meeting then relayed his most recent customer experience in which the customer referenced misleading marketing material.

As the team reviewed the entire process, it found that the marketing collateral was very vague with respect to service charges associated with heating coverage. The team recommended an immediate rewrite of the collateral, and this was distributed to existing and new customers. The complaints disappeared, and transactional customer satisfaction increased.

Survey results used for public relations

With the advent of J.D. Power and Associates in the utility research arena, utilities are more aware of the public relations impact of their satisfaction results. When scores have dropped, or are low, utilities look to their customer research department for data to respond to a reporter's questions or inquiries.

One researcher lamented about the increase in his workload just prior to and after the release of the J.D. Power survey results. Prior to the release, utility clients pressed the researcher for predictions on the outcomes and their utility's placement in the rankings. After the survey results were posted, utilities sought information with which to justify their utility rankings or to poke holes in the actual research quality. In his opinion, these utilities unfortunately treated the results more as a beauty contest than as an opportunity to truly gain customer insight or overcome management inertia to address key problem areas.

Lack of expertise in utility to analyze results

Those in management who believe that customer research is core to their business planning process will staff their research department accordingly. Too often, it is either understaffed, or staffed with people whose background is something other than customer research. It might be an engineer who needed a change in roles, or an accountant. Sometimes the person in charge of customer research is also in charge of a variety of other functions that may run the gamut of regulatory interface, community relations, or other combined duties. In this situation, the person may not have the time or expertise to get into the research to really identify key opportunities. Often the amount of resources and talent a utility customer research organization has in place is in alignment with the level of importance customer satisfaction takes at the top of the house.

Some best practices include having on staff a person with a background in customer research in order to effectively manage various customer feedback tools and to ensure effective analysis that is linked to business plans. Another option is to subcontract research out to various consultants. This works well when the utility has someone on staff who can effectively serve as a liaison and understands the key decisions that need to be made in conducting the research.

Lack of integration with other feedback mechanisms

Survey data is not linked to measures, focus groups, and complaint data. The implementation of a listening post is a great way to bring about this integration, but listening posts are very rare in utilities. In fact, one utility polled investor-owned utilities across the nation to learn about customer listening posts in utilities. There were no responses to the poll. The utility asking the question then expanded its survey to other types of organizations to learn about listening posts.

Lack of communication of results to all employees

Employee feedback can enrich the understanding of the results. But perhaps a more important reason to communicate to employees is that it engages the employee team. They take personal ownership to work to improve the results.

Al Destribats, executive director of the Telecom and Energy Group for J.D. Power and Associates, highlights the success of Arizona Public Service. This is a large utility that was not satisfied with their results in the J.D. Power survey a few years ago. The utility engaged employees in identifying and implementing improvements to customer service. The result is that six years later, they are one of the most improved utilities in customer service. This is a classic case, Al points out, where "employees rallied around the effort. The employees felt proud to work for Arizona Public Service."[5]

Customer-focused cultures have business plans that highlight customer-focused activities and measures. Engaging employees in achieving these plans creates alignment and successful improvement in customer satisfaction results.

Customer research used for evaluation rather than strategy

Customer research is a lagging indicator for utilities and is most frequently used to evaluate their success. Utilities with a stronger customer focus will have customer satisfaction built into their compensation plans. Additionally, some utilities have performance-based customer facing measures that drive utilities to be more proactive. Successful utilities are moving customer research to the forefront and linking it to forward thinking strategy.

Duquesne Light is an example of linking customer research into strategic initiatives. This utility used customer research to develop a series of customer promises and the processes to support achieving those promises. One of those promises is that customers will have questions answered in the first contact. With process improvements, the number of calls not handled on the first contact was reduced by 35%. And customers noticed the improvement, as transactional satisfaction increased by 5%.[6]

This chapter has reviewed the basic mechanisms to gain customer feedback and has delineated some common pitfalls to avoid when doing customer research. Customer-focused utilities are adept at avoiding the pitfalls and bringing all the various forms of customer feedback together in a manner that enables them to improve service, quickly identify service failures, and offer new products and services. These successful utilities essentially have created a customer listening post.

ESTABLISH A CUSTOMER LISTENING POST

The objective of the listening post is to increase customer satisfaction by addressing issues causing customer complaints. The listening post is responsible for identifying and communicating the customer issues, tracking and trending customer feedback, identifying top customer improvement opportunities, and sponsoring improvement projects. Many times listening posts will meet quarterly to review the aggregated data and identify trends.

A customer listening post is simply a cross-functional team that meets on a regular basis to review customer feedback. The objective is to increase customer satisfaction by addressing issues causing customer complaints. The listening post is responsible for identifying and communicating the customer issues, tracking and trending customer feedback, identifying top customer improvement opportunities, and sponsoring improvement projects. Diversity in participants is important on a customer listening post. A best practice is to include representatives from various departments and various levels in the organization. The champion or chair of a customer listening post may be the leader of customer service or public affairs. Listening posts often have a direct line to the senior management of the company, with scheduled updates on customer research, feedback, and associated initiatives. There are some areas of expertise one should consider on a listening post, including:

- **Customer care representatives.** One should consider including one or more representatives who bring information to the customer listening post around current customer complaints that are coming into the call center or are represented by customer letters. If complaint data owners have been implemented, as described in chapter 3, the results of their review of complaint data are important to bring to the listening post. Feedback from results of call monitoring also may offer insight on current issues.

- **Community relations.** Understanding the hot issues in each community is an important factor for the listening post to consider. Sometimes issues are very pervasive and span multiple communities. The community relations and account executives can provide insight on the large customer or political issues. One utility community relations team uses a Green Board, which is a system map showing each town. The community relations manager is responsible for designating a community status as green, yellow, or red. The goal is that the entire board be green. Areas in yellow and red are reviewed at a listening post meeting.

- **Regulatory.** Representatives from the regulatory area can share trends in commission complaints and feedback from the consumer affairs area on customer feedback.

- **Marketing.** Representatives from marketing can provide insight into current promotions or upcoming promotions. Listening posts are a great arena for marketing to *trial balloon*, or test, new ideas and marketing collateral, as this group is more in tune with customer expectations and issues.

- **Operations.** The operations folks can provide valuable insight into what is really happening from the customer's perspective. Sometimes there are differences between what is mapped out in a process and what actually occurs in the field. As in the gas story above, the field technician was able to provide insight as to why the customer believed the charge was not valid.

- **Support groups.** The business planning and customer research groups can provide needed support to analyze the information. Business planning provides the analytical support to link the feedback to various performance measures. Customer research shares insight gained from the transactions or any other various targeted customer feedback initiatives.

Establishing a customer listening post or a cross-functional team to review customer feedback on a regular basis is a powerful tool for identifying trends, improving customer service, and identifying new products and services. Customer feedback is a leading indicator of results that will later flow from customer research.

Duke Power implemented a customer listening post, which I facilitated. At one of our listening post sessions, the issue of outdoor lighting was raised. Community relations managers noted that key town leaders were calling them expressing concern at the number of outdoor light outages. The complaint data revealed that outdoor light complaints were on the rise at Duke Power. Performance measures on time to repair supported the complaints. Additionally, the slow response to repair was creating additional billing work. CSRs were processing lighting credits for customers who had been without their outdoor lights for several weeks.

The listening post established a cross-functional team led by electric operations to identify a solution. Their recommendation included a combination of changes in how and to whom light repair work was issued. They also recommended a shared measure between customer care and electric operations on lighting repair cycle time.

As they say, what gets measured gets done. This was true with the lighting repair. Cycle time was reduced to less than one week, and the customer response was very positive.

One should listen to the voice of the customer by gathering feedback from multiple sources and by using the feedback to identify improvement opportunities. Destribats observes that the utilities that consistently perform well with respect to the J.D. Power survey "do not sit back and relax. Rather they identify two to three opportunities each year that will enhance the service to their customers and they ensure these are implemented."[7]

REFERENCES

[1] Smith, Dennis. "Customer Satisfaction in the Utility Industry: An Overview." Chartwell Customer Satisfaction Audio Conference, August 19, 2004.

[2] Keating, W. Robert, Commissioner, The Commonwealth of Massachusetts, Department of Telecommunications and Energy; Interview, August 10, 2004.

[3] National Residential Customer Monitor, Spring 2004, Edison Electric Institute, p. 87.

[4] NSTAR Customer Post Transaction Surveys, April 2003, Research International.

[5] Destribats, Al. Executive director, Telecommunications and Energy Group, J.D. Power and Associates; Interview, August 2004.

[6] Belechak, Joe. "Managing T&D Cost and Performance." Duquesne Light, EEI Operations Conference, June 2004.

[7] Destribats, Al. Interview, August 2004.

5   OFFER PRODUCTS AND SERVICES TO MEET THE CUSTOMERS' NEEDS

Many utilities are continuing to look for the call-waiting equivalent for the electric, gas, and water business. This may be coming, but in the interim, progressive utilities are not waiting. Instead, they are finding success, profit, and increased customer satisfaction by strategically focusing on core products and services expected from a utility.

Utilities are wise to consider products and services from a strategic perspective. Product and service offerings should align to support corporate strategic goals. Utilities with a focus on customer service may choose products and services that enhance the customer's experience while reducing costs. Utilities with this strategic focus will tend to concentrate on products and services based on automation, like Web-based services. Other utilities have a corporate focus to increase revenues and profits. These utilities will identify income-producing products to augment revenues, like surge suppression and fixed bill options. Each utility will make unique decisions for products and services based on its strategic focus, customer base, and regulatory environment.

This chapter will explore the basics around the product and service development cycle, core products and services, and some innovative ideas that are just now being offered that improve customer satisfaction, reduce expenses, and in some cases, add profit to the bottom line.

PRODUCT AND SERVICE DEVELOPMENT CYCLE

One of the most important elements in the product and service development cycle is to adopt a disciplined approach. A disciplined approach guides a utility through an objective evaluation of the product or service under consideration. Using the four-step process outlined in figure 5–1, a utility can make an educated decision whether or not to proceed. Such a decision, called a *go/no decision*, may be made at key intervals in the product and service development cycle. A disciplined approach ensures that there are controls around the amount of funds and resources to produce a product or service, and that the company is able to react to market changes by introducing products and services in a timely manner.

An objective go/no decision is enabled by identifying up front some key attributes and/or metrics for each stage. Some companies will have thresholds established for a new product or service. For example, on a revenue producing service, a company may indicate that to proceed, it must be capable of bringing in a threshold amount of revenue. These types of metrics help prioritize the many product and service opportunities.

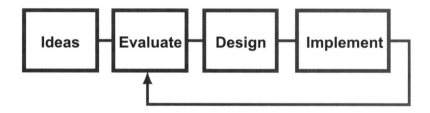

Fig. 5–1. Product and service development cycle

Ideas

There are many ways to generate ideas. One of the best ways is to leverage the customer information from a customer listening post. As discussed in chapter 4, a listening post integrates customer feedback from multiple sources, including performance against key metrics, customer survey data, complaint data, community feedback, regulatory feedback, and employee feedback. Organizations with listening posts often find that this forum will generate ideas for new product and service offerings.

For example, a utility listening post surfaced the idea of Saturday availability of service connections and disconnections. The utility typically completed hard disconnects when customers moved out of their residence, unless the unit was under agreement with the landlord for service to be placed in the landlord's name in the interim. This meant that the new customer moving in had no power until he had applied for service and a connect order had been completed in the field. While most customers called early to schedule a connection or disconnection, some would wait until the last minute to call for service. Often this was on Friday as they completed their plans for moving over the weekend. This created a resource constraint, sometimes resulting in protracted delays for customers desiring a connection. Along with the delays were distressed customers and repeat phone calls.

Complaint data revealed that long delays for service were a top concern with customers. Customer research indicated that offering Saturday service would positively impact customer satisfaction. Indeed, once Saturday service was implemented, transactional customer satisfaction surveys validated that customer satisfaction with the turn on/off process increased.

If a listening post is not in place, ideas can be generated and screened by simply bringing in a diverse team representing multiple departments and areas to brainstorm and evaluate ideas. Since many ideas will be generated, it is necessary to prioritize them to identify the best opportunities for product and service offerings. One technique to do this is to rank the ideas against key criteria, such as their fit with the corporate strategy, customer interest, and feasibility. This screened list can then be moved to the evaluation phase.

The go/no decision here should be based on some key attributes established for any product or service under consideration. At this stage, the attributes are rather general. As the process progresses, the go/no decision becomes more rigorous. This is to be expected as the resource allocations to the new product or service will increase as one continues through each stage. Some considerations for the idea stage for go/no decisions might include:

- Does the product or service fit with corporate strategy and objectives?

- Does this product or service improve customer satisfaction?

- Does this product or service reduce operations and maintenance expense?

- Does this product or service increase profits?

- Where will profits flow—into increased earnings or reduced retail rates?

- Does a regulatory authority require this product or service?

Evaluation

Product and service ideas meeting the initial criteria move to a more formal evaluation. The extent and time spent on each idea in the evaluation stage is relative to the complexity of the service offering. A simple offering of customer selection of a payment draft date will require less time in evaluation than reviewing a fixed bill offering, which has a revenue component. Some key areas to consider in evaluation include product design, pricing, and a market assessment, among others.

Product and service design specifications. The devil is in the details. This first step requires identifying the exact product and service offering. This is not as simple as it may appear, as people on the same team often have differing ideas on what the product or service will look like in production. A good project manager can navigate a diverse team through this step. This will provide the foundation for the next step of financial review.

When I was at Tampa Electric, my team was always on the lookout for product and service offerings. One idea that surfaced from employee feedback was to offer direct debit customers the option of selecting their payment draft date. Direct debit offers customers the convenience of having their payments debited directly from a designated checking account.

A team reviewed the various options of providing this service. Their analysis indicated that the customer-selected due date could be offered with some limitations very quickly at a low cost. A more robust offering would require more programming resources. The recommendation was to implement the more simplistic approach, which still provided the option to Tampa Electric to enhance the offering at a later date. As a result, Tampa Electric offered the option of a selected due date six weeks later, with great customer response.

Market assessment. The market assessment should identify the market size, customer segments, potential growth, competitors, competitive products, and impact on customer satisfaction. Benchmarking other companies offering the proposed product or service is an excellent tool in the market assessment to develop product and service goals.

In the example of customer-selected draft dates for direct debit, customer service representatives indicated that the most common reason customers gave for not going on automatic bank draft was the inability to select a draft date. A market assessment included a benchmark review of bank draft participation in other utilities offering draft date selection. For the benchmarking, Tampa Electric turned to the EEI and the American Gas Association (AGA) DataSource.[1] Vicky Westra, director of customer service for Tampa Electric, indicates that the customer-selected due date offering has been a great success and that draft participation almost doubled with the introduction of selected due dates.[2]

Financial assessment. Understanding the marginal costs of implementing the program is fundamental. If this program also has financial benefits, then some form of return on investment (ROI) analysis is required. Each utility has economic analysis models that should be referenced for this assessment. It is important, though, to determine all potential cost impacts, including technology, labor, and marketing. In the example of customer-selected draft dates, the programming costs were nominal, and marketing was planned through existing channels promoting the various payment methods. So the financial assessment was very simple. A more rigorous analysis would be required as the complexity increases.

Success measures. It is important to define in this stage key metrics that will be monitored to evaluate the success of this product or service. These measures often include elements of total cost, customer participation rates, customer feedback, and specific process measures like cycle time to fulfill customer request.

Prior to moving into the design phase, it is important to pause and evaluate whether to proceed or to stop the effort with the go/no decision. With the evaluation stage completed, more specifics can be detailed on the impacts of the product and service offering on customer satisfaction, revenues, and expense. It is helpful to have thresholds established for each of these criteria. For example:

- Can the current IT systems support this product or service?

- Does this product or service meet the company's financial requirements?

- Is the product or service proven technology or very new? Some utilities have a specific strategy to be first to be second, meaning that they do not invest in products or services that are very new and unproven.

- Does the current regulatory environment support this offering?

If, after objectively evaluating these questions and others, the answer is to go forward, the next step is the design phase. It is often helpful at this point to go ahead and specifically identify the unique product and service metrics and thresholds expected so that the future go/no decisions will continue to be objective.

Design

By this phase, it is common to have a project manager in place and perhaps even a full-time team. This phase involves planning the product or service for implementation. There are several components to the design stage.

Business model. This first component involves getting very specific with respect to the business requirements. These requirements include specific technical specification and business process design.

Process mapping is a great tool to drive out detailed requirements. Process mapping will detail the people, process, and technology support requirements to market, deliver, and service the new offering. This effort should result in answering the basic questions of who, what, when, and where. If customer billing is involved, questions about using the utility's existing billing system or supporting with a more customized system must be resolved. How will the offering be serviced, and who will service it? If internal resources are planned for servicing the product, how will internal priorities be weighed against this new offering? Can internal resources support the new offering consistently?

It is also important that one does not overlook collections activities on the new offering. Utilities sometimes find out too late that a product or service offering that appears to be a success based on sales is a money loser due to the inability to collect. It is important to take the time to thoughtfully consider the entire life cycle of the product or service.

Surge protection offers a great example of some questions to consider from a life cycle perspective. If the payback on surge protection is one year, what is the collections process for a customer who moves prior to the one-year period? What is the success in collecting the remaining amount due on the device from the customer? Is it cost-effective to remove the device, or will the new customer gain the benefit for free?

From the business model stage, a request for proposals (RFP) can be issued. In conjunction with the RFP, evaluation criteria for the responses are developed in this stage. Evaluation allows objective analysis of the various potential vendor partner(s). Multiple partners may be required to support the various roles of marketing, customer service, customer fulfillment, installation, and credit and collections, to name a few.

Pricing. Pricing the product or service can be challenging. It helps to first clarify the purpose of the product or service into one of three categories: value added, for profit, or cost recovery.

Utilities offer value added services to enhance their brands. A Braille bill is an example of a value added service. Producing a Braille bill is more expensive than normal bill print. This did not prevent Citizens Gas from leading the nation in offering Braille bills back in the early 1980s. When asked why Citizens Gas offers this service, Greg Sawyers, director of customer service, replies, "We do it because there is a demand for it. It is a value added service for those customers who need it."[3] Braille bill, large print bill, and other services like this support Citizens' Gas vision, which is "to be the best at customer satisfaction in the eyes of our customers, and therefore become the local distribution company of utility services."

Successful for-profit products and services not only add dollars to the bottom line, but also increase customer satisfaction. Michael O'Shea, vice president, Christensen Associates Inc., led the development of Southern Company's fixed bill option. He states that the fixed bill product "contributes to earnings and improves customer satisfaction."[4] Not only do the customer satisfaction research results prove this, but also customers take the time to write letters extolling the benefits of fixed bill. He tells of one customer letter that typified the response of customers to this product. The letter was addressed to the vice president of marketing. The customer thanked Georgia Power and its employees for coming up with innovations, especially this fixed bill product. She explained that she lived on a fixed income, and when the bills varied seasonally, she had difficulty paying on time. The fixed bill, she explained, removed this problem.

Sometimes a service offering is designed to simply cover the costs of offering the product. Fee-based credit card payments are an excellent example of the cost recovery category. Utility rates are generally not designed to support the costs associated with credit card payments. But utilities find that customers not only want this option, they will pay a convenience fee to use it.

Marketing, sales, and communications strategy. This involves designing specific advertising and promotion initiatives along with supporting collateral and fulfillment processes. Additionally, this plan should map out the promotion campaign with targeted measures on ramp up.

Consumer research can be instrumental in designing effective marketing campaigns. NSTAR completed research in preparation to target perceived underserved ethnic populations. The research not only identified the various ethnic populations within the service area, but also determined the barriers to serving the market and offered recommendations on how to best reach the audience. In the case of ethnic outreach, providing marketing collateral in the native language was highly preferred. Partnering with local community organizations was noted as a best practice to reach the various ethnic groups.[5]

Consumer research will help ensure marketing dollars are used most effectively and will reach the target audience in ways that are meaningful. Bill inserts are the most commonly used marketing approach for utilities. The ethnic outreach consumer research at NSTAR indicated these customers preferred direct mail in their native language. Utilities also find success with telemarketing techniques, depending on the product. Other marketing approaches include billboards, radio, and television. Booths at trade shows and home shows are very effective ways to reach targeted audiences.

Training. It is import to consider what sales, operations, and service training might be required to support the product and service. The process mapping will have identified all the people who will have contact with this product. One should review each of the roles that affect the product and assess any gaps in the skills needed versus the skills available. This will map out the training plan. If partnering with vendors, one should consider how training will be delivered to their personnel, or this could be a part of the contract with the fulfillment vendor.

Business plan finalization. Once partners have been selected, and process requirements have been defined from a people, process, and technology standpoint, the business plan can be finalized with confident projections on costs and revenues. This leads naturally into the go/no decision, using the key metrics and thresholds identified in the evaluation stage. Some questions to consider at this stage include:

- Can the product or service be successfully delivered to the customers?

- Is the time frame for implementation achievable and reasonable?

- Can the product or service be successfully communicated and marketed?

- Can this product or service be supported once it becomes available?

- Does the product or service still meet its financial objectives?

If the decision is to go forward, then it is time to implement. This stage is completed by reviewing and refining the go/no decision criteria for the upcoming implementation stage.

Implementation

If the decision is a go, then the company is ready to launch the new product or service. Activities involved in this stage include:

Finalization of contracts. The contracts must be finalized with vendors, suppliers for the product, or fulfillment services.

Launch. Meg Matt, principal of The Matt Group, recommends that one test each customer-facing step privately before going public. "Gone are the days when utilities could afford to offer new products and services with a 'ready, fire, aim' approach," said Matt. "Utilities are much more sophisticated and disciplined in the development cycle, and they realize the importance of testing the concept and marketing materials with a small group of customers or a customer advisory panel prior to a full-scale launch."[6]

One utility had completed its product design and was ready to launch its electronic bill presentment and payment. The project team was concerned that despite the intense review and product testing, a customer might find some issues or problems with this online tool. In this situation, to fully test the product, the utility wanted to run a pilot test with experienced Internet users.

The team recognized that the target audience would also likely be the early users of the new tool. So the team crafted this disclaimer that was posted on the online service: "Welcome to our new online bill presentment and payment service. We are excited about piloting this new tool and would love for you to test drive it. Please give us feedback on your experience." As a result, they received some great ideas to fine-tune the application and created a buzz with customers about this new service. Three weeks later, this utility fully launched the new tool and communicated its availability in a variety of ways to encourage participation. The response was great, and customers did not experience any problems with the test-driven tool.

One should review the results of the soft launch and make adjustments if necessary. It is helpful here to pause and make a clear go/no decision to move to the launch stage. If the business plan was rigorously developed and detailed, the results of the soft launch should not be surprising, but should confirm expected plans.

Gain customer feedback. One should seek out customer feedback, either formally through focus groups or more informally through transaction surveys or close monitoring of customer service calls. This feedback can be incorporated into the evaluation stage to refine the product or service offering.

Tampa Electric Company completely redesigned its surge protection offering, which was launched in 1987 as a purchased system. Customers struggled to understand the value differentiation in buying a product from their utility versus purchasing from a local home store. Vicky Westra, director customer service for Tampa Electric, explains, "We had to differentiate our product. Our Zap Cap Systems is a behind-the-meter device that customers lease." This differentiated service met the need for enhanced surge protection with no up-front costs. Vicky believes that the tremendous success of the program is due to three attributes. "First and foremost, Tampa Electric has been a local, highly regarded utility provider for over 100 years. Customers associate this product with a utility. And of course, the unique weather phenomenon of Tampa, Florida, being the lighting strike capital of the United States doesn't hurt."[7]

After some time has elapsed, it again becomes necessary to evaluate the product or service offering with planned expectations relating to sales, costs, and impact on customer satisfaction.

Evaluation

Finally, the product and service development process comes full circle with an evaluation stage. Since specific measures of success have been developed, a program manager can monitor the product or service offering against specific program objectives. The evaluation process should be ongoing as the product and service matures.

One should not be afraid to pull the plug on a bad product or service. Continuing to offer a service that customers do not want or that is not cost-effective is simply not good business. So if the results are not as expected, one should take a hard look at ending the program or dramatically re-engineering the program. If the program is a success, then the process can move forward and ramp up as defined in the marketing plan, or the plan can be adjusted based on the feedback.

CORE PRODUCTS AND SERVICES

What are some basic product and services that customers expect from a utility? The following are some basic products and services that a utility should consider implementing for its customer base.

Outage information

Customers do not like to be left in the dark literally or figuratively. Utilities are continuing to invest in linking their outage and CIS units to provide customers with accurate information, like estimated time of restoration, outage cause, and status of the job. Customers need this information to make life decisions, big and small, from health considerations to whether to go out to dinner or wait for the power to return.

Telephony services

The first moment of truth for a customer who needs to contact a utility is finding what number to call. Many utilities are augmenting local phone lines with intelligent call answering via automatic phone number identification provided by inbound toll-free services or advanced local phone services. Using toll-free service numbers accelerates a utility's ability to identify the customer. This type of capability is critical in outage management as it enables customer self-service.

Additionally, toll-free numbers are a great tool for responding to specific customer groups or call types. The toll-free number has a cost associated with it, but the utility also gains the advantage of being able to reroute calls easily. Utilities often maintain local numbers to promote a local feel to their company or to reduce costs. However, augmenting with toll-free lines also is helpful for targeted types of phone calls. Many utilities offer toll-free numbers for outage calls or direct connection to a specialized service team, like the business or credit teams. At an average cost of around $0.04/minute, toll-free numbers are often very good options for customer service.

High call volume answering systems are a critical service from a customer satisfaction perspective and from an operational performance perspective. Potomac Electric Power Company (Pepco) states, "Knowing who is out and the density of the damage shortens restoration times by as much as 50%."[8] A high call volume answering system eliminates busy signals for customers. Additionally, the utility's outage management system can provide timely, accurate outage information and status. The system that Pepco has in place, in partnership with a third party, is designed to handle 100,000 incoming calls and 180,000 outbound calls per hour.

Language line services are great tools to assist in situations where English is not the first language. There are several services available now for a nominal fee that can provide translation skills. Most of these services can translate more than 50 languages. Pricing for the service is based on volume and a per-minute charge. The language line service provides the side benefit of measurement of the growth of various languages used by the customers. This can be useful in analysis of whether to staff internally for language services. In Florida, for example, most utilities have Spanish-speaking customer service representatives on staff. The language line data can assist with analysis about internal staffing needs and also monitor growth in various languages.

Payment convenience

Offering a variety of payment options is now expected by utility customers. Most utilities today offer a combination of face-to-face, phone, Internet, and draft options. The face-to-face payment options are provided via utility storefronts or payment agents. Chartwell research indicates that between 20% and 30% of utility customers are paying their bills by some other means than the postal service.[9]

Customers are vocal about wanting payment convenience. A Methodist minister shared his frustration with the lack of payment options offered by his utility. A member of his church was attempting to have service connected, but did not have the funds to pay the deposit. The church was going to provide the funds. At this point the minister called the utility company to find how he could pay this deposit. The CSR replied that he could mail in a check or visit one of the conveniently located utility offices. The minister explained to the CSR that he was out of town on a business trip, so visiting the local office was not an option, nor was mailing in the deposit, as the service was needed for the next day. He asked about other options, such as credit card payment or using an electronic check via the phone. The CSR responded that the utility did not offer any phone payment services but added that Western Union was an acceptable way to make a payment.

The minister then tackled the challenge of finding a Western Union office. Since he was out of the state in an unfamiliar town, he used the phone book to locate the nearest Western Union location. He was more than happy to pay the $15.00 to have the money wired and was relieved when his call to the utility confirmed they had received the payment, and the connect order would be processed. But he closed by asking why utilities did not offer a payment option over the phone.

Customers want payment options to meet their various lifestyle needs and situations. Payments via the phone or on the Web are increasingly popular and cost-effective if handled by automation. While payments over the phone can be handled manually by a CSR, this is an expensive option. Instead of a CSR processing the payment, many utilities are linking to third-party providers for this service. Generally, third-party providers complete the transactions via automation, greatly reducing the cost per stub. Some utilities are finding acceptance with charging a convenience fee for this service.

Direct debit is one of the cheapest ways to collect payments and is attractive to certain customer segments. Often the opportunity is merely how to make it simple for customers to sign up for direct debit and to offer customers incentives to increase participation. Public Service of New Hampshire models a simple approach whereby customers simply have to check a box on the bill stub to indicate they want to enroll, and pay with a check from the account they want to designate for bank drafts in the future.

Billing options

In addition to payment convenience, customers desire billing and pricing options. Some common options include statement or summary billing and electronic billing.

Statement or summary billing offers customers with multiple accounts one bill that aggregates the various accounts. For customers, this is a great service that simplifies their payment processing time.

Summary bills often are muscled through the billing system because the systems were not designed to offer this type of service. Utilities create manual workarounds to provide this to the customer. While this meets the customers' needs, it often results in a lot of resource requirements and specialized skills at the company. New billing or CIS units come packaged with summary billing capabilities.

Sam Turner, manager of customer services for Jackson Energy Authority, turned summary billing into a competitive advantage for the mass market. Jackson Energy Authority not only provides electric, gas, water, wastewater, and sanitation services, it also offers competitive services of propane, cable, telephone, and Internet. Amazingly, Sam and the Jackson Energy Authority team provide all of these services on one bill.

To combine these services on one bill took some customization of the CIS. Jackson's senior vice president and COO, Jim Watson, provided the vision for this CIS effort. "Our Jackson Energy Authority bill has to be easy to read, easy to understand, accurate, and capable of separating the various services." Five rewrites later, Turner believes that Jackson Energy Authority has achieved the vision set by Watson. But he cautions that to continue to be recognized as a preferred provider of utility and competitive services, Jackson Energy Authority will continue to listen to customer feedback and enhance the billing options.[10]

Electronic bill payment and presentment is rapidly gaining in popularity as more customers do business online. Internet billing is the delivery of periodic bills that enable customers to pay the bills via the Web. There are three models for delivering electronic bill payment and presentment. The first is *biller direct*, where the customers directly access the biller Web site for bill presentment and payment. The second is through a bill consolidator, where presentment of bill information is through a third-party consolidator. The third is by e-mail, where the bill is presented to the customer via an e-mail message as opposed to the Web site. Chartwell's 2003 research determined that 2.8% of customers subscribe to online billing. There are many service providers and service options available to assist a utility in offering this capability.

Self-service options

Increasingly, customers want the flexibility to do business with their utility on their own time via self-service options. Utilities are increasingly meeting this need through self-service via the Web and interactive voice response (IVR) options. Chartwell indicates the most common self-service points offered via these mediums are account information, outage reporting, bill payment, appointment scheduling, and service connect and disconnect.[11] Self-service options can be a win/win situation for customers and the utility as processing requests via the Web and VRU are significantly less costly than by live voice answer.

Energy management services

There are a variety of energy efficiency and demand side management programs and services offered by utilities. Chartwell's 2004 research reports that 12% of utilities surveyed state that load management is their most popular offering.[12] The most common load management offering for residential and small commercial is air conditioning cycling programs. Energy management programs are even more popular with commercial and industrial customers. Chartwell's 2004 research indicates that 60% of utilities rank their commercial and industrial energy management programs as the most popular with this customer segment.[13] Commercial and industrial energy management programs and services include energy audits and consultation, energy usage information, load management, and energy efficiency programs, among others.

Additionally, utilities are offering energy management tools on their Web sites. For residential customers, energy calculators are valuable in understanding and controlling their energy usage.

Some of the most common and appreciated offerings are utility calculators. This tool, typically available on the Web, allows customers to evaluate their energy usage and test changes to energy usage on their bills. Energy audits are a more personalized method to identify energy savings and create customer goodwill. NSTAR transactional feedback on energy audits reveals a 97% satisfied and very satisfied response rate with these audits. Other programs and services can be designed by customer segment and can range from motor offerings, heating, ventilation, and air conditioning (HVAC), windows, and rebate programs.

Specialized support teams

Creating specialized service teams can be a real boost to specific customer segments. A best practice is to establish a team to serve the commercial and industrial accounts. These accounts have unique needs, and these customers generally believe they deserve a better level of service than the mass market. While most utilities have account executives to handle the large accounts, this still leaves a large number of accounts that have unique business needs and expect more personalized service.

At NSTAR for example, out of 1.3 million customer services, 55,000 are commercial or industrial accounts. Of those, only 1,000 are represented by account executives. That leaves 54,000 industrial accounts going through the call center like a typical residential customer. Only 12 months after I arrived, we had implemented our Tech Center to service these accounts. The response has been amazing. I also implemented this at Tampa Electric with similar results. In talking to utilities across the nation, this segmentation is definitely a best practice. Anaheim Public Utilities offers their major customers a single point of contact.[14]

EMERGING PRODUCTS AND SERVICES

Utilities recognize that customer expectations continue to rise. As such, utilities are continuing to expand on the product and service offerings. Brad Kates, vice president for Opinion Dynamics, suggests that utilities should exercise caution as they consider expanding products and services, particularly competitive products and services. Customer research reveals that companies with a strong reputation with their customers for providing high-quality service are in a better position to consider competitive service offerings. Interestingly, customers express concern about a utility that offers competitive services if they perceive the utility does not provide its core services well.

Emerging products and services can impact customer satisfaction, reduce costs, or provide revenue enhancement opportunities. Using a defined product and service development process as discussed earlier will ensure that the offering will align with the utility's brand but will also appeal to customers.

Speech recognition

This technology is developing exponentially in capability. I can remember studying this in college and thinking this was many years into the future. Then in the early 1990s, companies offered speech recognition in a limited way, with directed dialog of "press or say 1." Now speech recognition is more free-form, with natural language offerings allowing customers to speak their requests. Gartner research shows that 47% of customers were much more satisfied with voice recognition than touch-tone.[15]

Pepco has been a leader in this area, implementing natural language speech recognition in early 2004. The business case indicates a payback in 25 months for the investment in voice recognition. The early finding from this service offering is that it has increased the call completion rates on the VRU by 35%.[16]

Prepayment

Prepayment technology is not new and is actually very mature in the European markets. Acceptance and implementation in the United States is taking some time. Chartwell's 2004 research reveals that only 3.4% of U.S. utilities are offering prepayment. Most U.S. utilities, 71.4%, are not considering it.

Salt River Project (SRP) was the first U.S. utility to implement prepayment, and it currently has more than 30,000 customers participating. SRP has identified customer and utility benefits.[17] Its customer research indicates that 85% of customers were satisfied or very satisfied with the service, and 70% of participants have a better perception of SRP. The utility benefits from improved cash flow and reduced credit and collections costs.

But as Chartwell's research indicated, most utilities are not considering prepayment due to significant hurdles from a technology, process, and public acceptance standpoint. Jerrold Oppenhiem, nationally recognized low-income advocate, listed prepayment as one of the top five things utilities should not do. Prepayment ranked high on this list, along with price increases, poor reliability, misleading customer communication, and dirty power plants. Oppenhiem's concerns are not unique and are a formable obstacle to overcome in offering prepayment.

There are also considerations from a technology, administrative, and billing perspective. There continues to be flux with respect to technical providers of prepay. Utility processes and CIS units are designed around collection after product use. It is no small undertaking to re-engineer these systems to support prepayment.

New mover programs

Utilities recognize that the first impression is a lasting impression. Because of that, more utilities are offering services targeted at the new mover segment. New mover services are designed to simplify the new mover experience and to orient customers to the services provided by the utility. Examples of new mover services include concierge services, in which a customer can initiate service with an electric utility but also with other service providers, like phone and cable and welcome packages.

Welcome packages are packages that are delivered to the customer's homes that inform the customers of various programs and services. The welcome packages may include coupons for discounts on energy-efficient products, or even magnets listing key utility phone numbers. One innovative utility is using the new mini business card CD technology. This CD, which is the size of a business card, is inserted into a welcome card. The card welcomes the customer to the utility and contains highlights of the various services offered by the utility and links directly to the utility Web site.

Concierge services are growing in popularity with electric utilities, not only because there is often a revenue-sharing opportunity, but also because customers find this to be a value added service. Concierge services basically offer a new mover customer the ability to sign up for other utilities or services at the completion of their utility application. There are third-party aggregators that represent a variety of new mover service providers, like phone and cable companies. Since 70% of customers contact their new electric utility first when setting up service, it is a natural extension for electric utilities to offer customers the ability to connect their other services in the same phone call.[18]

For utilities offering concierge services, it is as simple as transferring the phone call directly to an aggregator of concierge services, or directly to another new mover service provider. Customer satisfaction research shows that more than 90% of customers would recommend using the concierge service again.[19] Research data from a new mover service provider that uses a direct link from the utility indicates similar satisfaction results, with 79% of customers responding that they were satisfied or very dissatisfied with this service.

Bill options

There are a variety of bill options available today, such as Braille, large print, and special language bills. Utilities are sometimes constrained in what can be offered due to limitations in the CIS. As will be further discussed in the chapters on outsourcing and grading the CIS, partnering with third-party providers to offer enhanced bill services is one way to mitigate constraints with the CIS.

The Braille bill option, for example, is offered by 45% of investor-owned gas and electric utilities.[20] Citizens Gas has offered Braille and large print bills for more than 20 years. While not very many customers have selected the Braille bill option, the fact that Citizens Gas offers this type of service appeals to all of its customers. Of Citizens Gas customers, only a small percentage receives Braille bills (0.02%) or large print bills (0.1%).

Fixed bill

One of the newest offerings for utilities is the fixed bill, which provides customers with a flat fixed-amount bill. Southern Company led the way in developing a fixed bill option. Michael O'Shea, vice president for Christensen Associates Inc., led Southern Company's effort to design a fixed bill product. The idea came from customers. O'Shea tells of conducting focus groups in the late 1990s to learn why a residential time-of-use offering was not being readily adopted. In each focus group, one out of four or five would say, according to O'Shea, "I don't know why the electric company can't make it simple for me, like cable TV. You can give me a time of use option, if you want, but I am not going to change my behaviors to save energy." O'Shea challenged his team to meet this need. The result was a pilot program in June 2000. The success supported unanimous commission approval in 2002 for a permanent tariff. Currently more than 200,000 residential customers are on the fixed bill plan, which is approximately one of every nine Georgia Power Customers.[21]

Green energy

The definition of *green energy* can vary from state to state, but most often it refers to electricity generated from renewable resources such as solar, wind, or hydro. Green or renewable energy products have risen dramatically in popularity. Chartwell research highlights this growth from only 22% of utilities offering it in 2001 to 54% offering it in 2004.[22] Customer acceptance has been slow for green power, with an average of 1%. Customer education and understanding of green power continue to be challenging.

This challenge was highlighted to me as I listened in on focus groups on green power. In one focus group, a participant could not understand how green power could be delivered to his home without building new power lines. Research on customers in Massachusetts indicates that customers want to do their part for the environment, and that it needs to be easy for them.[23]

Utilities are responding to this customer desire by offering a variety of green energy products. These range from consumers supporting the generation of electricity through renewable sources via renewable certificates to supporting a specific utility plant that is powered with renewable resources. With all green products, consumer education and communication is vital to the success of the programs.

Live chat

This service offering is for Web site users and provides them real-time access to a customer service representative to respond to their questions. From a utility perspective, this is an interesting offering that may require some new skill sets. Utility customer service representatives are hired and screened for their speaking skills. The challenge with Web service is that the responses are written, and therefore also available as documentation from a utility or customer perspective. It is important that what is communicated in written form is accurate and professional. Some utilities approach this conundrum with specialized training for representatives responding to Web inquiries, while others are hiring specifically for this skill set. One benefit to live chat is that one CSR can support several customers concurrently.

Virtual hold

This relatively new technology creates the Disney effect for telephone queues. Disney's early customer research indicated that if customers knew how long they could expect to be in line, their overall experience was better. This model has been copied by most amusement parks, with many enhancements. Virtual queue offers utility customers this same experience with respect to a phone queue. Virtual queue indicates to customers how long the estimated wait time is and offers customers the choice of continuing to hold or leaving a number and time for a call from the utility. City Public Service, located in San Antonio, Texas, reduced its call abandonment rate from 20% to 4% with the implementation of virtual hold.[24]

Utilities that apply a disciplined approach to product and service development will be successful in offering customers products and services that meet market demands, increase satisfaction, and are financially viable. A fundamental key is listening to customers and gaining an understanding of their expectations.

REFERENCES

[1] EEI/AGA DataSource provides benchmarking data on customer service processes. This tool is available to participating members of EEI and AGA.

[2] Westra, Vicky. Director of customer service, Tampa Electric Co.; Interview, August 27, 2004.

[3] Sawyers, Greg. Director of customer service, Citizens Gas; Interview, September 8, 2004.

[4] O'Shea, Michael. Vice president, Christensen Associates Inc. (retired Georgia Power executive); Interview, August 26, 2004.

[5] "Reaching Out to NSTAR's Ethnic Customers: Commercial and Residential Populations." Opinion Dynamics Corporation; Cambridge, MA, May–September 2004.

[6] Matt, Meg. Principal, The Matt Group; Interview, September 2004.

[7] Westra, Vicky, Interview, August 2004.

[8] "New Solutions for Customer Self-Service; Potomac Electric Power Company." CIS Conference, Miami, FL, May 5, 2004.

[9] Chartwell Research. 2003 Industry Survey.

[10] Turner, Sam. Manager Customer Service, Jackson Energy Authority; Interview, August 2004.

[11] Chartwell Utility Marketing Research. Web-based customer service. August 2003.

[12] Chartwell Utility Marketing Research Series. "Residential and Small Business Load Control and Demand Management." June 2004.

[13] Chartwell. "C&I Products and Services Data Summary and Report." 2004.

[14] Anaheim Public Utilities. "Romancing the Customer through Innovative Retail Programs and Products." Presentation, CIS Conference, June 12, 2002.

[15] Gartner ScanSoft Customer Satisfaction Study, 2002. This was referenced in Pepco's presentation at the CIS conference, "New Solutions for Customer Self-Service." Miami, FL, May 5, 2004.

[16] Chartwell. "Speech-Enabled Customer Service." February 2004.

[17] AESP Brown Bag Presentation on Prepayment. John R. Soeth, Salt River Project. May 2003.

[18] Chartwell New Products and Services Research Series. "Marketing Utility Products and Services." pp. 63–98.

[19] All Connect customer research from 2001.

[20] American Gas Association and Edison Electric Institute 2004 DataSource. Annual Benchmarking Survey (percentage based on 60 participating companies).

[21] O'Shea, Michael. Vice president, Christensen Associates Inc. (retired Georgia Power executive); Interview, August 26, 2004.

[22] Chartwell research, 2001, 2004.

[23] NSTAR Green Power Focus Group Analysis. June 2003.

[24] "Dominion and CPS Take Customers Off Hold." Customer Care Research Series, July 9, 2004.

PART II

Reduce Business Costs

6 REDUCE UNBILLED LOSSES IN THE METER-TO-CASH CYCLE

The combination of low customer growth, pressure to maintain or reduce rates while improving service, and the Sarbanes Oxley Act has resulted in renewed interest by utility leaders on the meter-to-cash cycle. Specifically, leaders want to ensure that revenue losses are minimized and solid controls are in place. Industry experts estimate that utilities are losing on average between 2% and 4% in revenues from losses in the meter-to-cash cycle. Utility executives with an eye on earnings growth are anxious to make sure that the losses are reduced, if not eliminated.

Utility executives are paying attention. Richard Taglienti, vice president of marketing and revenue assurance for Peoples Energy, says he is concerned about "what I don't know. Do I know where 100% of the meters are? Do I know the meter pressure correction factor is working properly?"[1]

This chapter will review the key components and goals of the meter-to-cash cycle and will discuss prevalent utility challenges and mitigation strategies. This chapter will identify a process to prioritize and minimize meter-to-cash losses.

WHAT IS THE REVENUE CYCLE?

The revenue cycle involves a series of subprocesses that ensure all revenue is received and accurately documented and recorded. Each subprocess must be tightly integrated and well controlled to minimize or eliminate revenue losses. Figure 6–1 reviews the subprocesses and the associated goals:

| Record all customers in CIS | Read all meters | Account for all usage | Bill all customers on right rate | Collect all receivables |

Fig. 6–1. Revenue cycle subprocesses and goals

Achieving the goals identified in figure 6–1 represents a meter-to-cash cycle with zero defects. However, utilities have not achieved this level of perfection. The most successful utilities are identifying the defects in their meter-to-cash cycle, prioritizing, and implementing strategies to minimize the losses associated with the defects.

Recording customers on the CIS involves processes and controls to accurately identify and record customers who are using energy. Ideally customers contact their utilities to notify them that service needs to be initiated. This does not always happen, particularly in situations where the service remains on after a customer notifies the utility of the need to close the account. Utilities also face challenges due to fraud, transient customers, customer data changes, and technology limitations. Having a database with a high integrity of customer data will minimize revenue losses due to unaccounted for usage and bad debt write-off.

Reading meters involves accurately reading and recording usage. Potential problems include access issues and meters not coded into the system. Utilities may use encoder receiver transmitters (ERTs), which are radio-based modules that fit on electric, gas, and water meters. Unresponsive ERTs hamper meter reading. The combination of targeted employee, process, and technology initiatives can be instrumental in improving the meter reading percentages.

Accounting for usage involves ensuring accurate usage data and mapping usage to the appropriate customers. Accounting for usage is challenged by deliberate theft, defective meters, and processes that inherently incur some usage, like soft disconnects.

Billing customers on the right rate involves accurately billing based on usage, billing determinants, and appropriate rates. The billing department is challenged to ensure customers are on the correct rates due to customer changes, inaccurate customer information, or order backlogs.

For a utility to collect all receivables will involve offering a variety of payment options, reporting and tracking of receivables, appropriate application of payments, and audit trails. The collections process is challenged by *can't pay* customers and *won't pay* customers.

With a common understanding of the key subprocesses involved in the revenue cycle, it is time to turn to common utility issues with each subprocess. Many utilities have focused efforts on minimizing revenue leakage by appropriately using technology, process improvement, and employee engagement. The next section looks at each subprocess and addresses the common challenges and strategies others have used to reduce or mitigate revenue losses associated with the subprocess.

RECORD ALL CUSTOMERS IN THE CIS

To accurately record all customers in the CIS involves a combination of well-engineered processes and technology. There are several processes involved with ensuring a high level of customer data integrity. The customer application process, new service connection process, and account maintenance process are all important to maintaining accurate customer data. Robust and tightly integrated CIS and construction work management systems provide a platform to minimize errors due to the lack of timely, accurate data transfer or employee input. The combination of process and technology limitations creates exposure to utilities for inaccurate information. The good news is that there are effective strategies to mitigate this exposure (table 6–1).

Challenge	Strategies
Record customer at premise	Complete hard disconnect process Use controlled soft shutoff process Partner with landlords Control new service connection process
Minimize inaccurate customer data	Secure key customer information Provide technology to support accurate data entry Prevent fraud
Maintain customer information	Update customer data Append customer data
Monitor and reduce order backlog	Automate paper processes Monitor aging reports

Table 6–1. Challenges and strategies to accurately record all customers

Record customer at premise

Ideally customers contact their utility to inform them of the need for service. Utilities with a hard disconnect policy have a built-in incentive for the customer to contact the utility, since the service is not available otherwise. This places a high degree of control with the utility. Revenue leakage is clearly reduced with a hard disconnect policy.

Utilities that have a hard disconnect policy are staffed to support this policy from a call center and field perspective. Hard disconnects will result in increased calls to the call center requesting service. Utilities encourage customers to call early to request service initiation, but unfortunately many customers wait until the last minute and then want service immediately.

Repeat calls are also an issue when the customer-requested connection is not completed in the time frame that the customer expected. They can also be a problem if there was some issue that prohibited the field technician from initiating service at the premise. The utility faces a resource issue of being able to respond to the number of inquiries. The requests for service turn on often increase at the beginning of the month and towards the end of the week, creating a peak in work and increased call volume.

Utilities are finding that real-time field updates with mobile data are helpful in situations where the service could not be turned on. The CSR can access the field orders and see the disposition of the order. For example, if the field technician was unable to initiate service due to access or safety issues, the CSR can inform the customer of the reason for the delay. Customers are more reasonable if they understand the reason that service was not connected. The CSR can inform the customer of the steps he needs to take to get the service initiated.

From a resource perspective, utilities can extend their hours of service to include weekends and evenings so that service connections can be completed when the customer requested the connection. Often a fee is charged for connections during these extended hours. Utilities may also encourage the customer to be ready to take service by charging a fee if a repeat visit is required. This is helpful in minimizing *can't get in* situations, in which access is unavailable to the field technician.

Utilities may use a controlled soft disconnect policy to avoid some of the resource and customer issues associated with hard disconnects. A well-controlled soft shutoff policy is customer friendly and reduces fieldwork, but it does present increased exposure of unaccounted for usage.

Utilities using a soft shutoff policy need to have a very controlled policy in place. This is often a rich area of opportunity to minimize revenue leakage. Controlled soft shutoff policies usually include a combination of targeted hard shutoffs and clear thresholds of usage or time that will result in a hard shutoff.

Utilities with a soft shutoff system will identify accounts with which they will continue to complete hard disconnects. For example, a utility may use soft shutoffs for residential accounts but hard shutoffs for commercial and industrial accounts. Utilities may segment the residential accounts. In the situation of commercial and industrial customers, savvy utilities are contacting the premise via phone to inform them of the pending hard disconnect. Most commercial customers do not want service interrupted and are very quick to initiate service. This practice minimizes the field work associated with targeted hard disconnects. At NSTAR, 70% of commercial customers scheduled for hard disconnects complete the application via phone, avoiding the field visit.

Strong reporting that quickly identifies premises where either the usage or time frame has exceeded acceptable thresholds is a mainstay in a controlled soft shutoff process. Utilities may automatically create field orders based on exceeding thresholds. The key in a well-controlled soft shutoff process is to complete these orders promptly. It is critical to establish tight thresholds and staff appropriately to complete field activity to minimize revenue leakage in a soft shutoff environment.

Timely, comprehensive meter reading is critical in a well-controlled soft shutoff environment. If consumption is registered on the inactive meter beyond an acceptable threshold, a hard shutoff work order is processed to encourage the new customer to apply for service.

Utilities operating with hard shutoff and soft shutoff systems will aggressively pursue partnerships with landlords. Such partnerships can be arranged when the landlord agrees that once a tenant closes an account, the service is automatically placed in the landlord's name. Any usage during the period between tenants is the landlord's responsibility. Landlords therefore are encouraged to ensure their new tenants apply for service.

Progressive utilities are even providing the landlord with access to initiate the customer's service at the time of signing the lease agreement. This may be accomplished through a Web site that easily allows the landlord to notify the utility of a new customer and to update the information.

New service requests create exposure for a utility to ensure that once the new service is built, the customer of record is then metered and billed. External forces that are somewhat out of the utility's control can further challenge the new service request process. An example of this is the permitting process, which can vary from town to town. Sometimes contractors do not follow the process or are not aware of the appropriate steps needed to secure service.

One of the best methods for a utility to identify where there may be exposure in its new customer connect process is to talk to its frontline employees. They sometimes are aware of electricians and plumbers who bypass the system and connect customers. They also are the eyes for the utility in spotting temporary services that are now serving a permanent facility.

Ensuring that there is strong, timely linkage between the work management system and the CIS can enhance securing a customer of record. Having controls in place that match new meter sets in the work management system with CIS active accounts is a best practice. Minimizing reentry of data from the work management and CIS units will reduce errors.

Minimize inaccurate customer data

During the application process, utilities secure key customer information. This customer information is important to ensure that customers are on the appropriate rate and to document customer contact information. This is a problematic area, as it often relies on customers providing accurate information. Addressing this through both process and technology is a sound approach.

From a process perspective, utilities need to identify required key customer information. Capturing accurate information up front as the customer applies is a first and critical step in mitigating bad debt write-off. This key information includes customer data, contact information, employer, and household information.

The single most important item of customer information is the social security number. Interestingly, even though social security numbers are a fundamental data element to ensure a more robust recovery cycle, some utilities choose not to request social security numbers in order to reduce call handle time. Unfortunately while this move may save dollars up front, in the life cycle of the account, it will cost more due to reduced recoveries and increased back office costs in skip tracing and returned mail.

Well-designed CIS or CRM systems can increase the accuracy of customer initiation by requiring key customer information and including edit checks to ensure accurate entry. CIS units with required address entry corresponding to U.S. postal requirements are a best practice.

The lack of edit checks in the work management was highlighted for one utility when it sought ways to reduce the instances of bad addresses in its CIS. The team's research identified that a majority of the incorrect addresses on account initiation occurred when the account was associated with new construction. This mail address information was passed from the work management system to the CIS. However, the work management system did not have automatic edit checks to ensure that addresses were in the correct U.S. mail format. The short-term solution was improved training. The long-term solution was to add the edit checks into the work management system.

During service initiation, ensuring that the customer on the phone is in fact a legitimate customer is a growing concern. Utilities are implementing processes to identify and mitigate fraud up front during service initiation. To this end, third-party services and data repositories are available to confirm identification.

Identity verification is available through the credit bureaus for a nominal fee. The bureaus will provide to the CSR either affirmation that the identity is confirmed or a flag that suggests additional information is needed for confirmation. The flags are generated when the information provided by the customer does not match information in the credit bureau. For example, if the customer provided a social security number of a minor, the bureau would send a flag.

Some innovative utilities address these mismatches with a fraud prevention team. These teams have procedures and links to external databases that enhance their ability to confirm identity. As will be discussed further in chapter 8, "Reduce Bad Debt," an up-front fraud team is an excellent tool to mitigate write-offs by catching problems early in the life cycle of the account.

Maintain customer information

While securing accurate information up front is a key step, it is also important to maintain accurate information on customers. Information initially gathered in the application process degrades with time. Phone numbers, mail addresses, and contact information will change over time. Even the customer of record may change status, as when the customer passes away. Hence it is important to have processes in place to maintain accurate, current customer information.

One easy way to maintain accurate customer information is to update the information every time the customer calls. A utility can create a culture where CSRs automatically confirm key contact information. Prompting CSRs with highlighted fields is a more robust method to ensure information is updated. Credit card and catalog companies have updating customer information down to a science, with required confirmation built into their customer systems and scripting. A best practice is to highlight on the CIS screen key information to confirm, such as the customer's phone number, employer, and billing address.

Appending key customer information to the CIS database is another best practice. Utilities are surgically appending their CIS databases with external third parties. This means that utilities are not appending information on every account, but rather they are integrating their append strategy to their credit strategy, and appending at-risk customers. Commonly appended fields include: social security numbers, phone numbers, and addresses. More information on how a utility can maintain and augment customer data is included in chapter 8.

Monitor and reduce order backlog

Processing orders promptly is a key to ensuring an up-to-date CIS. Automation is the best solution here, where orders are processed in real time using field and office automation. But many utilities still rely on paper orders, which unfortunately can get lost, be entered incorrectly, or be significantly delayed for entry.

Best practices for utilities still relying on paper orders is to create a culture that has a passion for completing work orders promptly. If order backlog is an issue for a utility, one should consider creating an *aging work order report* and then target performance metrics around minimizing or eliminating aged orders.

One utility implemented an aging report and was surprised at the volume of orders that were in the 30- and 60-day categories. The utility launched a team to reduce the backlog and to identify key contributors to the backlog. A major contributor was the reliance on paper orders. This effort supported the implementation of mobile data. In the interim, the team identified areas that were most challenged with processing paper orders. The combination of process changes and reallocation of resources eliminated the 60-day category and reduced the 30-day category by 40%.

READ ALL METERS

Reading all meters is a challenging process from two perspectives. The most common is reading all the meters that are in CIS. The DataSource indicates that a select few utilities are achieving best-in-class performance of 99.99% of all meters read each month.[2] A second challenge is with meters or premises that should be read that are not on the CIS (table 6–2).

Challenge	Strategies
Improve meter reading performance	Invest in automated meter reading (AMR) Invest in meter reading systems Address access issues Address ERTs not responding
Ensure all meters are recorded on CIS	Engage employees Enhance controls in new customer connect process

Table 6–2. Challenges and strategies to read all meters

As one talks to utility professionals, one will hear many entertaining stories of meters that were not read for long periods of time, if ever. One revenue protection specialist relayed a story about a gas service on a new home that had been place for more than 10 years. The problem was that the new service was never recorded on the CIS, nor was the meter installation recorded. The customer had been receiving free gas for all this time. The meter was an inside meter on an AMR route.

This situation highlights the challenge with AMR in that there are no eyes in the field walking the route to notice that a premise is being skipped. Even with manual routes, this type of situation might go unnoticed as the meter reader may assume the premise is noted in another book.

I asked the revenue protection specialist how he found the account. Interestingly he said that the customer came forward and admitted having the service. A settlement was reached between the utility and the customer. The impetus for the customer coming forward was the pending sale of the home, in which an undocumented gas service might have created some issues for a clean transfer of ownership.

Situations like this make reading all meters problematic. This particular situation touches on several subprocesses, including recording all customers and reading all meters.

Improve meter reading performance

AMR is one of the most reliable ways to ensure that all meters are read. LeRoy Nosbaum, CEO of ITRON, notes, "The business case for AMR is quite compelling."[3] The opportunity that Nosbaum points to is to leverage AMR and meter data to transform the business, not just incrementally improve the business. More detail on the transformational opportunities and the business case for AMR will be explored in chapter 12.

At NSTAR, for example, our meter reading percentages have increased from 96% in 2002 to 98% in 2004, with one-third the resources. NSTAR faced some challenging customer dynamics serving the highly urban downtown Boston area, where 80% of the meters were inside the premise. Relying on meter readers to maintain, and gain access to, these meters each month was problematic. Meter readers not only braved dark cellars, narrow stairs, and the goodwill of the premise owner for access, they also dealt with customers who had no intention of allowing access.

Most utilities have some penetration of AMR in their meter population. Surgically installing AMR to lower costs and address access is a common approach. Fixed network AMR installations, which provide daily data, is a robust AMR platform. This platform provides data that can be used by many areas of the utility, but it is also more expensive. Mobile data technologies are more commonly deployed, with 40% penetration.[4]

With manually read meters, a culture where employees have ownership and are given incentives to secure accurate reads is a best practice. Solid meter reading programs have processes in place to quickly assess skipped or missed meters and to apply resources to secure reads. Utilities are linking meter reading rewards and pay to quality performance as measured by number of skips and meter reading errors.

Utilities are also investing in their meter reading systems. Many are upgrading their meter reading management systems to provide timely, easily accessed information for enhanced meter reading management. Robust systems provide this information at nearly real time from the point of meter reading data upload. This information is available to the meter reading supervisor, who is aided in planning the work for the following day.

This is a vast improvement from older systems, which only provided information on meter reading performance after an overnight batch process. This delay left little time for a supervisor to thoughtfully adjust routes to catch skipped meters, or even complete routes. One should remember that the supervisor will also be dealing with the unexpected situations that arise daily, like employees calling in sick or vehicles not working.

Proactively dealing with repeat access problems is an underutilized opportunity for many utilities. There are many reasons why meters cannot be accessed. For manual meter reading, this can range from dogs to terrain, construction, and customer prevention. Utilities too often do not actively address customer access issues and continue to allow the meter to be estimated. This is changing, though, as utilities put in place technology and processes that identify access problems and launch a series of actions to address these problems.

From a technology perspective, meter readers are provided information on their handheld devices, including data concerning the number of consecutive estimates. This prompts the meter reader to go to an extra effort to secure a read by perhaps going to the premise at a different time, or leaving instructions for the customer to call in the read.

From a process perspective, utilities are addressing accounts with access issues with soft reminders to the customers via letters or phone calls. If the problem persists, the utility will escalate the action up to and including service termination for a customer not providing meter readers access to the meter. In the extreme cases of service termination, utilities may choose to place some type of automated metering at the premise to mitigate further issues.

With AMR installations, it is important to have a process in place to address ERTs not responding. The ERTs encode consumption data and tamper data from the meter and communicate via radio to a data collection system. The most common reasons for ERTs not responding are battery failure and location. Early vintages of ERTs, installed in the late 1980s and early 1990s, had battery lives of seven to nine years. Current technology has doubled this battery life expectancy.

Utilities need to monitor, research, and address ERT failures. Reports that highlight repeat ERT failures are good tools to identify true problems. Utilities with mobile ARM installations should establish a threshold of repeat failures that generate a field order to investigate. The result may be that the location of the meter does not allow the signal to reach the mobile unit. This can occur with new meter sets and also existing services where renovation had occurred.

Escalating ERT failure rates may signal the need for a large-scale replacement of ERTs. The utility may have installed a large number of ERT-based meters that are nearing the end of their life cycle.

An urban utility was experiencing an increase in ERTs not responding. Their analysis revealed some common problems. The most prevalent reason was due to battery failure due to the batteries nearing the end of their life cycle. Another reason was premise renovation, such as a condo basement that had been renovated into a laundry area. After the renovation, the mobile unit could not read the signal from the meter. The utility also discovered issues when new services were initiated. The AMR meter was folioed into a mobile route. The problem was that the meter was in a tall building. The team discovered that the van signal had good reliability for only 10 floors. If meters were located above the 10th floor, the signal could not be recorded. In this case, a census of meters located above the 10th floor was completed, and these meters were moved to a radio-enabled handheld unit. A process was also put into place to ensure that new AMR meter sets were appropriately folioed into the right type of reader, mobile or radio-enabled handheld.

Ensure all meters are recorded on the CIS

Utilities that suspect there may be meters on the system that are not recorded in the CIS are using a combination of engaging employees and enhancing controls. Utilities encourage and even give incentives to employees who report any metering issues. This employee engagement is helpful with several of the subprocesses of the revenue cycle. A utility's field employees are its eyes on the cash register. Enhancing controls in the new customer connect process to ensure that all new services are metered and billed is also important.

Utility customer service leaders have a responsibility to ensure employees understand the linkage between the meter, billing, and ultimately the company's financial performance. Creating this line of sight is powerful in that employees will make better day-to-day decisions, be attuned, and take action with situations that are unusual. Utilities can tap into this alignment by asking employees to be on the lookout for unusual metering situations and report them, even rewarding employees who do so. It is important, though, that once a utility asks for the feedback that it has a process in place to promptly review, investigate, and resolve the situation.

Some utilities get into a trap in which administering the program from an employee perspective consumes more time than the benefits warrant. Some incentive programs create ill-will among the employees, which defeats the purpose. The most effective employee engagement programs are simple in design and easy to administer. These programs have the support of IT platforms, which automate much of the processing of the employee communication.

Reviewing and re-engineering the new customer connection process can be a very lucrative initiative from a controls and customer satisfaction perspective. The new customer connection process for utilities is often very complex and involves many handoffs. The systems that support the new customer connection process may not be as robust as needed.

Documenting the process for new customer connects and highlighting the control points on the process map is an excellent tool to improve the confidence associated with ensuring all new meter sets are recorded on the CIS. Another approach is to take situations where meters have been located and not recorded on CIS and backtrack to discover how the situation occurred. After tracking the steps of several occurrences, typically some areas will surface where there are issues to resolve, such as with the employees, process, or technology.

A powerful control report is one that compares meter set orders to an active account in the CIS. Exceptions noted in this control report should be tracked and researched to expose process problems.

ACCOUNT FOR ALL USAGE

Ensuring usage data is accurate and accounted for continues to challenge utilities. Losses are inherent in electric, gas, and water systems. Utilities address usage by having processes in place to ensure that recorded usage is the actual usage and that written-off usage is minimized (table 6–3).

Challenge	Strategies
Written off usage	Control the soft shutoff process Monitor and address issues promptly Control the flat rate process
Accurate metering	Maintain and test meters Use solid state metering Identify and fix defective meters
Deliberate fraud	Use AMR systems Mine data Engage employees Define and enforce meter security Establish a revenue assurance team

Table 6–3. Challenges and strategies to account for all usage

Written-off usage

The soft disconnect policy exposes utilities to written-off usage. Well-managed soft disconnect policies result in nominal written-off usage. Management reports that monitor and trend written-off usage associated with soft shutoff is one tool to ensure the policy is working as designed. Additionally, creating reports that monitor the soft shutoff process at key thresholds will identify when the policy is going adrift. For example, an aging report can review the backlog orders generated due to the passing of a certain time threshold from the final soft disconnect. If the threshold is 30 days from the customer closing the account, then at that 30-day point, a field order should be generated and completed for a hard shutoff. Sometimes due to workload, weather, and other priorities, the backlog may grow. Having a report that monitors the aging of these reports by time and by usage is a good tool to use to ensure priorities are appropriate.

Sometimes a utility is operating a hard shutoff process and is considering a soft shutoff process or is merging CIS units. It is important that the utility take time to clearly identify the key controls needed in the new or merged CIS. Legacy CIS units are generally designed for the process the utility was using at the time of implementation. For example, if a utility was using hard shutoffs, the coding will not be in place to provide control reports to support an efficient, controlled soft shutoff.

Meters that measure company use create usage that in some cases may be written off. A better approach is to apply the same process to company meters as would be applied to customer meters. The cleanest, most accurate approach is to establish the company as a customer and create a bill. This mitigates the exposure to written-off usage.

Flat rates, where a meter is not installed, but rather the customer is billed on an established fixed tariff, create exposure for unaccounted for usage and revenue. Flat rates are used by utilities for a variety of items, like cable attachments, streetlights, billboards, and temporary services. There are a couple of methods to ensure that the inventory of flat rate accounts is correct. A periodic field audit can be completed to validate that the locations noted in the billing system represent all the locations that require a flat rate bill. For cable attachments, utilities may include the cost of a periodic survey in the rate, along with penalties for attachments identified that are not being billed. Another approach is to match records with the customers to compare premises. In the case of streetlights, a comparison of the utility records against the town records on a regular basis keeps the billing system accurate. Periodically confirming and documenting that the flat rate is valid is also a good practice. This can be done by installing metering equipment at a sample of flat rate premises and recording the usage.

Utilities have found that if regular attention has not been paid to maintaining accurate billing records for flat rates, there may be revenue dollars leaking from the process. Because flat rates are an exception, the management time and control rigor are not always as strongly in place as they should be. The area of flat rates can be low-hanging fruit from a revenue enhancement perspective if diligence has not been paid in the past to maintaining accurate records.

Accurate metering

Utilities operate with a variety of meter classes and vintages on their systems. Ensuring that these meters are registering accurately involves proactively maintaining and testing the installed meter population and using solid-state metering.

Utilities monitor the accuracy of their installed meter base generally through sampling meters on a regular basis. Utilities will sample various types of meter classes and verify the accuracy of usage measurement in a meter lab. Utilities do this as a preventative tool or due to regulatory requirement. The benefit to statistically valid samples is that meter problems can be identified. This enables the utility to be thoughtful and deliberate in changing out known problem meters.

The best utilities have a deep understanding of their installed meter base. These utilities break down their installed meter base by vintage year, manufacturer, meter type, and load. These attributes drive the frequency of failures. For example, if a sample test yields results pointing to a unique year and manufacturer, a larger statistical sample will be pulled to verify this information.

Utility meter experts will share their knowledge and experience at various conferences and other venues. Savvy utility employees will be listening for any aberrations noted in a specific meter population, as the same issue may be true for their population.

Solid-state metering provides enhanced accuracy to record usage, particularly in situations of low usage, where electromechanical meters may not record. Solid-state metering brings another benefit in demand meters as it provides the capability for more accurate determination of the peak demand in a 15-minute period.

Electromechanical meters, while a mainstay for utilities, are prone to registering low in low-usage situations. These meters are gear driven, and when usage is very low, there may not be adequate inertia to generate movement of the gears. Electromechanical demand meters are limited to a 15-minute block to determine peak demand usage. The 15-minute blocks register average peak demand for the 15 minutes from 00 to 15, 15 to 30, 30 to 45, and 45 to 60.

For electric demand metering, a utility should consider enhancing the quality and accuracy of the average peak demand calculation by using solid-state metering. Solid-state demand metering enables the utility to calculate the average peak over 15-minute intervals more frequently. Utilities with solid-state demand metering are using 5-minute intervals to recalculate demand. This creates 12 periods within an hour. In the example of a 5-minute interval, a utility calculates demand from 00 to 15, 05 to 20, 10 to 25, and so on. The more frequent demand calculation more accurately captures the highest 15-minute average demand. Utilities that more frequently measure demand have seen increases on those accounts of 0.5% or higher.

Defective meters will not accurately record usage. A combination of reactive and proactive processes can minimize losses associated with defective meters.

From a proactive process, there are some types of meters, like large gas meters, that require additional care and attention to ensure they are. registering properly. A planned maintenance program is well worth the investment. The maintenance program will identify meter defects and correct them.

Utilities also need reactive processes in place for identified meter damage. Meter readers and other field employees are in a great position to spot and report issues. My experience is that meter reading employees have great ownership for noting meter reading issues, like damaged meters, access problems, or broken seals.

The challenge seems to be in following through with action on the reported damage. It is important to apply resources to review and correct the noted situations. This will create an environment in which employees take ownership in detailing an unusual meter situation with confidence that management will address the issue. If this is not true, employees will quickly quit providing feedback concerning what they see in the field.

Utilities that process the meter reading comments well have systems that automatically create orders or reports sorted for easy review. Automatic orders might be appropriate for any damaged meter reports. Broken seal information may be more effectively managed by creating an application that allows for instances of multiple broken seals to be highlighted. A single broken seal can occur for many legitimate reasons. It may not be cost-effective to send out field resources on each broken seal.

Deliberate fraud

Deliberate fraud is often very challenging to detect. Utilities lose an estimated 1%–2% of annual revenue due to theft. The most effective revenue protection programs today use a combination of predictive sophisticated analytical models and reactive processes based on employee or customer reports.

While some theft is fairly easy to spot, like knives put into an empty meter base or illegal overhead taps, other theft is more difficult to catch. The theft may not be clearly visible to an observer. Utilities are also getting more sophisticated in their approach to identifying theft. They use sophisticated data mining techniques to take customer attributes, like location and usage, and link this information to system load and weather data to predict potential theft.

AMR systems have tremendous potential to identify theft. Many AMR systems have tamper and current diversion detection capabilities that include alarms that signal meter tilts and rotations, the presence of magnets, and power outages. AMR alarms can trigger when there is usage on an inactive account or when usage falls below an established threshold.

The challenge utilities with AMR have is sorting which of the alarms are real issues. BG&E found that 80%–90% of the tamper flags were not related to theft.[5] Data mining and predictive analysis techniques aid in filtering the numerous AMR tamper flags to sort out the more credible areas of concern. For example, an AMR tamper flag can be compared with connect and disconnect orders. If the flag noted a meter removal, it likely does not need field investigation.

One should not underestimate the power of customer and employee leads in combating theft. Honest customers do not like the fact that others are getting a free ride. Providing a secure, anonymous way for customers to report suspected theft is a best practice. Periodically reminding customers about the dangers of theft in bill inserts, or through other existing media, is also helpful.

Employees will also be supportive in identifying potential theft. The utility should make it easy for employees to identify and report broken seals and other irregularities. Some utilities provide incentives to their employees who provide leads on theft. The challenge with incentive programs is in making them fair and simple to understand and administer.

Meter security is another proactive strategy to minimize theft or unauthorized usage. Utilities need to have a clear policy on which meters it will lock and seal and should be sure the locks are sufficient to deter theft. As a wise revenue protection person once shared, if one would not leave one's car unlocked in the city, why would a utility leave its meters unlocked? It is a good question. The most appropriate seal and lock policy will depend on the utility and its service territory.

An effective strategy to identify theft is to establish a revenue assurance team. The focus of this team is to identify and act on situations in which there is unaccounted for revenue. This team is most effective if tightly linked to field technicians who can investigate unusual situations. The revenue assurance team will use a combination of leads from employees and customers, along with data mining, to identify potential theft situations.

BILL ALL CUSTOMERS ON THE RIGHT RATE

Utility CIS units do an excellent job of accurately billing customers based on the customer rate information, usage, and billing determinants that are recorded in the system. The challenge occurs when the information in the CIS is incorrect. Utilities have a variety of rate structures, some more complicated than others. Each utility will therefore have its own unique controls and rate check processes that ensure the most accurate rate.

Utilities face challenges related to accurately determining a rate when customers are initiating service and when they initiate changes at their premises that impact the rate. Utilities with rates based on heating types are impacted when those customers change their heat source.

Utilities like Tampa Electric take pride in ensuring that their customers are on the best and most accurate rate for their business. They would challenge a rate consultant to find an account that met the requirements for a better rate. How do utilities create that level of confidence? They have a combination of several effective measures. These include effective controls in setting and recording meter constants, effective controls when implementing rate changes, and ongoing analysis of customers and rates using rate analysis applications (table 6–4).

Challenge	Strategies
Minimize inaccurate meter data	Establish sound field procedures Automate processes Complete field audits
Place customers on most appropriate rate	Institute controls on service initiation Institute rate change controls Complete rate reviews

Table 6–4. Challenges and strategies to bill all customers on the right rate

Minimize inaccurate meter data

Large customers have meter installations that are more complex and include key meter constant data that are integral for accurate billing. Most utilities today are still paper based when it comes to completing meter sets. There is inherent opportunity for error in writing down the appropriate meter constants and then entering these into the system.

A good field procedure is to note key metering criteria on a form that remains at the metering installation. For example, on a large electric metering installation, noting the potential transformer (PT) and current transformer (CT) ratios, the date of the installation, and the meter number would be key information. This is helpful when changes or replacements to the metering installation occur in the future. This minimizes the opportunity for error in the field.

Automation is also a great tool. Field installers with portable computers that have the most current meter and customer information are in the best position to enter updated information based on fieldwork. This eliminates the opportunity for error that occurs by routing and rekeying information. Robust mobile data systems will provide field technicians with additional information and edit checks that validate entry.

Utilities will complete field audits of metering installations to verify that the installation is working as designed and that all of the information appropriate to the installation is accurately recorded on the CIS. If the utility finds an issue during the field audits, then analysis can be completed on the common denominator of the problem.

Utilities also can use data mining to assess potential issues with metering data. For example, if meters have been changed out due to an AMR initiative, then an analysis of customer bills before and after installation can provide a quick scan of issues. At NSTAR, we have installed more than 25,000 demand AMR meters. We are using a combination of AMR flags and data mining to double-check customers impacted by the meter changes to ensure that their bills continue to be accurate.

Place customers on the most accurate rate

During service application it is important to have an up-front process that provides appropriate prompts and edits for CSRs to place customers on the correct rate from the start. Since business customers are more complex with respect to rates, having a dedicated business team can enhance billing accuracy and improve customer satisfaction.

CIS edits and procedures can mitigate to a great extent customers going onto incorrect rates. One utility found that in an effort to process a call faster, rate information from the existing premise would be copied to the new account. The result was bad rate data, among other items. For example, if the previous customer qualified for the low-income discounted rate, copying information to the new customer placed the new customer on the low-income rate, regardless of whether or not the new customer qualified for this assistance. While training and communication reduced the occurrence of this situation, it was not eliminated until a new CRM package was implemented. This package included input data controls and automatic edits to ensure that the CSR made a deliberate decision about the rate.

Many utilities offer customers special rates, like low-income rates, that require recertification on a periodic basis. Ideally, automated systems and processes are in place that routinely canvas CIS accounts for those due to be recertified and automatically initiate letters to the customer to complete an application for recertification. There can be a great deal of dollars associated with customers on the wrong rate.

Linking directly with various agencies that certify customers, versus waiting or relying on customer self-reference, can help a utility enhance rate accuracy and minimize extra work. For example, if a customer qualifies for a low-income rate as of November 1st, but does not notify the utility until January, some utilities are required to cancel the prior bills and reissue them on the low-income rate as of November 1st.

When billing rates must be adjusted or changed, it is important to ensure that the changes are completed accurately. Best practices include solid control and approval processes for any rate changes. The controls need to be jointly developed between the business and the IT organization completing the programming. Once the programming is completed, a solid testing process to ensure the rates are operating as designed is fundamental. This testing is most appropriately done by the business.

Utilities that have good testing procedures in place will map out a test plan that targets the various customer segments impacted by a billing change and identifies scenarios for each of those customer segments. Using a test database that mirrors the CIS data, testers can then complete the test plans to ensure the programming changes are operating as designed. Controlled sign-off procedures by the business and IT then permit the changes to be implemented with the actual customers. Utilities may also choose a final check of segregating the printed bills for a last check on the rate change.

Utilities with confidence in having customers on the right rates complete annual rate reviews. These reviews involve sampling customers on each rate to affirm the rate is valid. This sampling process will surface systemic issues if some customers are on an inappropriate rate. Solutions to correct the situation can be identified and implemented.

COLLECT ALL RECEIVABLES

Payment issues are dissatisfying to customers and result in a great deal of extra work. In the advent of the Sarbanes Oxley Act, this is an area where companies have reviewed their control procedures and enhanced them, if needed. From a credit standpoint, the utilities that are successful in lowering write-offs have a process in place that is consistent, proactive, and aligned with the entire organization. Collecting all receivables involves reporting and tracking of receivables and appropriate application of payments and audit trails (table 6–5). Collection activities are challenged by *can't pay* customers and *won't pay* customers.

Challenge	Strategies
Minimize payment issues	Offer a variety of payment options Resolve payment issues promptly Reconcile daily
Improve credit and collections processing	Use life cycle approach to credit and collections Establish shared goals

Table 6–5. Challenges and strategies to collect all receivables

Minimize payment issues

To ensure timely collection of receivables, it is important to provide customers multiple payment options. This convenience has very positive results as measured by customer satisfaction, improvements in receivables, and reductions in days revenue outstanding (DRO). A variety of real-time payment options, like prepay, credit card, and pay via phone can assist the utility when working with delinquent accounts. When efforts to reach a delinquent account are successful, the utility does not want to lose the opportunity to collect the required balance because of limited payment options.

Strategies to minimize payment issues include having strong controls and ensuring a timely reconciliation process. Companies offering multiple services with associated billing are more exposed to payment issues. Partial payments particularly become problematic in this case if the customer has not clearly identified the payment appropriation. The number of payment entry points also creates opportunities for problems.

At NSTAR, we were successful in providing our customers who are on both electric and gas service one bill with both stubs, although this change did create some issues on the payment side. Our remittance processor has enhanced its equipment to detect any situation where there is more than one payment or one stub in an envelope. These are segregated for manual review and then processed.

The most effective receivable processes identify and resolve misapplied payments quickly. Technology is aiding this process. If remittance is outsourced, many of these organizations now have the capability to create images of both sides of the check for each payment. This online file is available real-time to the user and is helpful in quickly researching a customer payment or completing daily reconciliations of misapplied payments. Utilities completing remittance in-house have the benefit of locating the team handling misapplied payments with the team processing payments.

Utilities operating physical offices have added challenges. Each office must complete accurate, timely reconciliation. The control of the process is now more dispersed. Additionally, utilities collecting cash must plan for and mitigate the potential of robbery and embezzlement. After a series of attempted robberies, one utility renovated each office to include bulletproof material from floor to ceiling. Paying for armored vehicle pickup for cash deposits must also be considered.

Reconciling the accounts daily offers the opportunity to catch errors quickly while they can be fixed without the customers or the financial statements being impacted. Listening to customer feedback is also a good predictor of payment issues. It is important to monitor the number of calls on misapplied payments and to watch for increases in order to quickly detect problems. One office manager told me about a customer complaint on the delay in posting the payment made in the local office. The office manager's investigation into this situation revealed an employee who was kiting money by postdating the transactions.

Improve credit and collections processing

Excellent utilities with respect to credit and collections are looking at the entire life cycle of an account from the point of customer application all the way through to finaling the account or to the sale of the bad-debt portfolio. These utilities have an aligned focus on credit and collection and have shared goals. Chapter 8 provides much greater detail on the strategies for collections on accounts that are active, delinquent, and finaled.

With current accounts, the strategies identified are low-cost, high-value strategies. These early interventions can have a major impact in downstream write-offs. The strategies range from the basics of capturing thorough and accurate information up front as the customer applies for service to having established processes in place to identify and mitigate fraud.

Collecting deposits is a good method to mitigate later receivables exposure. Having a good process to minimize and quickly process returned mail would aid in reducing DRO. Impacting both customer satisfaction and improving receivables is a strategy behind proactive outreach to customers offering energy assistance and energy saving ideas and services.

Strategies to process delinquent accounts are varied and range from low-cost reminder letters and bill messages to higher cost field visits. The savviest utilities use behavioral-based scoring to improve the cost-effectiveness of their collections process. A foundation in dealing effectively with delinquent accounts is to have a credit policy in place and to monitor various credit reports.

A dedicated team providing credit support to customers is an excellent strategy to ensure consistence adherence to credit policies and guidelines. Outbound notification of customers in arrears through calls and letters is a commonly used strategy. A powerful tool for the utility credit leader is the ability to physically disconnect service due to nonpayment. This practice requires expensive field visits and has its greatest impact when linked to behavioral-based scoring to surgically target field disconnections that are the most cost-effective.

Once an account is finaled, cycle time to reach the customer of record becomes important. With each day, the likelihood of collection diminishes, and the value of the debt portfolio also diminishes. Utilities typically complete in-house collection activities for a period of time before writing off the account. Many customers who final their account will reapply for service at another location within the utility's service territory. Some utilities partner with data exchanges where information on customer moves is shared. This aids in locating the customer for collections.

Once an account is written off, utilities partner with third-party agencies to complete skip tracing activities. Utilities may have primary, secondary, and even tertiary agencies that pursue debt. Legal collection involves pursuing legal action to either secure an account or pursue a collection. Another strategy is to sell bad debt. Additional ideas and information on reducing bad debt are delineated in chapter 8.

One excellent way to improve credit and collections is to establish shared goals between the credit team and field team. Common goals and measures using a shared scorecard highlight the importance of credit with other key functions. This drives the right behavior.

IDENTIFY AND PRIORITIZE
METER-TO-CASH OPPORTUNITIES

Utilities find that there are many opportunities to improve their meter-to-cash cycle. The key is to identify those with the greatest potential for impact and to address those first. This section explores a process to identify and prioritize meter-to-cash opportunities (fig. 6–2) and includes a template that can be used to document and evaluate opportunities.

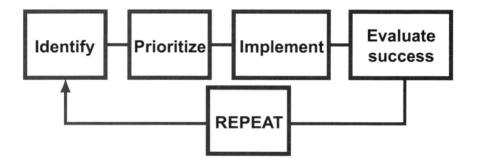

Fig. 6–2. Process to identify and prioritize meter-to-cash opportunities

To have success in reducing revenue loss, support needs to be in place from the top and from within the organization. LeRoy Nosbaum, CEO of Itron, has observed many utilities transform their business with key initiatives and automation. He notes, though "by far the most successful have top-down and bottom-up support for the activity. If you do not have support, you will get minimal to no benefit. If you have support from all levels for transformation, you will achieve significantly more benefit in hard dollars and soft benefits."[6]

If the support is in place to address revenue loss, then a cross-functional team can be launched, with representatives from various areas of customer care and operations along with subject matter experts in data analysis and data mining. With a dynamic team in place, a utility is ready to tackle the process of identifying, prioritizing, and addressing revenue loss. Chapter 13 will explore the keys to successful project management in more detail, including scope definition, management, organizational support, and change management.

Identify

In the first stage of identifying areas of loss, it is important to gather information and perspectives on the current revenue process. An interview of key stakeholders and subject matter experts is an excellent method to not only communicate and gather support for the project but to also develop ideas and hypotheses on areas of key exposure. Focus groups with frontline employees are another tool to generate ideas on where losses are occurring. Our employees see our system and implement our policies and procedures every day. They are some of the most knowledgeable people in determining where breakdowns occur, as they often are the ones that must repair the errors. Completing brainstorming sessions with stakeholders is yet another way to generate ideas on areas of opportunity. At this stage, the objective is to identify as many ideas as possible. These ideas can be later sorted, filtered, and analyzed with other data points to prioritize key opportunities.

Summarizing the key thoughts and ideas from the various interviews, focus groups, and brainstorming sessions will be revealing in identifying trends and areas of opportunity. The next step will be to gather intelligence and data that begin to give a scope to these various ideas.

For example, if broken meters are a key area, the utility's team should gather data on how many meters annually are reported broken and are fixed. Other utilities can be contacted to compare performance data in this area. Additionally, the team should gather information on key metrics currently in place to monitor the problem and identify the current owner of the process, if there is a clear owner.

To fully assess the current state, the team will also need to secure appropriate policies, procedures, and tariffs. If there are process maps existing, the team will need to secure these.

Prioritize

As the team enters the prioritization stage, they will have gathered and sorted through potentially hundreds of ideas to reduce revenue losses. These ideas will have been analyzed, sorted, and grouped into a more manageable number of potential areas for focus. One approach that is very effective in prioritizing is to evaluate each idea with respect to ease of implementation and value. In evaluating ideas, one should consider documenting responses to the following common attributes.

Description of potential problem. It is helpful to describe the problem and include available data that give a scope to the problem. Data on the transaction volume, customer counts, average dollar values, and external benchmarks are helpful.

Employee impacts. This describes any employees involved in the process and potential challenges to changing the process. This section identifies change management issues.

Technical issues. Technical issues may include lack of information or reports, any needed enhancements to various programs, and any new equipment.

Process issues. These issues pertain to potential regulatory policies or procedures that would need to be revised, and metrics that are currently in place to manage the process.

Value. This describes the estimated value or benefit to the utility of addressing the issue.

Implementation considerations. These include the needed actions to address the problem. This description will include key owners, resources, change management, and training issues.

With these and any other common attributes reviewed and addressed, the team can assess all opportunities by looking at the value and the relative ease of implementation. This sorting will clearly and quickly identify quick hits versus more transformational opportunities (fig. 6–3).

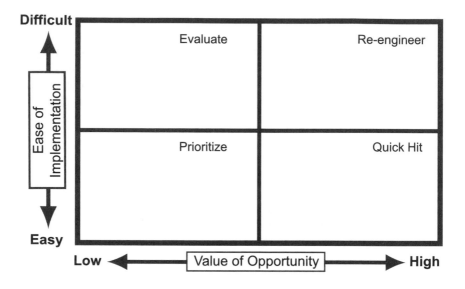

Fig. 6–3. Template for opportunity assessment

Implement

With the prioritization complete, one can then finalize which ideas will be implemented. The template will have identified the key resources and business owners. The final step is to put the plan into place and monitor the success.

Evaluate

Each template will have identified success measures that can be used to evaluate the implementation. Linking the success measures to corporate goals and individual performance is key to successful implementation. Implementation, unfortunately, is where many companies fail. They have the right ideas but lack the discipline to put the appropriate resources into place and ensure successful implementation.

One technique to ensure that focus stays with the implementation initiatives is to put a steering team into place that includes the key executives and appropriate team leaders. This team will monitor the implementation progress and address issues that arise along the way. This steering team can also take on the role of assessing overall success and identifying the next tier of projects, if applicable.

A disciplined approach to understanding the revenue cycle, identifying areas of opportunity, and implementing needed changes will minimize the losses associated with the process. Ideally, the re-engineered revenue process can provide reassurance to utility executives that they do know where 100% of their meters are at and that they are operating as designed.

REFERENCES

1   Taglienti, Richard. Vice president of marketing and revenue assurance, Peoples Energy; Interview, December 6, 2004.

2   AGA/EEI DataSource. "Percent of Reads Estimated." 2004.

3   Nosbaum, LeRoy. CEO, Itron; Interview, December 13, 2004.

4   "AMR Fixed Networks: Wireless vs. PLC." Chartwell Inc., August 2004.

5   Johnston, Garrett. "Taking a Crack at Revenue Robbers: Utilities Use AMR to Detect Theft." *Electric Light and Power.* June 2003.

6   Nosbaum, LeRoy. Interview, December 13, 2004.

7 OUTSOURCING

Outsourcing in general is on the rise, both in the utility industry and in the private sector. META Group Inc., a consulting and research firm, says that the outsourcing trend will grow by 20% per year though 2008 as more U.S. firms focus on cutting labor costs.[1] Outsourcing of utility customer service processes is also more prevalent. Chartwell research shows that in 1999, 8% of utilities outsourced some customer contact. The number has grown to 35% in only five years.

There are several components of utility customer service that can be outsourced, including the people, processes, and technology. Some utilities approach outsourcing with a surgical approach, only outsourcing specific transactions or functions. Others have outsourced the entire customer care business process. The right answer for each utility will be unique and will be predicated on its specific financial, technology, regulatory, and labor situation.

Investor-owned utilities (IOUs) are most likely to use outsourcing. Chartwell research indicates that more than 40% of IOUs outsource some aspect of customer contact. Municipals and cooperatives are less likely to outsource.[2] Jon Brock, CEO of Utilipoint, predicts increasing interest in outsourcing. He says the reason is the "increased visibility of high-profile deals like TXU, a Dallas Texas based energy company, and Capgemini, a consulting, technology, and outsourcing company. When TXU went to Wall Street highlighting a savings of $140 million, it caused leaders and owners of other utilities to pause and take note. Utility boards of directors have a fiduciary responsibility to ask the question of their company, 'Can we do this too?'"[3]

While the trend may be increasing, many customer service leaders at municipalities and co-ops share the sentiments of Mark Bolton, Coastal Electric Membership Corporation. He says, "The argument I'll give you is that we're very proud [of our setup]. When you call Coastal EMC, your call is answered by a real, live person, hopefully on the first or second ring, who's right here, who lives in the area and knows the area."[4]

Utility employees also have strong sentiments around outsourcing. They often point to the lack of pride and ownership an outsourced provider will have towards a customer. Carl Blevins, a union president at Tampa Electric, observes that "when you outsource, you get the level of service you pay for. With your own staff, you have the opportunity to create loyalty. You have the opportunity to create a team that will go above and beyond to serve your customers."[5] This chapter explores why utilities outsource and what services they outsource. It will demonstrate how to evaluate outsourcing opportunities at a utility, explain steps to take when outsourcing, and offer a review of business process outsourcing.

WHY DO UTILITIES OUTSOURCE?

The decision to outsource is a utility-by-utility decision. Utilities will consider outsourcing with alignment to their strategic plans and goals.

Lowering of customer service delivery costs is the top reason cited by utilities for outsourcing.[6] Utilities continue to look for ways to reduce the cost to provide service or avoid capital expenditures. Utilities have traditionally offered a very rich benefit and compensation package versus other unregulated companies. Because customer care falls under the same corporate umbrella, the costs for these functions has increased over the cost of providing call services or other back office functions at nonregulated businesses. Outsourcers are in a position to offer lower costs as they leverage the benefits of scale, investment in technologies, and degrees of freedom with respect to labor management.

Outsourcers can aggregate several clients. This increased scale improves their operating costs, resulting in lower costs per transaction for the client. Outsourcers will invest in state-of-the-art technology that is core to their business. A remittance-processing firm will be very knowledgeable about the best in available technology and equipment.

Outsourcers will locate in areas that support their labor needs. Call center outsourcers, for example, will locate in markets where there is availability of a part-time workforce and supportive education systems to prepare workers. Outsourcers will also quickly pick up and move if the human resource costs are no longer competitive in a given market. Utilities are challenged with moving because of the need to maintain a presence in the service area.

The second most common reason cited is focus on the core business, thereby minimizing internal resources on noncore functions.[7] The danger for a utility spending time and resources on functions that are not fundamental to its purpose is that inadequate time may be spent on the core functions. Utilities are engineering, capital-intensive businesses. Customer care is often viewed as a function that has to be done but is not critical to the basic business of poles, pipes, and wires. Noncore functions can actually become distractions, taking valuable management time away from other aspects of the business.

Increasing cash flow for strategic investments is another consideration. Utilities are constrained on capital. When evaluating whether to spend capital on needed transmission or distribution infrastructure, versus a customer service capital request for a new bill insertion machine, the nod generally goes to transmission and distribution. This is linked to the first strategic driver of a focus on core business functions. Electric, gas, and water utilities have the core responsibility of delivering service through a system of pipes and wires to the customer. Bill print and insertion, on the other hand, is required by all types of companies, from credit card companies to department stores to mail-ordered products. In fact, according to Jim Jossie, a utility industry consultant specializing in bill print and Internet billing solutions, "There are several hundred potential providers in the market to provide bill print and mail fulfillment services. These outsourcing print providers range from national players to local players."[8]

The value proposition they provide is that bill print and insertion is their core business and hence they spend the capital dollars on investments to ensure they provide state-of-the-art service. Because of economies of scale, these outsourcers are able to provide savings, such as discounts on postage, that would be unavailable to the single utility.

Utilities sometimes cite labor issues as a reason to outsource. The utility may not be in the position to spend the needed time to find qualified workers and provide training. If there are unique skills involved, like those required for computer application support, there may be difficulty in recruiting and training personnel. One human resource director for a utility in a more rural service territory lamented the challenge of enticing qualified technical candidates to move to their more remote service territory. Another challenge utilities face is resistance from internal employees when implementing new technology.

Utilities with a plan to continue to grow their customer base through mergers and acquisitions are interested in outsourcing to create a scalable platform that supports customer growth and expansion. Utilities desiring to grow revenue and improve service are outsourcing to increase speed to market with customer-valued products and services.

Utilities have partnered with a couple of entities to deliver products and services to the customer, like Tampa Electric and its surge protection offering. Vicky Westra, director of customer service for Tampa Electric, notes, "With surge protection and other products, we find that speed to market can be imperative. For example, we offered surge protection before it was commercially available in local stores. We established our position as a trusted supplier of this service, and that our whole house surge protection is a much higher value concept than simply protecting individual appliances with plug-in strips." Vicky goes on to say that theirs is a "true partnership with the surge suppliers, contractors, and outsourced call center, and as such, Tampa Electric is benefiting from the continued innovations in the product offering."[9]

WHAT DO UTILITIES OUTSOURCE?

Utilities outsource a variety of components, including people, processes, and technology. Chartwell research indicates that the main areas utilities outsource are credit and collection calls and high call volume overflow (table 7–1).

Technology Perspective	People Perspective	Process Perspective
Customer information systems hosting	Credit and collections	Bill production
Application management and support	Meter reading	Payment and Remittance processing
Web-based applications	Call center	Energy services
Telephony	Payment centers	Returned mail

Table 7–1. Outsourcing opportunities

Technology perspective

From a technology perspective, outsourcers provide a range of services from complete CIS hosting to support of specific applications. Outsourcing the entire CIS is an attractive option to new entrants providing service to utility customers or to a utility facing a decision on a major capital investment in advancing its CIS. Implementing a CIS can range from $20 to $80 million, depending on the size of the utility. Less-robust packaged software solutions are available from a range of $9 million to $50 million.[10] Beyond the initial capital expenses, there are the ongoing maintenance expenses.

An outsourced solution offers a lower front end cost with an ongoing monthly fee for maintenance. The contracts can also build in dollars for enhancements. Kinder Morgan, a natural gas company, says outsourcing its CIS has saved the utility at least 15% in annual operating costs.[11]

Southern Company Gas is an example of a utility that outsourced its entire customer service business process, which included the CIS engine. Southern Company Gas was entering the new deregulated gas market in Georgia. They chose to outsource to allow them to concentrate on their business of providing their customers with exceptional levels of customer service at competitive prices. Outsourcing allowed them to avoid the large up-front costs of a new CIS and to minimize the risk associated with entering this market. The outsourced model provides predictability in operating costs, ability to scale technology as business grows, and flexibility as the newly deregulated gas market changes.

Other utilities are outsourcing application management and support of various IT systems, including the CIS. NSTAR is using this model. Our CIS application is hosted and managed by a third party. The benefit NSTAR has seen is the continued reduction in costs to maintain the CIS. The outsourcer can leverage technology platforms, offshore programmers, and shared production support to reduce operating costs. In this model, the utility still owns the strategy, definition of process controls, contract management, identification of business priorities, and definition of business requirements.

Utilities are looking to outsourcers to provide application design, management, and support for Web-based applications. Outsourcers in this space may have a dedicated focus to create easy-to-use, innovative Web-based services. Some examples of Web-based applications that utilities are outsourcing include energy analysis tools. Lewis Walton, manager of marketing and energy services for Lee County Electric Cooperative, also points out that "by partnering with a third party, we were able to bring our new Calc-U-$aver to our customers within weeks."[12] Another creative offering is interactive Web-based energy education. There are several companies that specialize in offering educational and entertaining energy training tools.

Other hosted applications that utilities offer include bill payment and presentment offerings. These have become very popular with customers and utilities. The third party in this case provides a platform, expertise in the specific application, and compliance with various federal requirements for payment processing. This is an inexpensive way to provide the functionality to the customer.

Telephony is another outsourced service. Utilities are meeting increased customer expectations with respect to phone service by leveraging the robust platform of a third party. Electric utilities are particularly vulnerable to high call volumes following an outage. Twenty First Century Communications, a large service provider for high call volume solutions, has data that indicate that 20%–40% of all affected customers call. Of those customers, 76% will call in the first 30 minutes of the event. For example, in an event that impacts 100,000 customers, 15,000 to 30,000 customers will call to report their outage in the first 30 minutes.[13]

Unusual events, like hurricanes, present a strain on a utility's telephony infrastructure. It is hard, if not impossible, to justify a telephony infrastructure for an event that may only occur every 10 years. Third-party offerings of robust telephony platforms provide utilities with the ability to handle the unusual high call volume situations. This enables the utility to respond to all customer calls without telephony system constraints. The inability to reach a utility in times of natural disaster is a risk utilities cannot afford.

Telephony voice recognition services are also being provided in a hosted application model. There are a few very specialized service providers offering voice recognition technology. This relatively new telephony offering is continuing to evolve and develop. Utilities looking to offer this type of enhanced customer interaction may prefer to leverage a hosted model, since the technology is continuing to advance so rapidly.

People perspective

Utilities are sometimes a bit hesitant to outsource the people-based aspects of their business. They have concerns over whether a third party can service customers as well as their own employees. Dave Steele, vice chairman of IEI Financial Services, contends, "Customer service is about human beings applying the golden rule as they help other human beings find a solution to their particular dilemma. If you subscribe to that philosophy, then you become more comfortable with a company whose core business is providing exceptional customer care."[14]

Chartwell analysis indicates that nearly one-third of utilities outsource the task of collecting bad debt. Many utilities are partnering with third-party outsourcers to handle credit calls. These companies bring knowledge, robust technical platforms, and lower transaction costs. Savings estimates on a transaction basis range from 15%–30%.[15]

Utilities also will outsource the credit skip tracing and final bill collections to third-party companies. These companies have the advantage in they have a core skill set in tracking down customers and encouraging payment. Companies providing skip tracing and final bill collections services are linked to various databases that give them the edge in locating a customer. Additionally, they stay current with the credit rules and regulations that are in place.

Meter reading is another labor-intensive practice in which outsourcing may be considered. Utilities vary widely in their costs to read meters, depending on their service territory and labor rates. Some utilities are finding that outsourcing meter reading offers cost advantages. A third party has the opportunity to read multiple meters that may be at a premise and offer the respective utilities a price break for this aggregation.

There can be issues associated with outsourcing meter reading from a route integration perspective. This is particularly acute when the utility CIS links the customer account number to the meter reading cycle and route. This linkage of meter reading folio information to the customer account was a common practice in utility CIS units. Newer or re-engineered systems have decoupled the account number from the meter reading folio information. Utilities with newer systems can more easily take advantage of a third-party meter reading aggregator, as route changes will be transparent to the customer.

Call center operations continue to be an area of outsourcing opportunity. A third-party call center has expertise in managing call volume, staffing, and recruitment. The vendors in this space also have the flexibility of locating in regions where labor costs are lower. With the advancement of telephony systems, it is very feasible to route calls to another state or country. India, for example, is a major player in the global call center industry. United Utilities, a water utility in the United Kingdom, outsources part of its call center operations to India.

The conservative nature of utilities will likely limit the amount of total customer care outsourcing to other countries. However, the financial savings opportunities associated with this outsourced model will only serve to increase pressure on senior executives to reduce costs through this method.

The senior executives are getting sales calls regularly touting the savings opportunities of an offshore outsourced model. One such solicitation went to our CEO and was forwarded to me. This firm was based in India. The e-mail highlighted their value proposition of 24/7 "superior quality outsourced customer support at highly competitive prices." The head of business development for the firm added, "Leveraging our low-cost base in

India, we have access to a large pool of English and European languages speaking, computer literate and technically skilled graduate workforce."[16] Note that there are grammatical errors in this quote, apparently contradicting their value proposition of "superior quality."

For utilities in the United States, it is more common to outsource to call center operations that are located in lower cost states versus offshore locations. Some utilities are using vendors who provide support from call centers in Canada.

More than one-half of utilities are outsourcing face-to-face payments through pay agents.[17] Authorized pay agents, who may be located in convenience stores, grocery stores, or other retail business, will process utility payments for a small transaction fee. The pay agent gains the benefit of increased traffic to its location by taking utility payments. For the utility, pay agents offer customers the convenience of a number of payment options and extended payment hours in the evenings and on the weekends.

Utilities can contract with a third party for pay agent services. The third party will manage the various individual pay agent contracts. They will also provide the equipment and associated training for the pay agent on the equipment and process.

Utilities can set up their own pay agents on an individual basis. For this option, the utility takes on the burden of installing cash processing equipment, training, and contract management.

There are also many unauthorized bill payment vendors that provide this service to the customer, collecting their fee from the customer for processing the payment. While not sanctioned by the utility or regulatory body, these vendors offer the utility an outsourced provider in areas that are willing to pay for the convenience.

Process perspective

Some of the strongest business cases for outsourcing are around niche process opportunities like bill production, remittance processing, and energy services. Third parties that provide these niche services invest in the technology, equipment, and technical expertise to be able to offer very low cost alternatives for utilities.

Third-party bill production and remittance processing firms often secure the cost advantage in their ability to spread investments over several clients and optimize their operations. Some bill production and remittance operations are running three shifts, maximizing the facility and technology investment. Providers in this space may also offer the utility billing flexibility, including enhancements of customized bills, bills in other languages, links to electronic bill presentment, and online bill exception processing. There are a number of common springboards for evaluating bill print and remittance services. These include the need to replace print and insertion equipment, document composition software license upgrades, merge print operations, and reduce postage costs.

Energy services are another area for outsourcing and partnership. Utilities that provide energy conservation management services can partner with third parties that specialize in the labor, talent, and tools to deliver this service to customers in a cost-effective manner.

Returned mail is a relatively new service offering. The interest in this area is due to the increases in returned mail. An EEI study noted that retuned mail grew from 17% in 1991 to more than 24% in 1998. For EEI members, this equates to $2.5 million in associated revenue being returned monthly.[18] Vendors that are licensees of the U.S. Postal Service's FASTforward technology are in a position to offer a service that locates the new addresses of people who have moved.

Understanding why utilities outsource and what services they commonly outsource from a customer care perspective is a first step in looking for opportunities at one's company. This next section explores how to evaluate whether outsourcing is right for one's utility.

HOW TO EVALUATE OUTSOURCING

The first step in considering outsourcing is to honestly evaluate whether outsourcing is right for one's company. It will also be necessary to clarify the objectives of outsourcing and complete a financial analysis to fully evaluate outsourcing as a viable opportunity for one's organization.

Outsourcing fit with the company

There are some key questions to consider when evaluating a fit with outsourcing:

- Is the function a core competency of the business?

- Are there benefits to speed the product or process to market?

- Are there providers for this service?

- Does outsourcing provide cost reduction opportunities?

The first question is whether this is a core competency. The printing of Braille bills is an excellent example of a business process that is probably not core to a utility. There are firms and service providers, however, that do specialize in Braille print and have the infrastructure and business processes in place to provide this service at a competitive cost. Successful Web application providers have a core competency in Web design with a bent towards innovation. Braille bill production and Web design may not be core competencies of a utility.

Are there benefits to speed the product or process to market? Utilities considering offering a new product or service often partner with an outsourced provider to fulfill delivery of the produce or service. Services like credit card processing or establishing a payment agent network can be quickly implemented by using an established partner with the technology, process, tools, and infrastructure in place. Wayne Norris, a former utility manager and now executive vice president with Global Express notes, "Once a contract is signed with Global Express, the service can be initiated within 60 to 90 days."[19] Global Express provides networked pay agent services. Norris notes that his company can do this because they have in place a series of agents that can easily be trained to handle a company's payments, and technology to upgrade electronic bill payment processes in a timely and efficient manner.

Are there providers for the service? For the commonly outsourced services, like call center, credit, and payment processing, there are numerous service providers. At the other extreme would be services such as the concierge services described in chapter 5. The customer is offered the opportunity to be connected to other local service providers, like cable and phone, at the conclusion of his service initiation request. There are only a few organizations offering concierge services. Companies offering concierge service may not have secured sufficient contracts with local providers in the utility's service territory to make this a viable option for the utility.

Does outsourcing provide cost reduction opportunities? Third-party providers can often bring economies of scale that are not possible within the utility. The high call volume answering telephony infrastructure is an example of an economy of scale. If a utility is facing expensive equipment replacement or upgrades, outsourcing may offer financial savings. Remittance processing and bill production are both examples of capital-intensive operations that require unique skills. Companies that bring exceptional people management skills can offer lower cost labor options. Call center operations are examples of this value proposition.

Objectives of outsourcing

It is important for a company to be very clear about its objectives for outsourcing. Will outsourcing reduce costs, improve service, increase flexibility, or accomplish a combination of all of these? At Tampa Electric, we partnered with a third party to set up payment agents to improve service and increase flexibility. Previously we had managed individual contracts with various local retailers. The benefit to partnering with a third party was improved service to our customers, as the third party was able to offer additional locations. There was increased flexibility to add or discontinue a payment location quickly. A major side benefit was the savings in management time that had been devoted to the individual contracts. The billing manager was thrilled to be rid of the daily issues that came up from the individual payment locations.

It is important to document the specific objectives expected from outsourcing. These objectives may be included in the final contract as service level agreements. For example, objectives at NSTAR in partnering for application management and hosting of our CIS included high CIS availability and continued reduction in costs to maintain the CIS. Both of these objectives are built into the final contract in the form of service level agreements that include incentives and penalties related to the overall performance.

Financial analysis

A financial analysis is fundamental in evaluating outsourcing. It is critical that a utility fully understand its costs. In the example of producing a bill, it would be important to know the costs of supplies, equipment maintenance, labor, and contingency recovery. It is helpful to understand the fully burdened costs of completing the service in-house, but one should apply caution when comparing this to an outsourcer. Fully burdening the in-house cost can make outsourcing look quite attractive. In many cases, however, the overhead costs are not removed once a process has been outsourced. Determining the costs that are relevant is important to the analysis.

For the financial analysis, it is sometimes helpful to review the costs in a variety of formats. For example, the total cost of the process could be expressed in cost per therm, cost per kWh, and cost per customer, among others. Having multiple views of the internal costs is helpful in comparing them to outsourced providers.

One utility manager with whom I worked experienced this when evaluating outsourcing of meter reading. The comparison of outsourced providers to our fully burdened meter reading cost was very compelling, and we were on a path to outsource. We went the next step, though, and asked ourselves which of those overheads would truly go away. The employee benefits overheads would be eliminated, but other corporate overheads would not go away. "When have you reduced legal staff once you outsourced?" asked the manager. The business case looked much different after this more rigorous financial review.

As one evaluates an outsourcing opportunity, it is important to consider what additional investments will need to be made over the next five years to support the process. Will customer expectations be changing, requiring new investment or innovation? Will additional contingency recovery be needed? How stable and experienced is the potential outsourcer? What contingency plan is in place if the vendor goes out of business? Bill presentation is an example of an area in which customer expectations are rising. A third party can provide the flexibility to update and change a company's bill presentment more dynamically to meet customer needs.

As one evaluates whether outsourcing is right for one's company, it is important to take the time to honestly assess the key questions around core competency, speed to market, provider availability, and cost reduction. Gaining clarity on the specific objectives of outsourcing, along with completing the financial analysis, will serve as the platform for outsourcing. If one finds that outsourcing is right for one's company, then the next step is implementation. There are a series of steps to follow that will ensure successful implementation of outsourcing.

STEPS TO OUTSOURCING

If outsourcing appears to be an option, there are a series of steps involved in finalizing a partnership (fig. 7–1). Experts agree that utilities that are successful with outsourcing create a partnership. Outsourcing a business process is a marriage, not a divorce. To ensure excellent customer service, it takes a strong commitment from the utility and the outsourcer to work as partners.

1 Prepare a business case

2 Create a request for proposal

3 Identify providers

4 Evaluate the proposals

5 Settle on a contract

6 Manage the relationship

Fig. 7–1. Steps to outsourcing

Prepare a business case

Utilities will generally have a standard format for business cases. This format will touch on the financial, strategic, customer service, and labor aspects of outsourcing. Typically hurdle rates for net present value or internal rate of return are identified by the utility as benchmarks of viability.

The business case will often include strategic and soft benefits of outsourcing. From a strategic perspective, a partnership with an outsourcer may support rapid growth and expansion that might occur with a merger. Soft benefits include items like increased flexibility, improved customer satisfaction, and improved employee satisfaction, among others.

In order to complete the financial evaluation, benchmark data of typical costs of outsourced providers will need to be secured. A request for information (RFI) is sometimes used to gain an understanding of pricing. Talking with other utilities that have outsourced the function may provide insight. Research organizations may have benchmark information on typical outsourcing costs.

Create a request for proposal

If the business case is compelling and approved, the next step is to complete a request for proposals (RFP). The RFP needs to be very specific in the minimum scope of services required, along with the detailed current requirements. If service levels are a requirement, those should be noted in the RFP. One should consider incentives and key measures of performance that will be used to manage the future relationship. Quality and numerical performance criteria must be established up front in order to fairly compare the responses.

One way to expedite the development of an RFP and ensure that the RFP is comprehensive is to secure a consultant that specializes in that area. I have used consultants on a couple of key outsourcing RFP developments and have found this investment to pay tremendous dividends in ensuring the final outsourced solution meets all the company's requirements. A good consultant will have strong experience in the particular area one is pursuing.

There is a danger of not fully documenting one's requirements. Sometimes utilities have experienced problems in outsourcing bill print even though the outsourcer met the specified requirements. For example, the requirements might not have been sufficiently comprehensive and may not have specified an important item, such as the quality of the paper required for the bill statement. The vendor might have bid low based on a lower quality of paper. The unfortunate result for the utility in this situation could be increased payment posting exceptions, as the remittance processing equipment might not be able to effectively process the lower grade of paper.

The RFP may also include additional services that may be of interest for future enhancements. Some key elements beyond basic pricing include time frame for implementation, provisions for disaster recovery, financial viability of the company, and references.

Identify providers

To identify providers of the services, one should review the exhibitors at various customer service exhibitions and conferences. Trade magazines and research firms can also provide insight on providers. Surfing the Web for service providers is also a good tool.

Evaluate the proposals

Evaluating the responses to the RFP is best done using a team approach with a clear set of criteria established for evaluating them. Applying weights that indicate the relative importance of each criterion is helpful in the final analysis. Often vendor demonstrations can provide insight on the company. Once the team has narrowed down the finalists, it may be helpful to visit the provider on its own site. Reference checks are important to identify how the providers perform with other clients.

Settle on a contract

Once the outsourced provider has been selected, it is time to negotiate the contract. This can be quite time-consuming depending on the complexity of the outsourced arrangement. In the example of outsourcing the CIS, the contract will need to include service level expectations, rewards, and penalties for nonperformance. One should include a change control process in the contract so that both parties are clear about the steps and definition of a potential scope change.

Other items to consider in the contract are payment schedules that may be linked to various milestones in establishing the outsourcing arrangement. With applications, it is important to clarify the intellectual property rights. It is also important to define what will constitute a breach of contract. A utility's purchasing and legal staff can provide excellent insight to finalizing a contract that works for both parties.

Manage the relationship

The final and perhaps most important step is to manage the relationship. Utilities that have successfully outsourced maintain a close relationship with the outsourcing partner. Regular feedback on how the process is working along with monitoring of performance metrics is vital. The best partners, I have found, continue to enhance the value proposition they are providing to one's company. If their core business, for example, is remittance processing, they keep abreast with the latest innovations in equipment, processes, and regulations. Since this is their core business, one may find that their costs reduce over time as they further optimize their operation. Establishing regularly scheduled meetings between the vendor and the utility to discuss the relationship, performance, and suggested areas of improvement is vital to creating a true partnership. Communication of company changes on a regular basis will keep the relationship profitable and provide a seamless process flow between the utility and vendor.

CUSTOMER SERVICE BUSINESS PROCESS OUTSOURCING

Business process outsourcing (BPO) is a powerful tool for creating transformational change in a company. BPO for customer service involves delegating the back office business processes to a third party to manage. The BPO arrangement supports a clear focus on the core business operations of the company. Innovations and process improvements in the core business that will drive shareholder value can be the focus of the company's executives. The BPO provider, on the other hand, has incentives to continually use best practices, reduce costs, and improve the overall service. The combination of business focus with a strong BPO partner can result in providing a company a strategic advantage over other competitors.

For some utility leaders, BPO seems extreme and perhaps leaves on the table the best-in-class providers in each segment of the meter-to-cash cycle. High-profile BPO deals like the one between TXU and Capgemini, where savings of $140 million annually were touted as a benefit, have elevated the interest in BPO. It is important as a utility manager to understand the value proposition of complete customer care outsourcing.

For new retail companies entering the deregulated utility environment, customer service BPO allows the company to focus on its core business. Gartner research indicates that the focus on core business is the primary driver for a BPO arrangement.[20] This is true for Southern Company Gas, which has a BPO partnership that allows it to focus on gas sales in the deregulated gas market in Georgia.

Managing multiple contracts for each segment of the customer service cycle becomes daunting. Securing a BPO partnership with a single vendor with the appropriate incentives to provide quality customer service minimizes the management challenges of multiple contracts. Having one vendor can provide predictability in the operation and maintenance cost streams.

Risk management is another reason to move to BPO. The outsourcer takes on the risk associated with ensuring an accurate CIS, along with timely and accurate billing and service. CIS investments are very costly. Many companies offering BPO arrangements come to the table with a CIS platform in place.

If a utility is considering outsourcing the entire customer service business process, it is important that it look for a partner with a strong basis in process design and delivery. A utility wants predictability in the service provided to its customers. It is important that the utility recognize that it still owns the strategic decisions with respect to the future direction of customer service. The third party will handle the transactions, but the strategy on future developments needs to be aligned to the utility's corporate business plan.

Overall outsourcing is a very individual decision for a utility. Wayne Norris suggests that "successful partnerships are ones in which the customer experience is enhanced at a price the client can afford and where the vendor will make a profit."[21] Companies that have been successful at outsourcing have created strong partnerships with their outsourcers.

Successful companies are clear about their reasons to outsource, and they leverage the partnerships to allow more intense and productive focus on their core businesses.

REFERENCES

1 *The Boston Globe.* "Twenty Percent Annual Rise in Off Shoring Seen." October 13, 2004, p. C2.

2 Chartwell. June 2003.

3 Brock, Jon. CEO, Utilipoint; Interview, November 23, 2004.

4 Chartwell. "Outsourcing Gains Partial Inroad in the Call Center." June 2002, pp. 98–99.

5 Blevins, Carl. President, OPEIU, Local 46, Tampa Electric Company; Interview, August 6, 2004.

6 "How to Outsource Business Process for Competitive Advantage." Navigant Consulting. April 2003.

7 Ibid.

8 Josie, James J. Principal, James J. Jossie Consulting, LLC; Interview, January 24, 2005.

9 Westra, Vicky. Director of customer service, Tampa Electric Co.; Interview, August 27, 2004.

10 "Should You Outsource Your Customer Information System?" *American Gas.* May 2003, p. 25.

11 Ibid.

12 Walton, Lewis. Lee County Electric Cooperative; Interview, January 15, 2005.

13 Twenty First Century Communications Web site: http://tfcci.com HVAC page; Accessed January 15, 2005.

14 Utilipoint International PowerHitters, 2003. David Steele, vice chairman of IEI Financial Services, LLC; May 8, 2003.

15 Ibid.

[16] Correspondence via e-mail. September 29, 2004.

[17] "Chartwell's Guide to Bill Presentment and Payment 2003." Chartwell Inc., March 2003, p. 27.

[18] Maloney, David. DMC Consulting. "Returned Mail: An Analysis of Industry Trends and Process Enhancements." March 2000.

[19] Norris, Wayne. Executive vice president of client development, Global Express; Interview, February 3, 2005.

[20] Gartner Dataquest. "BPO Users in Large Enterprises Become More Demanding." Rebecca Scholl, December 3, 2003.

[21] Norris, Wayne. Interview, February 3, 2005.

8 REDUCE BAD DEBT

Reducing the write-offs associated with bad debt is a top priority these days with utility executives as they continue to improve earnings while keeping rates low for customers. Estimates vary in the industry on the annual dollars lost due to nonpaying customers, with some as high as $1 billion annually.[1] This chapter will explore strategies at each stage of the receivables process, from current to delinquent to finaled accounts (table 8–1), and will examine common utility mistakes.

Strategies to Minimize Bad Debt

Current Accounts	Delinquent Accounts	Finaled Accounts
Secure customer information	Establish a credit policy	Collect final bills
Process fraud	Monitor credit	Use collections agencies
Provide payment options	Use behavior based scoring	Pursue legal collections
Secure deposits	Maintain customer information	Sale of bad debt
Process returned mail	Provide a dedicated credit team	Mitigate bankruptcy
Provide energy assistance outreach	Complete strategic call and letter campaigns	Mine data
Offer a business team	Complete field disconnects	
	Forgive arrears	

Table 8–1. Strategies to minimize bad debt

There are several factors that impact a utility's bad debt write-off. Credit experts concur that even excellent utilities with respect to credit and collections processes will have variations in their levels of write-offs. This is due to the three key factors of regulatory environment, geographical characteristics, and socioeconomic factors of the utility's assigned territory.

Regulatory and government requirements vary from state to state. States that are more consumer friendly are likely to have more restrictions on collecting deposits, customer contact, and termination procedures. Certain geographical areas are more prone to extremes in weather seasonality, resulting in higher-than-average variability in customers' bills. For example, utilities serving the New England region can experience extremely cold winters, driving energy bills to seasonal highs. The large variation in energy bills brings challenges for customers on limited or fixed incomes.

Extreme heat or cold also poses concerns for consumer safety. Hence many states with weather seasonality will require moratoriums during which energy service cannot be disconnected. This is more commonly thought of in cold areas with winter moratoriums, but it is also true for states with unusually hot weather. Disconnections for nonpayment are discontinued in Nevada when the temperature reaches 110°F.

The economic viability of a utility service territory can also impact a utility's write-off. In the Carolinas, a key industry was textiles. Due to competition, many textile-manufacturing plants moved, closed, or went bankrupt. Utilities were wise to mitigate this exposure by asking for securitization of key accounts.

Excellent utilities with respect to credit and collections are looking at the entire life cycle of an account, from the point of customer application all the way through to finaling the account or the sale of the bad debt portfolio. Credit experts agree that a common mistake made by utilities is to focus energies on delinquent and finaled accounts. George Pollard, a credit expert with telecom and utility experience, states, "Most credit managers are spending time on inactive collections versus active collections. The problem with inactive is that it costs more to locate the responsible party for payment."[2] This mistake costs in increased write-offs and cost of collections. Up-front and aligned strategies through the life cycle of the account are critical.

STRATEGIES FOR CURRENT ACCOUNTS

With current accounts, the strategies identified are low-cost, high-value strategies. These early interventions can have a major impact in downstream write-offs.

Secure customer information

Capturing accurate information up front as the customer applies is a first and critical step in mitigating bad debt write-off. Bruce Gay, president of Monticello Consulting Group, suggests the added cost in call handle time to secure quality information up front pays for itself in increasing recoveries and reducing costs associated with skip tracing and returned mail. Concerning this information, Gay recommends, "Get as much as you can get. The more the better, and maintain it."[3]

The key information to secure includes customer data, contact information, employer, and household information. The level to which this information is obtained depends on the utility and the capabilities of the CIS. The accuracy to which the data is entered can be enhanced through edit checks on the CIS and standard entry methods.

Customer data can include name, social security number, credit score, and driver's license number. Contact information can include current address, previous address, and telephone numbers. Employer information can include the employer's name, phone number, and address, and previous employer. Household information includes landlord or mortgage holder name and phone number, and roommate or spouse names.

Social security numbers are the most critical piece of customer information. Interestingly, even though social security numbers are a fundamental data element to ensure a more robust recovery cycle, some utilities have chosen not to obtain them in order to reduce call handle time. While this move may save dollars up front, in the life cycle of the account, it will cost more due to reduced recoveries and increased back office costs in skip tracing and returned mail.

Gay has seen utility bad debt portfolios with inaccurate social security numbers range from as high as 30% of accounts to as low as 2%. Since a social security number is a fundamental data element needed for collections, the portfolio, Gay indicates, drops in value due to missing or incorrect social security numbers. In the extremes above, the difference in the value of the portfolio would be significant.[4]

Securing accurate addresses and inputting them correctly can mitigate delays in customers receiving their first bill. CIS units with required address entry corresponding to U.S. postal requirements could mitigate inaccurate data. Phone numbers can be problematic due to lack of data fields on a CIS to record more than one phone number and due to the customer's lack of having a phone number at service initiation. In fact, 70% of customers contact their electric utility first to apply for service, before phone or cable service.[5] This increases the challenge for electric utilities to secure a phone number.

Many utilities do not collect employer or household information. This may be due to limits on the CIS to store this information or desire by the utility to reduce call handle time. This information is helpful if the account requires intervention to encourage payment and in skip tracing. Additionally customers are sometimes reluctant to provide this information. Bill Zdep, former director of customer relations for General Public Utilities and now president of Forward Thinking, said he always had success in securing alternate contact information by reminding the customer that if they were due a refund check for some reason, the utility needs to have alternate contact information in order to ensure that the customer receives the check.[6]

If the customer is renting, the apartment agent information is helpful. If the customer skips on a utility payment, they may have also skipped on the apartment agent. The apartment agents can be very helpful in providing information needed for skip tracing. For homeowners, the mortgage holder is excellent information but is not very often secured. Additionally, e-mail addresses are emerging as a valuable tool in the life cycle of an account. Unfortunately, utility CIS units sometimes limit the amount of information that can be stored on an account, and a balance is needed between critical information and storage space available.

Process fraud

During service initiation, ensuring that the person on the phone is in fact a legitimate customer is a growing concern. Bob Hall, former general manager of credit and collections at Duke Power Company, commented that at Duke Power, he saw "consumer fraud grow by leaps and bounds. It was growing at an exponential rate"[7] Many utilities are thus implementing processes to identify and mitigate fraud up front during service initiation and to comply with the Fair and Accurate Credit Transactions Act. To this end, third-party services are available to confirm identification.

The Fair and Accurate Credit Transactions Act, signed into law in December 2003, provides for additional protection for the consumer and also helps the utility to minimize fraud. Consumers can now place a notice on their credit report to warn potential creditors that they will not authorize credit under their name without written authorization. Identify theft has increased the risk of fraud, and this new law will be a step in protecting the rights of the consumer.

A first step in fraud processing for a utility is to confirm the identity. Identify verification is available through the credit bureaus for a nominal fee. The bureaus will provide back to the CSR either affirmation that the identity is confirmed or a flag that suggests additional information is needed to confirm the identity. The flags are generated when the information provided by the customer does not match information in the credit bureau. For example, if the customer provided a social security number of a minor, the bureau would send a flag.

The challenge comes in how to process the account when a flag appears. Some utilities request the customer fax in information. This is an imperfect solution, as faxed copies are not always legible. Utilities with field business locations may request the customer come on-site to confirm identity. This option is an expensive option and not an option for some utilities that have closed business offices.

An innovative process that is being used is to route the caller to a fraud team that is equipped with additional information from the credit bureau. The fraud team CSR can ask the customer a series of questions called *wallet questions*. The answers to these questions could only be provided by the actual customer. The questions may be along the lines of what kind of car the customer drives, the amount of his monthly car payment, or the amount of his monthly mortgage payment. There is a cost associated with providing this specialized team with more robust credit information, but the benefit is to more clearly identify the correct customer. Some utilities have been successful in gaining regulatory support to deny service if the identity cannot be confirmed.

Provide payment options

Offering a variety of payment options is not only good for customer satisfaction, as was discussed in chapter 5, but it is also good for credit and collections. Offering bank draft and budget billing are both excellent tools to help customers maintain current accounts. The budget billing assists customers who are at risk for credit issues by levelizing their payments. The option of bank drafts assists a utility with its DRO. Companies with late pay fees have a built-in encouragement to pay on time. Customers who wish to avoid late pay fees will be anxious to use pay-by-phone, e-pay, or credit card options to bring the account current. A variety of real-time payment options, like credit card and pay via phone, assist when working with delinquent accounts. When efforts to reach a delinquent account are successful, the utility does not want to lose the opportunity to collect the required balance because of limited payment options.

Recognizing good pay customers is an excellent approach that supports continuance of the behavior and increases customer satisfaction. Some utilities accomplish this by simply sending letters annually from the CEO thanking customers who have paid all year on time. This simple thank-you letter always elicits return letters from customers expressing their appreciation to the utility for noticing their good payment behavior.

Prepay is another payment option that minimizes credit issues. Telephone companies have had great success in offering prepaid phone cards. For utilities, offering prepay is a bit more challenging. The prepay offering requires special metering, upgrades to the utility CIS to accept payment prior to usage, and payment process changes. The prepay technology is not new and has been used in European markets for many years. In the United States, very few utilities (3.4%, according to Chartwell's 2004 research) offer prepayment.

Secure deposits

Deposits are significant in mitigating write-offs. Utilities able to secure deposits should avail themselves of this opportunity to the fullest extent. However, this is often not the case. Some utility CIS platforms make administering deposits very labor intensive. Other utilities are prohibited from securing deposits on particular customer segments.

Utilities will link credit scoring with their deposit strategy. The customer is given the choice of paying a deposit or potentially having the deposit waived by a quick credit check. To complete the credit check, the customer's social security number must be provided. This is valuable information, as was discussed earlier, for collections activity down the road. Generally, by obtaining an accurate credit score, most utilities can waive 60%–70% of new applicants' deposits. This increases customer satisfaction while decreasing fraud, interest, and write-off costs to the utility.

If a utility is facing a huge administrative or cost burden with deposits, they may want to be selective on securing deposits on the most critical accounts. Credit scoring can assist to determine the most important accounts to secure. Also, offering customers alternative ways to secure the account in lieu of a deposit can reduce the administrative burden and cost associated with an unusually high interest rate on deposits.

Like customer information, it is necessary to monitor accounts on a regular basis to ensure that deposits are secured. Utilities that fail to monitor customer account activity may miss important flags that indicate additional security is required. These flags include disconnection for nonpayment, returned checks, and excessive late notices.

Many utilities have good processes in place to secure a deposit up front when initiating service. Often they will delay service initiation until a deposit is received. The opportunity is to continue to monitor accounts that have had a deposit refunded, or perhaps never required a deposit. When flags appear that raise the need for additional securitization of an account, prompt action needs to be taken.

On commercial accounts, political issues may be a factor in securing an account. There may be reluctance by utility leadership, marketing, or others to request a deposit from certain key accounts. Utilities are finding that a best practice on sensitive accounts is to have the account executive work with the customer to secure the deposit. To do this effectively, educating the account executives on why this is important is a first step.

While commercial accounts are challenging, they also represent potentially huge losses to the utilities if warning signs are ignored. The past decade has seen several companies once considered leaders in their industries in bankruptcy court. Enron and MCI are two examples that quickly come to mind.

Leading edge utilities have individuals dedicated to monitoring their commercial portfolio. A review of annual and semiannual financial statements often identifies potential problems before they are apparent to the utility. Utilities also review commercial accounts for increases in consumption or late notices. When any of these flags are raised, the deposit is reviewed to minimize risk of default. While the challenges are significant to securing a deposit on a commercial account that is experiencing a deteriorating financial profile, the risk of not doing so is significantly greater.

Process returned mail

Bill Zdep, president of Forward Thinking, suggests, "Handling all return mail is a best practice."[8] Returned mail alerts the utility that there is something wrong with the customer's address. With new accounts, an incorrect address can add months to the receipt of payment. Interestingly, Zdep finds that most utilities do not effectively process returned mail. This is due to resource constraints and the lack of understanding of the cost benefit to processing returned mail on a timely basis.

Zdeps experience with clients has revealed a return on investment on effectively processing returned mail to from a low of 7:1 to a high of 14:1. The return is based on the reduction in DRO by quickly securing an accurate address on initial bills, reducing the postal service charge for return mail processing, and locating a final customer more quickly for prompt credit processing.

Several companies have had between $20 and $100 million in lost and delayed revenue tied up on return mail, according to Zdep.[9] Research by EEI on returned mail indicates that 0.72% of utility mail is returned.[10] Returned mail impacts DRO, arrears, and collections effectiveness.

Provide energy assistance outreach

Proactive outreach to customers regarding energy assistance and energy saving ideas is an excellent tool to help payment-challenged customers maintain a current status by connecting them with funding assistance and reducing monthly usage through conservation. Unfortunately, some of the most credit-challenged customers also face the most daunting energy bills due to lack of proper insulation and conservation efforts.

Proactive customer communications regarding home energy assistance programs can help customers maintain or achieve a current payment status. For example, NSTAR has been nationally recognized for its outreach efforts to customers on energy efficiency management programs. NSTAR is successful in reaching out to low-income customers because of partnerships with other utilities and local community action programs (CAPs). This partnership has resulted in a comprehensive low-income energy assistance and management program, which offers a discount rate, energy efficiency improvement measures, and funding assistance through CAP agencies.

Additionally, NSTAR does a proactive outbound call campaign to customers with arrears who have qualified for fuel assistance, based on NSTAR records, but have not applied. Included in this message is information on NSTAR's energy efficient programs available to low-income customers. Interestingly, only 25% of customers indicate that they had awareness of this assistance. This highlights the need for proactive and aggressive communication campaigns.

Offer a business team

A team of representatives servicing business accounts is an excellent way to mitigate exposure to write-offs. Nonresidential accounts are more complex, and the issues vary significantly from the residential accounts. By having a team focused on the business account, a utility is more likely to be consistent in applying security deposit requirements and collecting accurate account information.

Utilities generally use account executives to manage the very largest accounts. It is important that the account executives understand the importance of the revenue life cycle so that they can encourage prompt customer payment. Account executives can monitor arrears on their assigned accounts and prompt customers for payment. Since engaging our account executives at NSTAR in ensuring that their customers pay in a timely manner, the arrears for the assigned accounts have reduced significantly.

STRATEGIES FOR DELINQUENT ACCOUNTS

Strategies to process delinquent accounts are varied and range from low-cost reminder letters to higher cost field visits. The savviest utilities are matching strategies on delinquent accounts to payment patterns using robust behavioral-based scoring methods. A foundation in dealing effectively with delinquent accounts is to have a credit policy in place and to effectively monitor reports. Segmentation to a credit team, whether in-house or to a third party, is an excellent tool to focus efforts on credit.

Establish a credit policy

A fundamental question each utility should ask is whether it has a clear credit policy in place, or if it is vague and thereby creates exposure for the utility. The credit policy should include clear guidelines on the following key areas:

Criteria for granting credit extensions. The policy should describe how credit extensions are granted. Many utilities use a table format that details the degrees of freedom with respect to agreement length, percent of payment up front, and payment method. The CSR will quickly assess the account and offer the customer appropriate extension agreements.

Credit scoring criteria. The policy will outline the external scoring criteria, score results, and customer disposition based on the score results. If internal scoring is also used, the policy will provide a similar outline for internal scoring results.

Notification process for pending disconnection. The policy should outline various notifications and the appropriate regulatory requirements that the notifications support, as well as detail the notification process.

Criteria for waiving a late pay fee. The policy should identify the degrees of freedom various levels of the organization have with respect to waiving a late pay fee and the process by which fees are waived. Some policies outline an exception approval process to document where and why late pay fees are being waived outside of the policy.

Criteria for waiving reconnect fee. The policy should outline the circumstances in which a reconnect fee may be waived and detail the process to waive the fee.

Utility credit policies may include other key areas. This highlights the basic areas that should be covered in a credit policy.

Monitor credit

Success with active arrears comes by diligent monitoring of arrears accounts. Online or printed reports that should be reviewed include DRO, monthly write-off, rolling 12-month annual write-off, bankruptcy trends, energy assistance fund application reports, and bankruptcy potential.

Other reports monitor the effectiveness of the process. Reports such as adherence to credit extension policies allow the credit managers to quickly address situations where extensions are being granted outside the framework of the policy. Notice effectiveness reports match customer payment activity as a result of a notice. This provides the credit manager with information on which notices are effective in driving behavior, and which accounts need to be addressed in another manner. Monitoring defaults on payment arrangements is also an important credit report. This is an early flag for accounts that may need additional securitization.

Use behavioral-based scoring

Behavioral-based scoring enables a utility to apply the right treatment to the right customers. Behavioral scoring models vary among utilities in terms of robustness. Some utilities simply do not have this capability built into their CIS or credit systems. The benefit to using or adding a behavioral-based component to a utility's credit system is that it can help ensure that the most cost-effective collections process is in place. Behavioral scoring should flag truly high-risk customers and identify early intervention opportunities.

While many utilities have a rudimentary internal behavioral-based scoring procedure, a best practice is to create a more robust customized behavioral-based scoring model using external and internal data. With a customized model using both external and internal data, the utility can more effectively manage terms of payment extensions, field visits, and issuing of reminder notices.

Bob Lalima, former gas credit manager for Brooklyn Union Gas, and now an executive with an outsourced credit organization, says that "behavioral-based scoring is one of the most robust, but underutilized strategies."[11] Customized behavior scoring is relatively easy to implement. A key first step is to partner with an external credit bureau. These companies have experts on staff who will work with the utility to build the business requirements. Once the requirements are in place, a model can be designed and implemented, typically within three to six months. The payoff is that the utility is now able to more effectively use limited credit resources on the most critical accounts. This is especially true when using field disconnects in a cost-effective manner.

Maintain customer information

While it is important to gather information up front, the accuracy of this information degrades with time. Bob Hall, former general manager of credit and collections at Duke Power, indicates that external credit-scoring information is only good for approximately six months.[12] Hence it is important to have processes in place to maintain accurate, current customer information. One easy way to do this is to ingrain with one's CSR team the need to confirm key customer information with every service contact. Catalog, credit card, and banking businesses have this confirmation built into their scripts. Excellent utilities also have confirmation built into scripts or processes. A best practice is to highlight on the CSR's customer information screen or GUI script any key information to confirm, like phone number, employer, and billing address.

I can remember early on in my utility career, I observed a credit clerk reading the newspaper. When I asked what she was doing, I learned that she was reviewing the obituary column to identify customers who had passed away. Fortunately today, we have much easier and more accurate ways of refreshing the CIS with information, even concerning deceased customers, by working with a third party.

Utilities interested in having a highly accurate CIS may append their systems on a six-month basis to identify deceased customers or to update phone numbers and contact information. Savvy utilities are identifying their riskiest accounts and appending key data to these accounts. There is a cost associated with this effort, but the benefits are tremendous from a collections perspective. Additionally, as will be discussed on the sale of bad debt, a portfolio is more valuable if it has been *scrubbed,* and deceased accounts have been removed or updated.

Provide a dedicated credit team

A dedicated team, either internal or external, that is focused on credit processing is a best practice. A common trap that utilities fall into when a team is not dedicated is focusing all personnel on incoming customer service calls during times of high call volume. Usually, the time taken away from credit processing is not reimbursed. A dedicated approach also ensures consistent, objective, and compassionate review of the account situation. Specialized training of a credit team on administering the credit policy, handling difficult customers, and negotiating with account holders will result in more effective collections and reduced costs associated with repeat calls.

Ensuring consistency in applying the credit guidelines minimizes customer shopping. Shopping occurs when customers realize that a company is inconsistent in the terms it offers on credit extensions. This situation often results in the customer calling repeatedly until he secures the arrangement he prefers. This unfortunately creates a great deal of unnecessary work for the utility. A better approach is to adhere to the credit policy consistently. A utility should ensure that its CSRs document all transactions immediately when granting credit arrangements or waiving of fees. This supports audit compliance and avoids the effects of the customer who continually shops for an answer.

At NSTAR, when credit was consolidated, the credit team not only reduced write-offs by 15%, but it also reduced commission credit related complaints by one-third. The main reason, cited by Tony Simas, director of credit and collections at NSTAR, was the consistency in applying the credit guidelines.[12]

Regardless of whether the credit team is internal or external, or credit is instead handled by universal CSRs, it is important to offer these employees incentives, communicate with them, and recognize good performance. This will create a positive environment in which desired behaviors with respect to credit and collections are reinforced and encouraged.

Complete strategic call and letter campaigns

Outbound notification of customers in arrears through calls and letters is a commonly used strategy. Many utilities are partnering with a third party to pursue active collections. Reminder notices and letters are most often generated by the utility's credit system. Both letter and phone campaigns can be more cost-effective and customer focused when combined with behavioral-based scoring.

Many utilities are partnering with third-party outsourcers to handle credit calls. These companies bring knowledge, robust technical platforms, and lower transactions costs. Savings estimates on a transaction basis range from 15%–30%.[13]

There are several measures that are helpful to evaluate the effectiveness of outbound and inbound credit processing. If one is using or considering the use of a third party, these are metrics that one may want to include in the contract:

- **Percent of outbound dialing completed in prime times.** The prime times are generally defined as: 8:00 am to 10:00 am and 5:00 pm to 9:00 pm on weekdays, and 9:00 am to 2:00 pm on Saturdays. A good percentage to strive for is to have 70% or more of outbound calling completed during the prime times.

- **Penetration rate.** This is used on outbound dialing and measures the number of passes to try to reach a responsible party. Some companies will have penetration rates of 250% or greater. That means that on 100 accounts, there were more than 250 outbound calls made on those accounts in an attempt to reach a responsible party.

- **Percent of outbound dialing that reaches the responsible party.** This measures the effectiveness of the outbound dialing. On active but delinquent accounts, generally a 20%–25% success is a considered a good level.

- **Percentage of calls referred back to the utility for further assistance.** It is important to make sure the outsourcers are not sending back the more challenging calls to the utility so that they can focus on the quicker or easy calls.

- **Quality.** A system is needed that will allow the utility to monitor the call to make sure the customer is receiving the type of experience desired by the utility.

- **Reward and penalty.** Setting up an incentive or penalty for the outsourcer based on the agreed-upon performance metrics creates a motivated vendor.

- **Percentage of credit arrangements paid.** This is an excellent metric to measure the overall effectiveness of the outsourced CSR's performance.

A utility can achieve success in credit and collections regardless of whether it outsources or handles credit internally, or has a combination of the two. The most successful utilities monitor and assess the performance of their credit process and link success to individual performance.

Complete field disconnects

Physical disconnection of active accounts, while costly, is probably the most powerful tool of all for credit managers. The best practice is to link behavioral-based scoring to surgically target field disconnections that are the most cost-effective. Even without behavioral-based scoring, it is more cost-effective to prioritize field forces on higher balance locations while moving lower balance accounts to phone and letter campaigns.

The percentage of customers disconnected for nonpayment varies widely among utilities. According to 2004 data from the AGA/EEI DataSource, the percentage of customers disconnected in relation to the total customer base ranged from less than 1% to more than 10%. In reviewing the data closely, it is clear that the some utilities are figuring out how to achieve low write-offs and avoid costly field disconnect activity. Among a subset of companies with extremely low write-off rates of less than 0.25% of revenue, the most effective were able to achieve the low write-off rates with eight times fewer field disconnects.[14]

The most effective utilities at reducing their bad debt are those that very closely follow their regulatory requirements for the collection cycle, billing, notices, and disconnection. By timely following up on those accounts identified as delinquent, sending the appropriate notification, and then disconnecting when not paid, the amount of bad debt is reduced exponentially. Customers quickly learn the collection practices of their local utility and adjust their payment habits to satisfy the most aggressive creditor.

Forgive arrears

Utilities in general are very skeptical of arrears forgiveness programs. Structured appropriately, and in partnership with other organizations, arrears forgiveness programs can be quite successful from a customer and bad-debt perspective.

Successful arrears forgiveness programs are very surgically targeted to customers who, given the right training, assistance, and support, can move from needing some sort of assistance to achieving self-sufficiency. Structurally linking the arrears forgiveness credits to key behavior milestones is another element of good programs. For example, at NSTAR, we participate in a very targeted arrears forgiveness program, administered by a CAP agency. In addition to our funds, the agency has secured governmental grants and energy efficiency funds to offer the customer a comprehensive package of training, energy management assistance, and financial assistance. The 18-month program has milestones involved that if successfully achieved allow the participants to receive a credit on the energy arrears.

Customer feedback on the program is overwhelmingly positive, as is the feedback from the administrating agencies. The benefit to the utility is taking a customer from poor payment behavior to good payment behavior, while avoiding expensive field disconnect and final bill activity.

STRATEGIES FOR FINALED ACCOUNTS

Once an account is finaled, the speed of reaching the responsible party becomes the key factor in collections. It is commonly understood that with each day, the likelihood of collection diminishes, and the value of the debt portfolio diminishes also.

Collect on final bills

Typically utility credit systems automatically produce the initial final bills and notices. The time in which utilities maintain in-house collections varies from 30 days to more than 100 days. Most utilities tend to maintain in-house collections until the point of write-offs.

A new trend emerging is called *early out*, in which a third party steps in, typically between days 30 and 100, to pursue collections. An early out program targets final bill collection at least 60 days prior to write-off. This work may be performed by a utility or a third party that specializes in this window of time when an account is finaled but has not been written off. The early out process involves using automation to check for a new service by phone number, social security number, contact information, and other information. Some credit experts estimate that a good early out process can reduce write-offs by 25%. The benefit to a third party completing this work is that they have refined the process and have the technological tools available to make the process more efficient and can thus work at a lower commission rate.

Use collection agencies

Utilities have varying strategies with respect to collection agencies. Typically, once utility debt is written off, the accounts are transferred to a primary agency. Some utilities also use secondary and tertiary agencies.

A recommended practice is to use several collection agencies in order to evaluate performance. Some utilities publish each month the recoveries by each agencies so that the respective agencies can see how they are performing against other agencies. In fact, the utility may also place more collection amounts based on the performance of the agency. Other utilities establish performance standards linked to incentives and penalties for their collection agencies. It is important to monitor the success of the collection agencies.

Credit experts recommend placing credit with a secondary agency after one year. The difference between primary and secondary agencies is generally in their area of expertise. Organizations that serve as secondary collectors have technology, processes, and techniques for evaluating and teasing out collections from old debt. Another way to handle secondary collections is to simply rotate the debt from one primary collector to another after a period of time. Since primary collectors have different approaches, a fresh look at the debt portfolio by the agent may produce results at a lower cost than formally securing a secondary agent.

Data mining is a great tool to understand which agencies are performing best with which types of accounts. This *drill down* data allows a utility to segment the accounts to the agencies based on their areas of expertise.

Some utilities use tertiary agencies. When considering secondary or tertiary agencies, it is important to analyze one's debt. For example, if the utility balances are small, $100 or less, and considering the yield rates and commission a utility is paying the agency, it may be looking at single-digit recovery. At this point, it may be more lucrative to sell the debt.

Pursue legal collections

A legal collection involves pursuing legal action to either secure an account or pursue a collection. In situations in which a customer owns property and has an outstanding balance, a lien is placed on the property. The lien remains on the property until the customer applies for financing or attempts to sell the property. At this point, the lien is paid in order to complete the transaction, with appropriate interest applied.

Sale of bad debt

Selling bad debt is becoming increasing popular. When debt is sold to a third party, the third party takes over the risk associated with the debt. The reason to sell bad debt is that the value and recovery from selling is higher than continuing in a traditional recovery program. This is why all major banks sell bad debt. At some point it becomes more valuable to sell.

The timing concerning when to sell varies from utility to utility. Bob Hall, vice president of InoVision, states that the "best time to sell nonperforming debt is determined by the potential purchaser and the utility. It takes some data analysis to identify the optimum point of sale."[15] For example, if a utility has good final bill process in place and a strong primary collections agency, then it may want to maintain the debt for 7–12 months with the primary agency before selling it.

There are several benefits to selling the bad debt. A key benefit is an influx of dollars to reduce current write-offs. But perhaps more importantly, selling the debt eliminates the utility's administrative work associated with a dispute. For example, if an account is with a primary agency and there is a customer dispute, the utility is front and center in researching the issue. Once the debt is sold, the risk and responsibility for disputes then belong with the new owner. They will likely choose to waive the bill and move on to another account.

Mitigate bankruptcy

In today's economy, bankruptcy is becoming more common. The primary area of focus for utilities with respect to mitigating the impact of bankruptcy should be on the commercial accounts. Some utilities will have a bankruptcy specialist on the credit and collections team. This person will monitor accounts and use external information to identify customers whose financial situation may be degrading.

The credit bureaus can provide customized analysis on a utility's commercial and industrial portfolio. One may find that a combination of information for several bureaus is needed to address different segments of one's customer base. Dunn and Bradstreet, Equifax, and Experian all provide services and models that identify accounts for closer monitoring. Once an account is identified, the utility will want to minimize exposure by encouraging payments, securing a deposit or some other type of security, or renegotiating a contract.

Mine data

A key strategy that is often overlooked is to analyze the accounts that are written off. Are these repeat customers? Are the customers residential or nonresidential, homeowners or apartment dwellers? Do they have good credit or poor credit? Utilities fail to recognize that many of the same customers are repeat write-offs. Hence it is important to mine the data to help a utility identify where delinquencies and charge offs are coming from and enable the utility to design specific actions to address the specific segments. The data will be compelling to sell internal management on the process change.

Data mining can increase the effectiveness of a utility's collections processes. By understanding the behaviors of its customers, a utility can most effectively apply the appropriate intervention. Data mining can identify customers who will pay based on a notice or phone call versus those who will require a field visit.

COMMON MISTAKES TO AVOID

Utility customer care leaders need to be aware of some common mistakes made with respect to credit processing (fig. 8–1).

1 Lack of integration of credit and collections with other areas of the business

2 Benchmarking performance without regard to differentiating factors

3 Lack of investment in credit and collections systems

4 Failure to capitalize on the policies, tools and technology in place

5 Culture that bad debt is not important as it is recovered through rates

6 Lack of talent and skills in leading credit processing

7 Hesitancy to partner with third parties

8 Assume charge offs will track history

9 Not challenging public utility commission rules and regulations

10 Lack of data mining or inability to data mine

Fig. 8–1. Common mistakes

Lack of integration

Lack of integration of credit and collections with other areas of the business is common. Many utilities continue to operate in a silo, not realizing the impact that upstream processes have on downstream processes. One new utility credit manager realized that write-offs were on the rise. Her research into the causes for the increase revealed poor data quality. The poor data could be traced to two specific years, 1998 and 1999. Her research into past practices revealed that during the late 1990s, the utility had foregone gathering customer information in an effort to answer more calls. The life cycle for credit is long, and in this case, the penalty for not gathering this information was revealed several years later when write-offs continued to rise.

The silo effect can work in reverse when a credit leader implements changes to a process without notifying the call center, billing, or other key areas. One utility credit manager learned a valuable lesson on this when, in an effort to address mounting arrears, notices were sent to accounts with very low balances. The problem was that the call center was not in a position to handle the flood of incoming calls. The result was many frustrated customers, employees, and regulators, with little impact on arrears reduction.

One excellent way to improve integration is through service level agreements (SLAs) with other departments that credit and collections depend on to complete fieldwork or investigations. Common measures using shared scorecards highlight the importance of credit with other key functions. Bob Hall cites the advent of SLAs as the most significant advancement for credit and collections during his tenure as Duke Power's general manager of credit and collections. Hall notes, "Duke was successful at getting charge-off related goals on all key individuals' annual performance reviews and/or incentive plans. This drove the right behavior."[16]

Benchmarking performance without regard to differentiating factors

If one moved a utility operating in the South to the Northeast, write-offs would increase due to economic, regulatory, and geographic factors.

In fact, the average difference in write-offs of utilities in the South as compared to utilities in the Northeast is significant.

I can personally attest to the differences. My credit teams in Florida and in Massachusetts reduced write-offs more than 20% in a two-year period. In Massachusetts, our write-offs as a percent of revenue were four times greater than the write-offs in Florida. Reasons for the differences included that in Florida, deposits were secured from both residential and commercial customers to mitigate losses. Late pay fees were in place to encourage prompt payment. Fuel prices at the time were rather stable in Florida, and terminations of service could occur year-round.

To successfully benchmark, it is more effective to select a peer group of utilities. At NSTAR, we have a peer group that serves a similar urban environment, with similar regulatory and regional challenges. We segment the write-offs into quartiles to measure our performance against peers.

Lack of investment in credit and collections systems

Enhancements to the credit and collections systems are often low priority for utilities. Even utilities that implement new CIS platforms often overlook upgrading the credit and collections portion of the system. The reason is that utilities often focus on ensuring the CIS meets regulatory requirements and supports customer interaction. For a credit manager, this means that adding programming to support the sale of bad debt may take months to get prioritized as an improvement. Enhanced reports that enable more targeted, cost-effective field collections or early customer intervention are sometimes ideas that never materialize. Data mining for credit and collections is an underutilized tool, in part due to the lack of available data or tools to easily access this information.

One effective strategy to mitigate this is to work with third-party vendors who often bring more robust technologies and processes to the table. Third parties will have sophisticated predictive dialer capacities and the trained staff to support and enhance the technologies. Additionally, the third parties have access to additional data to append to customer contact information, which aids in collections.

Failure to capitalize on the policies, tools, and technology in place

Some utilities are not fully taking advantage of the policies, tools, and technology they have in place. A very common example in the industry is failure to secure adequate deposits from customers at the time of service initiation. Additionally, requesting an additional deposit amount when an account is identified as a risk is sometimes overlooked.

Time is of the essence when pursuing collections. Some utilities diminish their collection opportunities by not tightly following the credit timeline afforded to the utility. For example, the utility may not proceed in a timely manner with late pay notices, disconnection, or referral to a credit agency.

Culture that bad debt is not important

A few utilities have a culture where credit and collections is not valued or considered important. One reason is the rationale that bad debt just rolls into the rate base. This rationale does not provide an incentive to reduce. The good news is that today, more utilities are realizing that focusing on credit and collections is a good practice. There is increased pressure by customers and regulators to maintain or reduce rates.

Support for credit and collections must come from the top. Companies with support from the top will have shared goals on write-offs with key departments and will invest the necessary resources into improving the entire process of the credit and collections life cycle.

Lack of talent leading credit processing

A retired credit and collections manager lamented that since his retirement, three individuals had been in the credit leadership role in a period of eight months. Bruce Gay shared the story of a credit manager who left hundreds of thousands of dollars on the table due to sole sourcing versus competitively bidding for a service.[17] The credit department can sometimes be seen as the dumping ground. It is sometimes viewed as a place no one wants to go and where people are moving in and out while finding a job that best fits. The danger with not putting experienced, talented employees in the credit department is higher write-offs and more expensive collections.

Utilities serious about write-offs are placing talented strategic leaders over credit and collections. Some are looking externally for credit expertise from the retail, credit card, or banking business. Additionally, these utilities support the credit and collections leadership by providing incentives to make improvements. These leaders are taking the process apart, step by step, understanding the point of integration, and improving the process.

Hesitancy to partner with third parties

Outsourcing credit and collections processes is on the rise. With that said, utilities continue to be hesitant to partner with third parties. Some utilities are limited due to labor contracts in their ability to outsource. Utilities may have imbedded costs that will not go away once an outsourcer is in place. This may make outsourcing look less attractive. Very often, utilities have a culture of wanting to do it themselves.

What a third party can bring to the table is a credit culture. Highly effective third parties have credit and collections as a core competency. They invest in innovation, technology, and process improvements to ensure they provide a competitive advantage. They also bring scale and contingency recovery to the picture.

Assume charge-offs will track history

When preparing budgets, a common practice is to use previous performance as an indicator of future performance. This can be problematic with respect to bad debt. If a utility has been successful at continually reducing bad debt, the danger is to project this forward to the upcoming budget. A better practice is to augment this forecast with other data, such as sales growth, economic outlook, and fuel price. Connecting with the experts in the utility's sales and load forecasting area will provide valuable insight into key economic data.

Not challenging public utilities commission rules

Utilities are hesitant to address existing rules and requirements with respect to credit and collections. Some of these requirements, which may have made good sense at the time, are outdated and do not reflect the advancements in consumer expectations or technology available today. An example of that was in North Carolina, where the commission guidelines on notifying a customer of a pending disconnect required a physical notice to the customer's home. When this rule was originally designed, many rural customers did not have phone service available. However, 50 years later, phone service is pervasive. Contacting customers via phone is an excellent technique and provides a win/win situation of giving the customer the opportunity to make arrangements with an agent while receiving the call.

Progressive utilities are reviewing and addressing existing rules and requirements where it makes sense in order to create credit processes that better meet customer and company needs. Another great example of this is the move by several utilities to establish tiered reconnect fees.

A tiered reconnect fee is based on cost of service during normal working hours and after working hours. Utilities with tiered reconnect fees can offer customers a choice when the customer is waiting for a reconnect. In a situation where the customer payment is after-hours, the customer is offered a choice of an after-hours reconnect at a premium fee or to wait until normal business hours for the lower reconnect fee. This choice is well received by customers and meets the needs of the utility.

Lack of data mining or inability to data mine

Utility credit managers often do not review written-off accounts for trends and use this to refine or change their credit strategies. Many times this is due to a lack of methods to assess information or a lack of tools to analyze credit accounts. A good investment for utilities is to start analyzing data for trends. If systems are not in place to do this, a great first step for the utility is to create the systems that support data analysis.

With more than $1 billion estimated annually being lost due to nonpaying customers, reducing bad debt will continue to be a priority with utilities. Successful utilities will use a blend of strategies that address active, delinquent, and finaled accounts. The most effective strategies use data and behavioral-based scoring to cost-effectively deploy customer intervention methods.

REFERENCES

1   Pollard, George. Vice president, major accounts, OSI; Interview, November 29, 2004.

2   Gay, Bruce. President, Monticello Consulting Group; Interview, November 29, 2004.

3   Ibid.

4   "Marketing Utility Products and Services." Chartwell New Products and Services Research Series; pp. 63–98.

5   Zdep, Bill. President, Forward Thinking; Interview, December 3, 2004.

6   Hall, Bob. Vice president of marketing, InoVision, and formerly general manager of credit and collections, Duke Power Company; Interview, November 30, 2004.

7   Zdep, Bill. Interview, December 3, 2004.

8   Ibid.

9   Maloney, David. DMC Consulting. "Returned Mail: An Analysis of Industry Trends and Process Enhancements." EEI, March 2000.

10 Lalima, Bob. Director of sales, RUI (a credit and collections provider); former credit manager, Keyspan and Brooklyn Union Gas; Interview, December 16, 2004.

11 Hall, Bob. Interview, November 30, 2004.

12 Simas, Tony. Director of credit and collections, NSTAR; Interview, December 2004.

13 Utilipoint International PowerHitters, 2003; David Steele, vice president of business development, First Contact; May 8, 2003.

14 "Credit Collection Net Write-offs." AGA/EEI DataSource. 2004.

15 Hall, Bob. Interview, November 30, 2004.

16   Ibid.

17   Gay, Bruce. Interview, November 29, 2004.

9 CREATE EFFECTIVE CHANNEL MANAGEMENT

Channel management is a deliberate strategy with respect to the various customer communications that range from highly personalized face-to-face interaction to completely automated service. Success for utilities in channel management is the ability to offer customers service in the way they want it, when they want it, at the lowest available cost to the utility. Since utilities serve diverse customer bases, this generally means offering a variety of channels in which to do business, along with deliberate initiatives to migrate customers to more cost-effective channels.

This chapter will discuss channels commonly used by utilities and examine channel management by customer service process. For each process, there will be a review of the most applicable channels, target customer segments, and strategies to maximize the channel.

COMMON CHANNELS

Utilities have historically relied on face-to-face, mail, and phone-based channels in order to bill and service customers. The advances in telephony and IT capabilities, the introduction of the World Wide Web, and changes in customer expectations are transforming the way utilities serve customers. It was not that long ago when telephony and IT systems started support of centralized call handling. Prior to that, representatives at local utility offices were in the best position to respond to a customer inquiry, as this often meant researching paper-based files.

Telephony advances of automatic call distribution (ACD) systems in conjunction with online customer information systems supported increased

CSR productivity in centralized call centers. For many utilities, this advancement supported the consolidation of customer service personnel and gained the benefit of the pooling principle so important in today's call centers.

Concurrent with the rapid advancements in IT and telephony were the increases in customer mobility and the concept of service 24 hours a day, 7 days a week. The phrase *24/7* became part of the vernacular in the 1990s. Customers were also becoming more accustomed to self-service. Banks introduced automated teller machines (ATMs), and gas stations introduced self-service gas pumps.

This combination of changing customer dynamics, rapid technology development, and increased pressure on utilities to reduce rates has resulted in utilities offering customers more options on ways to do business while lowering overall cost. The channels offered today by utilities have expanded beyond face-to-face, inbound phone, and mail options to Web, interactive voice response (IVR), outbound phone, and kiosk options.

Face-to-face customer service

Face-to-face service is still utilized by utilities for various key stakeholders. Most utilities have an account executive team in place to provide more personalized service and support for their largest customers. Many utilities also have community relations personnel who maintain relationships with key government officials and community leaders. Company owned and operated local business offices are still used by utilities to provide customer service. In fact, 27% of investor-owned electric and gas utilities continue to provide face-to-face customer service in local business offices.[1]

Mississippi Power, part of Southern Company, is an example of a utility that continues to maintain local offices to serve its 200,000 customers. These local offices process customer payments and provide full customer service, including answering account questions, initiating service, and completing deferred payment arrangements. Joe Gentile, manager of revenue accounting for Mississippi Power, says, "We have maintained local offices because we want to keep a local presence in the town. It is a rural territory." Interestingly, Mississippi Power has more payments come in via the local office than via central cash remittance. Clearly this option is popular for these customers.[2]

Mississippi Power, like other utilities with local business offices, provides full service in the office. Some utilities only offer collections services in the offices and direct customers to courtesy phones for customer service. Additionally, many utilities are upgrading the local business offices from a security standpoint to discourage a robbery attempt and protect employees. Utilities equip the local business offices with easy-to-use cash processing systems with real-time updates. Utilities also offer drive-through service at some locations to enhance customer convenience.

When installing courtesy phones, a utility should provide good signage directing customers to the phones in languages appropriate to the customer base. Arranging for some privacy while on the phone is appreciated, as is a small counter on which to make notes.

Another face-to-face option is the use of pay agents to handle customer payments. Authorized pay agents are third-party agents who process utility payments for a small transaction fee. Customers who deal in cash or money orders find pay agents to be a good option. More than one-half of utilities are taking payments through pay agents.[3] These pay agents may be located in convenience stores, grocery stores, or other types of retail businesses. The value proposition for the pay agent is to increase traffic to its location by taking utility payments. For the utility, it is offering customers the convenience of a number of payment options and extended payment hours in the evenings and on the weekends. Utilities can contract with a third party who then contracts with the individual pay agents and provides the equipment and training. Utilities also can set up their own pay agents. For this option, the utility takes on the burden of installing cash processing equipment, and providing training and contract management.

Duke Energy had yet another innovative solution to face-to-face service, and that is through utility payment centers. These payment centers, which are operated by a third party, are unique in that they process a variety of utility payments in addition to offering other services like check cashing, wire transfers, and payday loans. Many of these utility payment centers were located where Duke Power formerly had its business offices. The result has been continued high satisfaction ratings by its customers on the billing and payment transaction.[4]

For key accounts, face-to-face service is very common via account executives. Utilities vary in their definition of key accounts, but most commonly key accounts represent the largest customers based on revenue. Utilities segment key accounts into groups such as industrial accounts, national retailers, and municipals. Account executives typically handle 50 to 100 accounts. Finding the right personnel is the most critical factor in providing service via account executives to a utility's large customers. Account executives who have a solid understanding of the key utility processes and are adept at working with other departments to ensure service to the customer will be the most successful.

Inbound phone-based customer service

Inbound phone-based customer service occurs when typical utility calls on billing, credit, moving, emergencies, etc. are routed to a call center for processing. With the advent of call center technology, many utilities are moving away from providing face-to-face customer service in local offices. Amazingly, in the late 1990s, more than 75% of investor-owned utilities provided service via local business offices, as opposed to only 27% today.[5] Utilities like BG&E have successfully migrated customers from face-to-face to phone and other self-service methods without negatively impacting customer satisfaction.

At Tampa Electric, during my efforts there, 30% of the local offices were closed, but customer satisfaction, as based on a J.D. Power survey, rose for the billing and payment experience and customer service. Tampa Electric moved from 11th nationally in billing and payment satisfaction to 5th in three years. The improvement in customer service was more dramatic, and Tampa Electric improved from 20th place to 1st place.

Gentile points out that Mississippi Power "offers the best of both worlds. The call center handles over 500,000 calls annually. We offer our customers the fast-paced transaction options via the IVR, phone, and Web. We continue to offer the convenience of local business offices." [6]

A key to successfully providing customer service via a centralized call center is to ensure that appropriate service levels are maintained so that the services are easily accessed by customers. Additionally, re-engineering processes so that the transaction can be completed via the phone is important. One utility that was re-engineering customer service to support phone-based service identified six transactions that required the customer to physically go to an office to provide a signature. New designs and authentification processes had to be created to support phone-based service.

Having a sound telephony structure to support an efficient phone center is a centerpiece. Some key elements include adequate phone trunks to prevent busy signals, an ACD to more efficiently route calls, emergency power backup to ensure constant service, and an IVR system. As a utility designs the interior of its call center, it should make sure the atmosphere is positive, with adequate lighting and ergonomic design.

Mail

Utilities still use traditional mail to provide service and communicate to customers. Bills and notices are typically provided today via direct mail. Most customers still prefer to get information via regular mail versus the Internet, as evidenced by the low adoption rate for Internet billing of 2.5%.[7]

The utility bill is a very important tool for communication and branding the utility. All customers receive a bill, and for some customers, the utility bill is the only communication they have with their utility. J.D. Power survey data indicate that only 40% of residential customers contact the utility during a 12-month period.[8]

Billing design should be done thoughtfully and should involve many key stakeholders, including marketing, customer service, and regulatory staff, among others. Innovations in billing include personalized billing that includes relevant information for a segment of customers, and billing in multiple languages. Beyond bill design is the design of the envelope and return envelope for easy customer processing. Marketing with bill inserts continues to be popular, but utilities increasingly are placing marketing messages right on the bill, as this is where customers are more likely to read them. Utilities are also using the return envelope fold over for marketing messages, energy efficiency reminders, or customer service reminders. Offering bills in other languages or in Braille is becoming increasing important. Technology enhancements are making these options more cost-effective.

Interactive voice response service

Interactive voice response (IVR) became prevalent in the 1990s. The early versions of IVRs were not always well designed or user friendly. This quote from a bank customer summed up what many customers felt about early IVRs: "When I called in to authorize the card, they had one of those phone systems where it's all handled by the computer. It was annoying, like a bad start to the relationship."[9]

The combination of design enhancements to IVRs and changes in customers' expectations is resulting in increased customer utilization of IVRs, with some utilities achieving 30%–50% or more of all calls handled through IVRs. Duke Power won national recognition for its IVR redesign project.[10] After re-engineering the IVR, Duke Power moved from handling 39% of calls in the IVR to 50%. The changes by Duke included simplifying the menu, offering Spanish-language outage reporting, and offering payment processing.[11]

Public Service Electric and Gas successfully increased IVR from 5% in 1995 to more than 30% in 2000, while significantly reducing staff. Their analysis of inbound phone calls revealed that 68% of calls could have been handled via the IVR. Their focused initiative to re-engineer the IVR was founded on customer feedback.[12]

Some best practices with respect to IVR design include minimizing the number of options, offering customers *outs* within the menu to speak to a person, and designing it so the customer can quickly access the functionality desired. The innovation of voice recognition is transforming this technology and its consumer appeal. Research from Chartwell indicates that 17% of utilities now offer voice recognition technology.[13]

Utility IVRs today handle a variety of applications. High-volume, lower complexity calls are some of the best calls to move to the IVR. Some typical applications include outage reporting, account balance, payment plans, payment by phone, payment verification, bill copies, and meter reading.

Internet

Internet or Web-based services are becoming increasing popular. Overall, 63% of adult Americans use the Internet.[14] Utility Web sites are not the most popular with customers. Data shows that 83% of customers have never visited their energy company's Web site and 46% of those who did only visited once in the past year.[15]

Utilities have been working hard to improve their Web sites to attract the ever-increasing audience of Internet users. The result is that utilities are seeing growth in customers using the Internet for utility service requests. The functionality of billing and payment are some of the most popular features for Web-based service. Energy management tools are a hit with customers. The Web also supports other utility areas, like corporate communications and investor relations.

The most successful Web sites are both rich in function and useable. *Rich in function* refers to functions that customers want to see or might expect to see from an energy Web site. *Usability* refers to ease of use of the various functions.

From a functionality perspective, customer research by Platts indicates that there are key functions customers expect. These include an ability to check the account balance or the status of a payment, authorize an electronic payment, review frequently asked questions, ask general questions about a bill, or access customer service.[16] Utilities that have seen success with respect to their Web sites complete their own customer research to validate key functionality that their customers value. Some common functions that utilities are now offering on their Web sites include:

- **Account management self-service.** This feature allows customers to view their account balances, check on payment status, and pay their bills through automated payment options.

- **Contact the utility.** This feature provides customers an easy way to make service requests or submit questions.

- **Bill presentment and payment.** This feature offers customers the option of receiving their bills electronically and paying electronically.

- **Energy management information and online audits.** These features aid customers in understanding their energy usage. The most robust energy management tools link to the actual usage referenced in the customers' bills.

- **Frequently asked questions.** This feature offers a quick reference for customers on how to read their meter, how to read their bill, and moving or transferring service instructions, among many others.

- **General information.** This catchall feature offers the option of providing basic information on pricing, rates, products, and services offered by the utility.

From a usability perspective, the most successful Web sites make it easy for customers to do business with the utility online. The information on the site is relevant and up-to-date. Responses to inquiries or service requests are made in a timely fashion.

To achieve making it easy to do business, the utility should make sure the site has easy navigation with screens that are not cluttered. It is important to review the fonts to ensure they are sized appropriately and to reduce scrolling. Search time can be reduced by grouping information in meaningful ways. Another best practice is to display data clearly.

To ensure that content is relevant, it is important to have an ongoing content review process that includes all stakeholders with content on the Web. The most successful teams are very cross-functional and have clear ownership for specific content. Resources and support for timely update of the content are also available.

Many companies are providing instant responses to customers who have inquiries to reassure the customer that the inquiry has been received. Often this note will include information on when the customer can expect a response. For service requests, customers are also given more real-time information and confirmation numbers.

Outbound phone

Outbound phone customer contact is becoming increasingly popular. Research indicates that outbound calling is used by 72% of utilities.[17] By far the most common utility use with respect to outbound phone calls is with credit and collections. Outbound calling is used as a friendly reminder to encourage payment.

Other applications where utilities use outbound communications are for returning customer calls and for outage notification. Utilities will offer customers the option of leaving contact information for a return call as a call volume peak shaving option. There is technology available to offer this service in an automated fashion to customers.

The technology in outbound customer contact has evolved. Predictive dialers can in essence queue customers for service by the next available agent. The dialer screens out the busy signals and ring/no answer calls. Many of the dialers today can leave an appropriately scripted message on answering machines. Actual customers are then queued up for service by the next available agent.

Best practices with respect to dialer design are to complete calls when customers are available. This is sometimes referred to as prime time. Designing an outbound campaign with a low abandonment rate is a best practice. A rate below 2% is a good target. If the rate is higher, then customers are on hold much longer for a representative. It is this phenomenon that occurs when one answers the phone at home, as I do often, only to find that there seemingly is no one on the line. I am generally not patient to wait beyond saying *hello* three times, but apparently many customers will wait.

Outbound communications are being used not only for credit purposes but also for outage notification. The outbound communications can be automated to provide customers updated information on estimated restoration times, planned outages, and storm status. With outage situations, it is important to communicate with many customers quickly. This is why utilities often partner with third parties for high-volume outbound communications. The third parties bring a strong telephony infrastructure to play.

Because automated outbound communications are inexpensive, in the range of $0.15 to $0.30 per call if using a third party, and significantly less if using internal equipment, utilities are finding other applications for outbound communications.[18] Energy management or efficiency messages can be offered to customers in an outbound message format. Companies specializing in outbound messaging will offer this service in multiple languages.

Outbound communications are proactive in nature, and if targeted appropriately can offer the utility a cost-effective communications option. If the messaging or contact is well designed, customers will feel positive about the interaction.

Kiosk

A relatively new channel is the self-service kiosk. Modeled after ATMs, a fully functional kiosk can provide customers the convenience of paying their bills in a self-service fashion. Salt River Project has used payment kiosks for several years in conjunction with their prepay metering offering. Overall, this technology has not been heavily adopted by utilities. Only 13% of utilities offer bill payment kiosks.[19]

CHANNEL MANAGEMENT BY CUSTOMER SERVICE PROCESS

In order to design a channel management strategy for one's utility, it is helpful to look at the key processes with respect to each channel (fig. 9–1). For each customer service process, it is important to first identify which channels are appropriate for the process. To issue a bill to a customer, the most appropriate channels are regular mail and Internet.

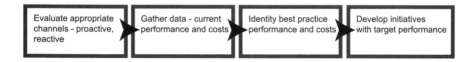

Fig. 9–1. Channel management development process

Once the determination has been made on appropriate channels, the next step in the process is to gather data on the utility's current state, including its performance and costs. Then it is necessary to research the performance of other utilities and companies offering similar processes. The objective here is to identify best-in-class performers. For example, if a utility's IVR is handling 15% of its calls, and best-in-class is 50%, while the average for the utility industry is 25%, this would indicate a potential area of improvement, and perhaps a targeted initiative to increase the usage of the channel.

This section demonstrates how a utility can get a head start on its channel management strategy development by matching utility customer service processes to appropriate channels and to the appropriate customer segments. The process evaluation tool highlights the typical costs per transaction using the following categories:

- **Practically free.** Costs range from $0.00 to $0.15.

- **Very low cost.** Costs range from $0.15 to $0.50.

- **Low cost.** Costs range from $0.50 to $3.00.

- **Efficiency opportunity.** Costs range from $3.00 to $10.00.

- **Premium.** Costs are greater than $10.00.

The process evaluation tool also notes the target customer segments for each channel and the opportunities the utility has to maximize the channel. Each section also will discuss successful migration strategies to move customers to lower cost channels.

Billing process

Billing is one of the simpler processes to evaluate. Billing is a proactive and one-way communication. Applicable channels to consider are mail and Web-based electronic billing (table 9–1). Mailing the bill is a mainstay to ensure that customers receive their bills. Electronic billing is becoming more popular with customers, with adoption rates averaging 2.8%. Some utilities are achieving as high as 4%.

Channel	Cost per transaction	Audience	Opportunity
Mail	Very low cost	All customers	Migrate customers to electronic billing
Web	Practically free	All customers	Expand use with marketing and incentives

Table 9–1. Billing channel evaluation tool

There are several options for billing electronically. The *biller direct* model is the option whereby customers directly access the biller's Web site for bill presentment and payment. The *bill consolidator* model involves the presentment of bill information through a third-party consolidator. A new arrival is the bill via e-mail, where the bill is presented to customers via their *Inbox* as opposed to the Web site.

Chartwell's 2003 research determined that 2.8% of customers subscribe to online billing. Using a combination of biller direct and bill consolidator can increase customer adoption rates to 4.1%.[20] There are many service providers and service options available to assist a utility in offering this capability.

The opportunity in the billing process is to encourage customers to migrate toward electronic billing. One of the most cost-effective migration strategies is to communicate frequently using existing channels. For utilities, these generally are the bill inserts, bill messages, e-mail messages, Web sites, and the bill envelope. A second part to migrating customers is to identify a target customer segment where this option may be attractive.

Leveraging existing communication channels is the most cost-effective option. For customers who are visiting a utility's Web site or those for which a utility maintains e-mail addresses, marketing through the Web site and e-mail messages is a low-cost or no-cost effort. A utility can place a promotion right on the homepage, or send out an e-mail with a link to a sample electronic bill. Using bill inserts and bill messages is another low-cost tool, and it is natural, as the customers are focused on the utility bill at the moment of opening their bill. Utilities have had great success with placing promotional ads on the back flap of the return payment envelope. Customers see this as they are making their payments. Others have used the actual bill envelope to note promotional messages.

With respect to targeting key customer segments, natural candidates are customers currently visiting the utility's Web site. Other customer segments are customers on automatic fund transfer programs or budget billing. Customers on these programs have expressed a desire for simplicity and ease of doing business. If the utility captures e-mail addresses, this becomes another segment of customers to target.

The IVR on-hold message is another low-cost tool to market this service. Utilities can also place an announcement on their Web sites or send e-mails, which are also low-cost options.

A more costly marketing technique is to identify customer segments that are highly likely to use electronic billing and target marketing efforts toward them either via direct mail or e-mail. Utilities can purchase e-mail lists for nominal costs. With direct mail, a postcard is a more cost-effective approach as the utility can eliminate the envelope costs and leverage reduced postage. A targeted postcard promotion can be done for less than $0.50 per customer. More elaborate direct mail pieces that require envelopes increase in cost on a per-customer basis, depending on the direct mail piece design.

Other innovative options include incentives and partnering with other stakeholders. Utilities can offer incentives or entice customers to enroll by giving them a chance to win prizes. Other utilities have partnered with bill consolidators or banks to complete joint promotion of the service.

Payment process

There are many channels to evaluate when considering payment options. The channels range from the most expensive, which are in-person payments, to the least expensive, which are electronic payments (table 9–2). Electronic payments refer to a range of alternatives from automatic bank drafts to online Web payments.

Channel	Cost per transaction	Audience	Opportunity
Face to face: Utility office	Efficiency opportunity	Unbanked customers, time urgent customers	Migrate customers to lower cost channels
Face to face: Payment agent	Low cost	Unbanked customers, time urgent customers	Migrate customers to lower cost channels
Inbound phone: CSR	Efficiency opportunity	Time urgent customers, customers wanting convenience	Automate so CSR does not need to process
IVR	Very low cost	Time urgent customers, customers wanting convenience	Expand
Kiosk	Low cost	Prepay customers, unbanked customers, customers wanting convenience	Migrate to lower cost channels
Mail	Very low cost	All customers	Expand
Web	Practically free	Customers wanting convenience	Expand
Electronic payments: bank draft, fund transfer	Practically free	Customers wanting convenience	Expand

Table 9–2. Payment channel evaluation tool

Utilities may choose to maintain local business offices for community, branding, regulatory, or other reasons. The opportunity is to reduce costs associated with maintaining the office. Some utilities have moved to only taking payments at the local office, and directing customers to courtesy phones, which connect directly to the utility call center. Duke Power has an innovative approach of converting business offices to utility payment centers, which are operated by a third party. The benefit to customers is that they can continue to pay their Duke Power bill as they have always done, but they may also pay other utility bills and take advantage of other conveniences offered in the utility payment center, like check cashing and payday loans. Duke has found this strategy not only successful meets customer needs, but also significantly reduces its operational costs.

Authorized payment agents provide support for cash-only customers. Payment agents are a critical component of a strategy to close business offices. Utilities may choose to overpopulate an area with payment agents in the early stages of closing a business office to provide customers with many options. The opportunity here with payment agents is to reduce low-use locations that are more costly to operate.

"If you build it, they will come" holds true when offering payment in person at business offices. When I was at Tampa Electric, I realized that to build support for a dramatic change of closing business offices, compelling data would be needed. Using the information from the DataSource, I widely shared the following chart highlighting the large percentage of walk-in customers when business office availability was denser (fig. 9–2). The graph, based on more than 60 utilities that maintained at least one or more business offices at that time, shows that utilities that averaged one office per 26,000 customers had a walk-in rate of 31%. The walk-in rate dropped significantly to 9% in the fourth quartile for utilities with one business office per 550,000 customers. When I combined this chart with cost data highlighting that the annual cost to maintain a business office for Tampa Electric was $250,000, it became a more compelling option.

The approach we took at Tampa Electric to close offices was slow and deliberate. The employees were involved in designing and implementing the customer communication plan, which was implemented 90 days ahead of the impending closure. Additionally, several payment agent locations were sited near the office to provide customers other options.

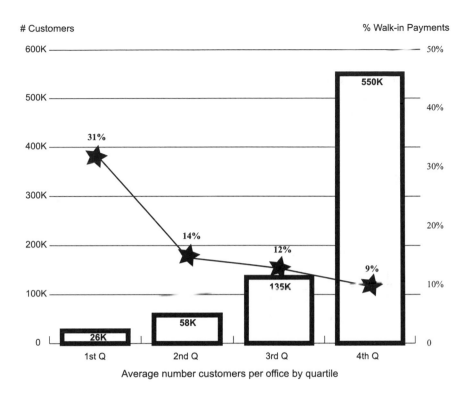

Customers

% Walk-in Payments

600K ——————————————————————————— 50%

550K

500K ——————————————————————— 40%

31%

400K —————————————————————— 30%

300K —————————————————————— 20%

200K ——————————————————————
14%
12%
9%

135K
58K
26K

100K —————————————————————— 10%

0 ———————————————————————— 0

1st Q   2nd Q   3rd Q   4th Q

Average number customers per office by quartile

Fig. 9–2. If you build it, they will come.

Interestingly, the most often asked question from customers was what was going to happen to the employees. Many of these customers had been coming to the office for years and knew each employee by name. It was very reassuring for customers to hear from employees about the new opportunities they would be moving to.

In the case of Tampa Electric, after business offices were closed, additional funding was provided to the call center to improve service levels along with payment agents. Not only did costs per stub reduce as customers migrated to bill payment by mail, but customer satisfaction increased. The vice president at the time told me long after the strategy had been implemented that it seemed counterintuitive to him that business offices could be closed and customer satisfaction could improve. He admitted he had serious doubts, but nonetheless, supported the strategy. In the end, he was very glad he did.

Best practices to migrate customers to lower cost options include closing physical business offices while concurrently offering other payment options, like more payment agents and payment over the phone. Credit cards and checks can easily be processed over the phone. This provides a great convenience to customers who want to avoid late payment fees or need to have a real-time payment processed.

The opportunity with payments over the phone is to automate the transaction versus handling it with a CSR. Handling payments over the phone with a CSR is time-consuming and costly. More cost-effective solutions include using a third party to provide the service. This can be done at a relatively low cost of approximately $1.25 per stub. Utilities may choose to offer phone-based payments with a convenience fee paid for by the customers. This is a very common approach for credit cards, but many utilities also use this for check processing.

Some utilities are designing their IVRs to provide check payment via phone at no cost to the customer. The cost to the utility is in designing the programming and ensuring that the processing follows all appropriate regulations.

The payment process is the most common one referenced in a kiosk strategy. Kiosks can replace utility business offices and can be located in customer-convenient locations, like malls or grocery stores. Few utilities have implemented kiosks. The ones that have done so have combined them with their office and prepay meter strategies.

Mail is still a standby for most customers to make payments. The opportunity utilities have in this channel is to continue to move customers to automated payment options and to reduce costs of remittance processing. The key to reducing remittance processing is to minimize payment exceptions, which add additional administrative costs, and if outsourcing, it is important to periodically re-bid the service.

Using automated services and offering customers payment options real-time on the Web are the lowest cost options. Automated funds transfer is ideal for residential and business customers who seek easy ways to do business with their utility. Offering Web payment is the natural complement to electronic billing. Customers expect that electronic bill offerings come complete with payment options online.

Some utilities have been innovative in migrating customers to automated services by offering incentives. A common incentive is to reduce or waive the deposit fee if the customer signs up for bank draft. Salt River Project offers a 1% discount to customers who pay via their SurePay automatic payment program. Other incentives include a reduced connection fee for automated pay selection and rebates on the electric and gas bill.[21]

Outage

Responding to outage or emergency calls will require a mix of channels. For gas utilities, responding to gas leak calls with a live CSR is a requirement. For electric and water utilities, some outages will require CSR knowledge and guidance to properly record the outage. While utilities will always need to provide live voice answer, many are managing and reducing the costs to handle outage calls by using technology. The IVR is becoming a major processor of outage calls. Some utilities are achieving more than 50% of outage calls processed via the IVR (table 9–3).

Channel	Cost per transaction	Audience	Opportunity
Face to face	Premium	Key accounts	Use on exception basis
Inbound phone: CSR	Efficiency opportunity	All customers	Move customers to self-service
IVR	Very low cost	All customers	Expand
Outbound phone: CSR	Efficiency opportunity	Key accounts, media, government officials	Use on exception basis
Web	Varies	Media, emergency organizations, local government, customers	Expand
Outbound phone: automated	Very low cost	All customers; customers wanting outage updates, planned outage customers	Expand

Table 9–3. Outage channel evaluation tool

While it is not ideal, there are times when face-to-face communication is needed during outage situations to deal with key accounts or highly upset customers. In a protracted outage situation, customers may seek out utility employees at various operations centers. Staffing these centers with customer care personnel to communicate with these customers is a good practice that enables the operations folks to maintain their focus on repairs.

Many emergency calls are handled via CSRs. While utilities are continuing to increase the number of customers to automated services via the Web and IVR by providing more robust outage information, some customers still prefer to speak to a CSR. With protracted events, customers who use automation may at some point wish to speak to a CSR. The key to handling outage calls successfully, whether via automation or with a CSR, is to give the customer information on the event that is relevant to his home or place of business. Utilities are finding success with this by linking CSRs and automated systems directly with outage management systems (OMS), which can give customers specific estimated times of restoration for their own premises, if available.

Proactive outbound notification is becoming more popular for key customer segments, like key accounts, or crucial care customers who rely on electrically powered devices. While utilities can do this in-house using a predictive dialer, for large numbers of customers, it is more effective to partner with a third party that has sufficient telephone capacity to make thousands of calls in minutes. Northeast Utilities, for example, previously used its outbound dialer to contact critical care customers, but this process took several hours. By partnering with a third party, the notification time is now in minutes.

Outbound notification is the most cost-effective when it is totally automated, including the message that customers hear on the emergency event. There are situations for particular customer segments, like key accounts or key community leaders, where a personalized outbound call to update them on progress is greatly appreciated. A good emergency plan will identify those key customer segments and identify appropriate personnel to make the outbound calls.

The Web is gaining popularity as a tool for customers to monitor the progress of outage restoration. I used to hear folks say that if the customer's power is out, he obviously cannot use his PC to find out information. In today's world with battery backup, this is no longer true. The Web is popular with customers who may be located with other family members or who are out of town, since it allows them to check on the restoration progress at their premises. This tool is also valuable to media and emergency organizations that need to be closely linked to the restoration progress during large outage events. Progress Energy has Storm Central on its Web site, which provides customers instant access to all aspects of outage restoration. Storm Central uses a map display of the total number of outages and the areas impacted by the outages.

Best practices to increase IVR utilization include providing a user-friendly IVR that links to the utility outage management system. This provides customers with more specific information on their premises. Establishing a high customer match rate via the phone number is a requirement for high IVR utilization. Some utilities are seeing upwards of 85% matches by using a variety of techniques to ensure updated phone numbers. These include completing regular updates, encouraging customers to update their information, and storing more than one customer phone number. Utilities that are achieving high IVR usage rates for emergencies provide their customers with information that is specific to their outage, including the cause of the outage and the estimated time of restoration. Providing customers with a confirmation number prevents repeat calls from customers to check if their outage was recorded.

Outbound phone messages offer another option with respect to outage management. Some situations where outbound, prerecorded messages are helpful include the following:

- Estimating time of restoration is not available, but when it is available, the customer can choose to be updated via outbound phone call

- Notifying customers of planned outages

- Notifying customers of major changes in the outage situation

Account information

Account information can be cost-effectively offered on the Web and by IVR. Utilities can also provide account information via CSRs in the phone centers or in local business offices (table 9–4).

Channel	Cost per transaction	Audience	Opportunity
Face to face	Premium	Large accounts	Exception basis
Inbound phone: CSR	Efficiency opportunity	All customers	Minimize calls to CSR that can be handled via automation
IVR	Very low cost	All customers	Provide accurate, real time account balance information
Mail	Very low cost	All customers	Information rich bill statements that eliminate the need for the customer to call
Web	Practically free	Business customers, customers wanting more robust information	Offer robust applications and information, i.e. energy mangement services

Table 9–4. Account information channel evaluation tool

For large accounts, or unusual billing situations, face-to-face meetings may be necessary. This should be the exception rather than the rule. A best practice with account information is to use automation to triage calls. The simple calls can be handled via the automated tool. Simple calls, for example, are questions on current account balance. More complex calls are routed to CSRs. The Internet is also an option that will be attractive to some customers who have more complex accounts, like business accounts. The most common strategy here is to provide account information via the Web and Internet, thereby screening out the easier calls and leaving the remainder for CSRs.

To encourage customers to use automated account information services, a utility should provide real-time information that records payments in a timely manner. On the Web, providing customers with easy links to applications like energy management applications is a great technique to not only enhance satisfaction but also create self-service.

Service request

Utilities field a variety of service requests, including simple rereads, service connection, and relighting appliances. Service requests can be handled by a variety of channels (table 9–5).

Channel	Cost per transaction	Audience	Opportunity
Face to face	Premium	Large accounts	Exception basis
Inbound phone: CSR	Efficiency opportunity	All customers	Minimize calls to CSR that can be handled via automation
IVR	Very low cost	All customers	Enhance IVR to support simple order placement and order status update
Web	Varies	Business customers, customers moving, customers needing order status	Migrate more customers to this self service channel

Table 9–5. Service requests channel management tool

Face-to-face handling of a service request should be an exception. This may be necessary with a key account or for a complicated service request. Otherwise, it is more cost-effective to offer customers self-service options and minimize service requests that must be handled by a CSR.

The business case for fully automating self-service requests is sometimes challenging to utilities. This is due to the complexity of business rules involved with many service requests, like new service, and the programming costs associated with automating to CIS.

Utilities sometimes choose to present the customers with self-service capability via the Web, but behind the scenes they still have a CSR who reenters the information into the CIS. It is easy to offer the form on the Web so that the customer has the Web option. The more difficult part is tying the form directly to the CIS.

By presenting customers with self-service options via the Web, the utility can gather data for a business case. The number of users of the application and the time for a CSR to re-key the request into the CIS behind the scenes can build the business case for end-to-end automation from the Web to the CIS. At NSTAR, for example, we offered customers the ability to request service connections, disconnections, and transfers. During 2003, more than 30,000 customers chose this option. The estimated labor savings of automating these requests was close to $200,000. This data helped move this to a priority IT project.

In the IVR strategy, it is very effective to program the IVR to support simple service requests or to gather information that will reduce the call handle time for the CSR. Some simple requests, like service disconnections, can be handled with the IVR. Information that will be needed by a CSR to process the order via phone can be secured in the IVR menu, expediting the call. This might include information such as the phone number or the date for service disconnection. Offering status information on a service request is another application that reduces calls to CSRs.

Energy management

Energy management is function that is valued by customers, and as such, it contributes to brand image. Energy management services also contribute positively to customer satisfaction.

Developing a strategy on energy management is aided by an understanding of the cost-effectiveness of the various services that a utility provides as based on the energy savings. Each utility will need to create its own unique strategy considering its customer base and services. Since energy management is a value added service, which impacts satisfaction and brand, there are other considerations beyond just its cost to provide that a utility must consider when evaluating the channels (table 9–6).

Energy management is an area where the channel selected needs to be matched carefully to the customer segment. Utilities will offer energy management to their largest customers through the account executive team. The account executives will match the business needs of the customer with the various products and services offered by the utility.

Channel	Cost per transaction	Audience	Opportunity
Face to face	Premium	Key accounts and all customers with large opportunties to reduce energy usage	Limit field visits to key accounts or qualifying customers
Inbound phone: CSR	Efficiency opportunity	All customers	Provide meaningful information; migrate to web
IVR	Very low cost	All customers	Provide energy management tips
Outbound phone: CSR	Efficiency opportunity	Targeted customers	Provide energy management tips and advice
Mail	Very low cost	All customers	Use bill inserts and bill messages for tips on energy management. Target direct mail pieces to key customers
Web	Varies	Customers wanting interactive process	Market and incent customers to this channel

Table 9–6. Energy management channel management tool

Utilities are becoming innovative with self-service offerings to customers via the Web. A tool like an energy calculator that helps customers better understand the energy usage in their homes is very popular with customers.

Utilities that do offer face-to-face consulting or home energy audits have an opportunity to triage requests so that the more expensive home visits are targeted to customers who will gain the most benefit. For example, a customer who is in a new home that meets the latest building codes may be thrilled with a home audit, but the identified savings from the audit will be small. Utilities that must prove the cost-effectiveness of programs like home audits will find benefits in offering these customers online tools like the energy calculator or handling them via a phone CSR.

Utilities are using IVR and mail to proactively communicate with customers concerning energy saving ideas and tips. These tools can direct customers to an interactive Web-based application that will enable customers to better understand their usage and opportunities to save.

Credit management

Credit management involves reminding customers of arrears, encouraging payment, and, if necessary, discontinuing service if payment is not forthcoming. Many utilities are turning to third parties to assist in the various segments of credit management, as was described in chapter 8. Clearly the opportunity with credit management is to reduce write-offs and the cost of collections. Hence low-cost channels and self-service are very attractive with credit management, as is highlighted in table 9–7.

Channel	Cost per transaction	Audience	Opportunity
Face to face	Premium	Key accounts needing credit advice	Tightly integrate credit and account management to review and address arrears
Inbound phone: CSR	Efficiency opportunity	All customers needing credit advice	Move to self service
IVR	Very low cost	All customers needing credit aggrangements, payment options, reconnects, account information	Offer robust self service payment arrangements, payment processing and reconnect order fulfillment
Outbound phone: CSR	Efficiency opportunity	Targeted credit customers	Move to lower cost channels
Mail	Very low cost	Targeted credit customers	Expand
Outbound phone: Automated	Practically free	Targeted credit customers	Expand

Table 9-7. Cost of collections by channel

IVR, Web, mail, and outbound messaging are the lowest cost channels to prompt and encourage customers to pay. Utilities have been successful in migrating customers to lower cost options by offering customer friendly, easy-to-use applications. For some credit customers, it is preferential to request payment extensions using automation, as they may be embarrassed about their situation. Proactive channels of outbound notices, phone calls, and outbound messaging are also excellent tools to reduce the cost of collections and improve satisfaction with the process.

While in-person help is a very expensive option, it is sometimes necessary in cases where there is fraud, theft, or a highly sensitive customer. One utility credit manager shared her story about a nursing home that had not paid its bill in more than two years. The credit manager enlisted the support of an account executive to meet in person with the customer and encourage a payment arrangement. The customer's response was that the utility "will not cut me off." No effort was made to pay. The credit manager worked then with people in community affairs, regulatory, media, and the legal department, along with the account executive, for the next six months determining the appropriate steps necessary to discontinue service. The steps included multiple customer notifications, arrangements with other health care organizations to handle the residents of the home, and notification of key government officials. In the end, the service was not disconnected. These steps indicated to the nursing home management that the utility was serious. The customer made the needed payment.

Successful channel management provides customers service in the way they want it, when they want it, at the lowest available cost to the utility. Successful utilities are very deliberate in identifying opportunities to migrate customers to lower cost channels. The tools presented in this chapter are designed to help utilities identify their key areas of opportunity.

REFERENCES

1   AGA/EEI 2004 DataSource; a benchmarking tool available to AGA/EEI members.

2   Gentile, Joe. Manager of revenue accounting, Mississippi Power; Interview, December 17, 2004.

3   "Chartwell's Guide to Bill Presentment and Payment 2003." Chartwell Inc., March 2003, p. 27.

4   "Reducing the Costs of Walk-In Collections While Keeping Customer Satisfaction High." Kevin Goodwin, Payments manager, Duke Power Company; EUCI conference, 2001.

5   AGA/EEI DataSource 1999 and 2004; a benchmarking tool available to AGA/EEI members.

6   Gentile, Joe. Interview, December 17, 2004.

7   "Chartwell's Guide to Bill Presentment and Payment 2003." p. 17.

8   Destribats, Alan. Executive director, Utility Group, J.D. Power and Associates; Interview, August 21, 2004.

9   Lloyd, Jack. "A New Approach to In-Depth Voice of the Customer Research." Presentation at EUCI conference, December 6, 2004.

10   Duke Power received Electric Light and Power and Chartwell's Projects of the Year Award in 2004.

11   Davis, Kathleen. "SMUD, Duke Power win EL&P/Chartwell Projects of the Year." *Electric Light and Power.* September/October 2004, pp. 28–29.

12   Workman, Dave. "Maximizing Contact Center Value for Your Organization through VRU Technology." Presentation, January 2002.

13   "Speech-Enabled Customer Service Applications in the Utility Industry." Part of the Chartwell CIS and Customer Service Research Series, Chartwell, Inc., February 2004.

14 America's Online Pursuits Power Internet & American Life Project.

15 E Source Residential Market Survey. 2001.

16 "Customer Service using the Internet." Platts Research and Consulting; The McGraw Hill Companies; Andrew Heath, director, E Source E Business Service; Presentation, January 2003.

17 "Automated Outbound Communication." Chartwell Inc., September 2004, p. 7.

18 Ibid. p. 65.

19 "Chartwell's Guide to Bill Presentment and Payment 2003." Chartwell Inc., March 2003. p. 28.

20 Ibid, p. 18.

21 "Using Incentives to Move Customers to Self-Service Options, Internet and Bill Payment Methods." Chartwell Customer Care Research Series, Chartwell, Inc., July 2004, p. 4.

PART III

Maximize Technology, Processes, and Efficiency

10 MAP, MEASURE, AND BENCHMARK THE KEY CUSTOMER SERVICE PROCESSES

Hope is not a plan when it comes to delivering consistently excellent customer service. It is not enough to hope that one's employees know the right thing to do. It is not enough to hope that a customer's experience when calling one's company with a request will be satisfactory. Rather, excellent companies have a plan to consistently deliver quality customer service. This plan integrates people, processes, and technology.

The fundamental element in the plan is a set of clearly defined, measurable, and well-executed customer service processes. To the extent a company executes well-designed processes to deliver customer service, it will more frequently provide excellent quality. Process mapping defines the process so that it can be understood and well executed by all stakeholders. Process measurements help to manage the process and to identify when the process is not working as designed. Benchmarking helps to understand the gaps in delivering the process against others that are the best in their class. Robert Camp, with the Best Practice Institute, notes, "Before you can build strategies leading to world-class performance, you must first understand how world-class organizations operate; it's called best practice benchmarking."[1]

The opportunity in mapping, measuring, and benchmarking the key customer service processes is to identify areas of improvement. Dave Steele, vice chairman of IEI Financial Services, and former utility customer service executive, states, "Clearly the largest opportunity and the least understood is process improvement and the application of tools that help measure the activity and result."[2]   This chapter explores the tools and techniques associated with process mapping, process measurement, and benchmarking.

PROCESS MAPPING

Processes are no more than the steps by which work is done. Process mapping is a pictorial representation showing the steps involved in completing that work. It is a proven technique for creating a common vision and shared understanding for improving business results. Process mapping is most effective mapping the steps end-to-end from the customer's perspective. Process mapping offers several benefits:

- **Understanding of the process.** Process maps promote a more thorough understanding of the steps within the process. This can aid in gaining a consensus on how the process actually works.

- **Identification of process inefficiencies.** Process mapping amplifies where a process has multiple handoffs, or cycle time delays.

- **Communications tool.** Process maps provide a training tool to help employees understand their role in the process and how their role impacts the customer.

- **Definition of process measures.** By mapping the process, an organization can define the key metrics that are fundamental to that process.

- **Business case support.** Process maps are an excellent tool to highlight business case benefits of a proposed change.

Process map basics

Process maps can range from high-level maps to very detailed process maps. High-level maps are helpful to gain an understanding of a process from the big picture. The high-level maps provide a quick understanding of the process and areas of opportunity. Detailed process maps review each specific step, action, or decision point in a process.

There are common symbols used in process mapping. Commercially available software tools come equipped with the symbols and functionality built in to allow the user to quickly and easily produce process maps (fig. 10–1).

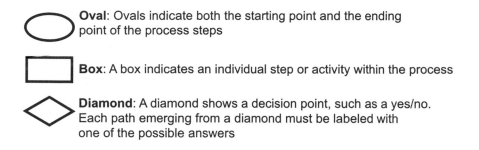

Oval: Ovals indicate both the starting point and the ending point of the process steps

Box: A box indicates an individual step or activity within the process

Diamond: A diamond shows a decision point, such as a yes/no. Each path emerging from a diamond must be labeled with one of the possible answers

Fig. 10–1. Symbols used in process mapping

Companies use both *linear* and *swim lane* process maps. A linear map is the most common. It details the sequence of steps that are involved in a process. Linear maps identify areas of rework or unnecessary steps in the process. A swim lane flowchart or process map depicts the sequence of steps. Swim lanes have the added benefit of identifying the people or groups involved in each step. Process maps using swim lanes are excellent for identifying the number of people or groups touching a process, and where handoffs can be avoided.

In customer service, processes often connect with other organizations. Utility outages or emergencies are examples of this situation. The customer service organization's role in the process is to provide the customer with easy ways to report a problem, along with providing the customer with available information about the problem resolution. Field organizations are generally responsible for diagnosing the actual problem and providing information on what the problem is and how long it will take to correct it. It is important when mapping processes that the final process map identifies the key connection points with other departments and the information needed from those departments.

To create accurate process maps, it is important to have participants familiar with the various steps in the process and to clearly define the beginning and end of the process. Without this up-front definition, teams can get bogged down mapping steps that are not germane to the project. Additionally, identifying whether the process map is a detailed, granular view of the process or a high-level perspective impacts the work of the team preparing the maps.

Using process maps

Process maps are integral to managing customer service processes and process re-engineering. Utilities delivering consistently excellent customer service maintain current process maps on all of their customer service processes. This process map reference becomes a tool to manage, train, and review processes. Process improvement and re-engineering efforts are jump-started when a company maintains accurate process maps.

Process maps are sometimes most valuable when used to improve process effectiveness. To do this, a first step is to document the *as is* process, or the process as it currently functions. Companies that have maintained process maps will just need to pull out the applicable maps. If no process maps exist, or if the ones available are outdated, then a cross-functional team can put together a map of the current process.

Once the current state of the process is documented, the team can identify the *to be* process, or the future process. Success in this exercise occurs when the team overcomes its natural tendency to limit its thinking on the future state with constraints the process currently has due to resources or technology. The best future state maps are an ideal vision of how the process would operate with maximum effectiveness.

For process improvement and re-engineering, the team then identifies the gaps between the current state and future state process. The gaps can be defined along with recommendations to bridge the gaps. Often teams will sort the recommendations by ease of implementation and significance of impact on either cost or quality of the processes.

When preparing a business case to implement recommendations, it is helpful to remember that pictorially showing the steps that are eliminated with process mapping makes an impact. The process map in figure 10–2 illustrates high-bill complaints in a swim lane format.

The swim lanes highlight that, in addition to the customer, two different employees may be needed to complete the high-bill complaint issue. This example combines current state and future state process flows. The steps in grey are the ones that are eliminated with advanced AMR. With advanced AMR, the need to involve a field service representative is eliminated. Advanced AMR would enable first-call resolution and would greatly reduce cycle time. The efficiency gains are significant. This process chart highlights the benefits of process mapping to support business case development.

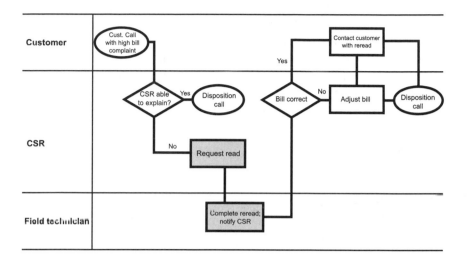

Fig. 10–2. Swim lane process chart for high-bill complaints

I was working with a team that was tasked with enhancing the process of initiating service to customers. The team started mapping the process. They were making great progress until they got to the point at which the customer is placed in a meter-reading route, and then the meter is read. The team then started to spend time detailing the meter reading process. I stopped in to check on the team, and they were frustrated with trying to map the meter reading function, as they did not have the experts in the room. I asked them to reflect on the goal of their project. When they did, they realized that their goal was not to identify how to improve the meter reading process, but rather to improve the process of initiating service. At this point, they adjusted the process map to identify how initiating service was linked to the meter reading process.

Clearly defining the key process steps will support the identification of key process and in-process measures. Successful companies measure the key processes and have these measurements linked to individual performance. In the case of processes that cross multiple areas, shared performance measures are powerful tools to ensure good delivery of service.

PROCESS MEASUREMENT

Defining process measures for each of the key areas in customer service is an important foundation for effective process management. Measures are leading indicators of customer satisfaction and business performance. Leading indicator process measures can provide important information about the health of a process and about the level of business performance. Furthermore, they can provide this information well in advance of other popular indicators, like customer satisfaction surveys. There is often a delay in customers noticing a change in their experience following the implementation of the process change. This section identifies some common utility measures grouped by the key areas in customer service.

In serving the mass customer service market, it is important to have a broad range of well-defined measures and to trust the resulting data from the measures. Aggregated information gleaned from well-designed measures is essential in the ongoing process of identifying necessary business change. When real data are not available, it is tempting to rely only on anecdotal data to identify a needed change. The downside of using anecdotal data is that this information often reflects the needs of a small number of customers, and as such, the resulting changes will not necessarily improve overall customer satisfaction.

From a macro perspective, utility customer service can be broken down into five areas of responsibility:

1. Read meters accurately and in a timely manner

2. Deliver timely, accurate bills

3. Process payments accurately and promptly

4. Provide quality customer service and information

5. Manage credit and collections effectively

There are common utility measures used to evaluate the cost and quality of each of these areas.

Utilities review costs of customer care processes to improve decision making. E Source notes, "Utilities can make better-informed decisions about customer care investments and operational matters when they are fully aware of all the costs and benefits involved."[3] Utilities need cost information to manage the daily business and to evaluate business options, such as transforming with automation or outsourcing to a third-party provider. Direct costs associated with labor and administrative support are reviewed. Another view of costs is the *fully burdened costs*, or indirect costs, which include overheads or other allocations. Savvy utilities thoroughly understand the cost structure of their customer service processes in order to make the best strategic decisions on investment or business opportunities.

Reviewing costs alone is not sufficient. The quality of the process must also be evaluated in order to make the best business decisions. Poor quality processes result in lower customer satisfaction and increased costs due to increased cycle time and rework. An error in meter reading, for example, can mean a second field trip to read the meter, additional administrative effort to correct the bill, and a delay in billing. This rework adds costs to the overall meter reading process.

Read meters accurately and timely

Effective meter reading involves accurately reading and recording usage on time and at the lowest possible cost. Meter reading includes the activities involved in securing usage data and the associated activities to record the usage. Meter reading cost is largely driven by labor, so utilities with a high penetration of AMR technology gain the dual benefit of lowering costs and improving quality. Automated systems, for example, do not need sick days or engage in *curbing*, a term used to describe a meter reader who inputs an estimated meter read rather than going to the meter for an actual read (table 10–1).

Cost Measures	Quality Measures
Meter reading cost per customer	Meter reading accuracy
Meter reading cost per meter	Percent of meters read

Table 10–1. Common meter reading measures

From a cost perspective, meter reading can be looked at by customer and by meter. Meter reading costs are impacted by access issues, skipped meters, poor route management, the population of automated meters, and customer self-service. Typically the costs included in the meter reading measure are the labor, vehicle, and administrative support costs. Utilities will monitor submeasures that impact cost, like the percent of meters read electronically and customers per meter reading employee. AMR costs can be impacted when ERTs do not respond.

From a quality perspective, utilities will measure meter reading accuracy and percent of meters read. Utilities completing manual meter reading will want an accuracy measure to monitor effectiveness of the field resources. Improving the percent of meters read reduces the customer issues associated with estimated bills or no bills at all. This percentage is also used in some states as a service quality index measured by the public service commission.

Utilities will calculate meter reading accuracy in a variety of ways. It is often difficult to compare meter reading accuracy numbers between utilities, since definitions of what is included in the accuracy measure vary. One of the easiest definitions is to measure when a second meter reading determines the initial reading was not accurate. However, this measure does not pick up every meter reading error, as some errors do not get intercepted by a CSR or even by the customer before the error self corrects on the next read.

The percent of meters read is another quality measure that is a predictor of estimated reads. Utilities use further measures, such as meters skipped and meters that could not be accessed, to understand the driving factors behind the percent of meters read.

Deliver timely, accurate bills

Effectively billing customers involves billing accurately, on time, and at the lowest cost. The billing process includes bill calculation, print, and mail functions, and any back office functions associated with correcting bills, processing bill adjustments, or correcting other errors in the process. AMR has a tremendous impact on the accuracy and costs associated with the billing process. With manually read meters, billing is enhanced with quality meter reading and robust CIS bill processing designed to identify potential errors (table 10–2).

Cost Measures	Quality Measures
• Billing cost per bill	• Percent accurate bills
• Billing cost per customer	• Percent bills mailed on schedule
	• Billing complaints per customer

Table 10–2. Common billing measures

Billing costs are impacted by labor and postage costs. Generally a more inclusive measure is billing cost per customer, since it includes the cost of bill generation, exception processing, printing, and postage. Billing cost per bill is often more narrowly defined as the bill print and postage costs. Both costs can be reduced by increasing the percent of customers billed electronically. Utilities that eliminate the mailing of a paper bill save significantly on postage.

A submeasure impacting billing cost per customer is the percent of billing adjustments or exceptions. Billing adjustments measure the number of times an event during the billing process requires action by a billing specialist. This measure can be compared with other utilities to gain insight on quality of the billing process. A high percentage of billing exceptions increases the costs associated with the billing process. Billing specialists will request re-reads where the meter readings appear suspect, and then they will complete necessary reviews and adjustments. The percent of meters read electronically impacts the billing costs by improving the accuracy of meter reading and reducing estimated readings.

The quality of billing can be measured by billing accuracy and the timeliness of billing. Quality from a customer perspective can be measured using bill resolution cycle time and billing complaints.

The definition of billing accuracy will vary from utility to utility, but usually includes a component for known billing errors that customers received that were not caught by the billing team. Bill accuracy may have a component of estimated bills. The percent of bills mailed on schedule highlights the speed at which the billing process is completed. This percentage will be lowered when a utility is dealing with a high number of billing exceptions or is experiencing resource constraints to review exceptions.

Billing complaints per customer highlight not only issues with the accuracy of the bill, but also the readability and understandability of the bill. Billing resolution cycle time measures the time delay from a billing question to resolution.

Process payments accurately and promptly

Effectively processing payments involves updating payment status in a timely, accurate, and cost-effective manner. The activities in this process include the collection of payments and the review, processing, and recording of payments. This function has metrics that can be compared across utilities on cost and effectiveness (table 10–3).

Cost Measures	Quality Measures
• Payment cost per stub	• % Remittance completed on day recorded
• Payment cost per customer	• Percent manual exceptions

Table 10–3. Common payment processing measures

The cost of processing payments is largely impacted by the payment channels offered to customers. Face-to-face payments in utility offices, as outlined in chapter 9, are the most expensive method of payment collection. Payments where the customer pays a convenience fee are the least expensive for a utility.

The channels offered and the popularity of those channels impact costs per stub and costs per customer. Utilities successful with strategies to move customers to lower cost payment options, like automatic bank draft, self-service payment over the phone or the Web, or customer convenience fee options, will lower the cost per stub. Submeasures on percent of customers using each channel are important to understand the success in various initiatives to move customers to lower cost channels.

Payment processing quality measures center around the timeliness and the accuracy of posting. Prompt payment posting aids in reducing the average DRO. Manual exceptions are more costly to process. A transaction that requires special handling outside of normal production is considered an exception. Examples of exceptions are checking encoding errors, such as a check for $1,000 that is entered as $10,000, situations where checks and stubs are separated, and payments applied to the wrong account. Exceptions take additional time, and if using an outsourced vendor, will add to the processing cost. A misapplied payment is one of the exceptions that is often reviewed separately because of the customer and financial impacts associated with applying payments to incorrect accounts. The correction of misapplied payments by the utility can be administratively time consuming and extremely frustrating for a customer.

Provide quality customer service and information

Effectively providing customer service involves timely, accurate provision of customer information in the lowest cost fashion (table 10–4). Processing inbound customer calls, e-mails, or electronic orders are activities included in this process. The call center is the predominant channel used to service utility customers. Fortunately, metrics for the call center aspects of providing customer information are in abundance. Purdue University, for example, offers the BenchmarkPortal, which manages the call center database originated at Purdue University's Center for Customer-Driven Quality. According to the BenchmarkPortal Web site, "This data warehouse of call center best practice statistics includes thousands of call centers in 24 industry segments."[4]

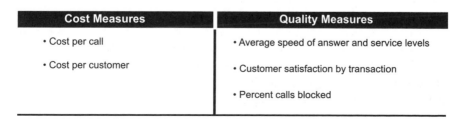

Cost Measures	Quality Measures
• Cost per call	• Average speed of answer and service levels
• Cost per customer	• Customer satisfaction by transaction
	• Percent calls blocked

Table 10–4. Common customer service measures

Cost measures around providing customer service and information include both cost per call and cost per customer. The cost per call is a measure on the most popular channel. The cost per customer is a more inclusive cost measurement that includes the costs associated with providing service via other channels, like face-to-face and e-mail.

On cost per call, factors that impact costs are CSR productivity, training costs, turnover rate, and calls handled via automation. CSR productivity is often measured by analyzing occupancy, average handle time, and adherence to schedule. The percent of calls handled by the IVR is the most common automation submeasure.

Occupancy refers to the percentage of time during a 30-minute period that those CSRs who are on the phone spend talking and completing after-call work. A high occupancy rate, such as greater than 90%, means that CSRs are processing calls with very little break in between calls. Service levels, which measure the percent of calls handled within 30 seconds or less, will decline in periods of high occupancy. Utilities experience high occupancy during emergency events, where call volume increases dramatically. High occupancy adds to the stress level of a call center. Prolonged periods of high occupancy lead to CSR burnout.

Average handle time is both the talk time and the after-call work time that a CSR spends in working with the customer. A user-friendly CIS can impact average handle time by reducing the time it takes to review an account and process an order. Training and coaching can aid a CSR in reducing average handle time by more effective screen navigation and proactive call management.

Adherence is the measure of time an individual is on the phone during the course of the assigned shift, available to take calls. Adherence to schedule may also be referred to as compliance to schedule. Call centers that are achieving high schedule adherence will more likely meet planned service level targets.

Companies experiencing high turnover will increase their costs due to additional training and lower productivity of new CSRs. It takes some time, from a few weeks to months, depending on the utility, for a CSR to achieve expected performance in call handle time.

Cost per customer includes costs associated with providing service via phone, in person, and over the Internet. Increasing the percent of calls handled via self-service will decrease the cost per customer. Understanding the costs associated with serving customers via each channel, whether self-service, face-to-face, or by phone, along with the popularity of the channel will impact the overall costs per customer. The annual number of calls per customer will impact staffing requirements. This is a submeasure that can be compared to other utilities to evaluate performance. Work practices impact the number of calls per customer. A utility that is aggressively addressing credit customers will see an increase in calls from credit customers, perhaps impacting overall calls per customer per year.

From a quality perspective there are two key drivers of customer satisfaction. The first is how easy it is for the customer to contact the utility. The second measure concerns the quality of the customer's interaction with the utility.

Common measures to gauge how easy it is for a customer to contact the utility include how often customers receive busy signals and how long they wait for a CSR once they reach the call center. These situations can be measured using telephony reports.

The number of times a customer hears a busy signal is measured through telephony reports on blocked calls. Companies generally aim for the level of calls blocked to be only 1%–3% of all calls. If a company is experiencing higher rates of calls blocked, this could indicate a need to expand the telephony infrastructure.

Service levels measure how quickly calls get answered. A common service level target is 85% of calls answered in 30 seconds or less. Another metric is the average speed of answer, which measures the time the average caller waits before the call is answered by a CSR. Most companies begin to measure average speed of answer from the point the customer exits the IVR and is in queue for a CSR.[5] An additional metric is the percent of calls abandoned, which is inversely proportional to the percent of calls answered.

The second element is the quality of interaction. First-call resolution is a key predictor to how satisfied customers are going to be with their transaction. NSTAR's transactional research illustrates the power of first-call resolution. More than 90% of customers handled in the first call are satisfied or very satisfied with their customer service experience. This percentage drops to 59% in situations where the customer had to contact NSTAR again.

At NSTAR, first-call resolution is measured using transactional surveys and is further reviewed using a repeat call measure. However, in the utility industry, few utilities measure first-call resolution, and those that do are not standardized in how they measure it. Research by Chartwell indicates that there is "no set standard for measuring first-call resolution in the utility industry. In fact, most utilities do not measure it at all."[6] As a result, companies have several methods of measuring first-call resolution. These include measuring just the percentage of calls transferred, measuring based on a sample of calls monitored, and asking customers during a transactional survey if their request was handled in one call. Utilities are creating databases that capture customer calls along with the disposition of the call. This database can be used to measure repeat calls, and to complete more detailed analysis into the reasons customers are not fulfilled on their first call to the utility. Customer transaction surveys are the most common way to measure satisfaction with the experience. These may be done via phone, mail survey, or by automated means using a post-call IVR application.

Manage credit and collections effectively

Effectively managing credit and collections involves implementing strategies with current accounts, past due accounts, recently closed accounts, and charged-off accounts such that the cost of credit and collections is minimized. The activities included in the credit and collections process include the creation and distribution of customer notices, field collections work, inbound and outbound collections calls, and post-write-off collection agency tasks. The cost component includes both the bad debt expense, which is comprised mostly of the actual write-offs from uncollectible accounts less recoveries, and the costs associated with the processing of credit customers. Quality is reviewed by looking at measures on the credit policy effectiveness and customer feedback (table 10–5).

On the cost side, the percent of bad debt represents the financial cost to the utility for uncollected revenue. The cost per past-due account is a different measure that provides a view of the resources spent to deal with credit issues.

234

Cost Measures	Quality Measures
• Percent bad debt write-off	• Days revenue outstanding
• Collections cost per past due account	• Credit complaints per 100 customers
	• Percent disconnects in error

Table 10–5. Common credit and collections measures

The percent of bad debt write-off is a common measure used to compare performance against other utilities. This is calculated from the net write-off versus revenue. The net write-off is calculated from the write-off dollars less recoveries on written-off accounts. If comparing percent of bad debt write-off to other utilities, one should use caution as varying service territory demographics and regulations impact bad debt tremendously.

Submeasures that provide insight concerning the percent of bad debt involve receivables and deposits. Aging receivables of greater than 90 days are a good predictor of future bad debt write-off. Intervention will reduce what is eventually written off from the 90-day arrears. Account deposits can mitigate the actual write-off associated with an account. Measuring the percentage of deposits secured on eligible accounts is a way to monitor that deposit guidelines are being closely followed.

The collections cost per past due account is the total collections costs as compared to the total accounts in collections. The collections costs include the costs of interventions via phone, letter, field visits, or agency fees. The percent of customers disconnected is a submeasure that can be compared to other utilities. A higher percentage of customers disconnected, which is the most expensive form of customer intervention, will lead to higher costs associated with past due accounts. The number of disconnects per field service representative (FSR) provides a productivity measure to ensure field resources are maximized. The credit calls per customer and percent of calls handled via automation are important submeasures to understand the office labor components.

From a quality perspective, DRO provides insight into management effectiveness. The measures of credit complaints per customer and disconnects in error are more customer-centric measures.

DRO is the average number of days from bill issue to payment. This metric is a good indicator of the overall effectiveness of the credit policy and processes. Credit managers can use 30, 60, and 90 days arrears trending to monitor and act on arrears in real time. The arrears trending provides insight to the DRO metric, which is often a rolling 12-month metric that is reviewed on a monthly basis. Submeasures impacting DRO include the percent of arrangements made, the percent of arrangements kept, average duration of an arrangement, and average arrears per customer. Measuring the percent of arrangements made, the percent of arrangements kept, and the duration of the arrangements is a method of monitoring the effectiveness of a credit policy. The average arrears per customer is an indicator of how high and how rapidly account balances are increasing. Credit managers have more success when they can keep the average arrears per customer low, as this means customers do not get so far behind that catching up is an impossibility.

Credit complaints are a customer-facing metric that is often monitored by regulatory bodies. Ensuring credit policies are applied consistently can greatly mitigate credit complaints. Call monitoring and sampling of credit arrangements are excellent tools to provide insight into the consistency in credit policy application

Disconnects in error are a terrible customer experience. Understanding the frequency of this occurrence is important to ensure that appropriate diligence is occurring before disconnecting a customer for nonpayment.

Selecting a final set of process metrics can be challenging. There is often the temptation to include every possible measure. It is actually more important to identify the critical few measures that truly indicate the effectiveness and efficiency of the process.

As one evaluates a series of metrics, it is important to consider the inherent value of the metric. Is the data available on an ongoing basis? How often is the data refreshed? If a metric is tied to an employee opinion survey, for example, it is likely that this metric is only updated annually. Is it possible to segment and stratify the metric? For example, if the metric is call handle time, one could segment this by type of call, CSR, or groups of CSRs. Is the metric subject to volatility? For example, call volume metrics are subject to seasonality changes.

Process measurements provide customer service leaders with information with which they can more tactically and strategically manage to achieve the best results. Identifying the right process and subprocess measurements for one's team is critical to managing performance. Additionally, process measurements provide calibration for a leader on whether the processes are running effectively as compared to other similar utilities. Benchmarking a utility's performance is a next key step in truly understanding where it has improvement opportunities.

BENCHMARKING

Benchmarking is a tool that allows companies to review, analyze, and compare key metrics to identify areas where performance can be enhanced. Benchmarking combined with process mapping is a powerful toolset to identify opportunities to improve the effectiveness, efficiency, and cost of a process. Effectiveness involves determining if all the process steps need to be done to deliver the service. Efficiency concerns the cycle time necessary to do the work. The cost structure of the process determines if there are lower cost alternatives to completing the work.

Benchmarking process

Benchmarking performance involves metrics and the identification of best practices. Best practices identify those factors that enable an organization to perform at its highest level. Robert Camp, Best Practice Institute, suggests when benchmarking that it is important to "choose leading companies that are good at what you need to be better at; it's a learning process."[7]

When embarking on a benchmarking effort, it is first critical to clearly define one's purpose and scope. Benchmarking, done thoroughly, takes a great deal of time and resources. Some benchmarking efforts require up-front fees in order to participate. If a utility is going to spend the effort and dollars, then it should be clear about what specific areas it is going to benchmark. Will the utility benchmark call center performance, billing, credit and collections, or some subset of these?

It is also important to determine with which companies comparisons will be made. Often utilities benchmark against other like utilities with similar demographics and customer bases. Benchmarking against peers identifies how a utility stacks up against them. Another avenue is to benchmark against other types of companies. Benchmarking against retail, banking, or other industries can reveal transformational ideas and practices.

If a utility does select companies with similar processes, it should seek out those that are well regarded. It is important to screen the potential companies for their real commitment to the effort. If the company is not going to take the benchmarking seriously, then the data provided may not be accurate. One way to screen for commitment is to find out why they are interested in participating.

Once a utility has selected a group of companies with which to benchmark, it is time to identify the important metrics and the definitions of each of those metrics. One should keep in mind that the more metrics there are, the more comprehensive the analysis will be of a company's customer service performance. The more robust the benchmarking study, the more resources will be needed to complete the comparison.

First-call resolve is a great example of a metric that needs a common definition used by all benchmarking participants. Different companies measure first-call resolve very differently. Some measure first-call resolve by measuring the percent of calls transferred. Others measure it using a question on a customer transactional survey or based on evaluation of calls monitored. Each of these methods yields an answer that is appropriate for the individual company, but it may not be comparable with other companies that measure differently.

Unit cost measures are another area to ensure a common definition. When looking at a cost per customer, one should make sure that the utilities participating in the benchmarking survey counted customers in a similar manner. For example, a dual service utility, such as gas and electric, may count a dual service customer as one customer, while others may count this person as two customers. This makes a tremendous difference in the cost per customer calculations.

When selecting the metrics, it is also important to ensure there are metrics around cost, quality, and customer satisfaction. Each of these areas is important to measure individually and corporately. For example, if a company is trying to understand how important service levels are to customer satisfaction, it is good to have the metrics on both customer satisfaction and service levels to determine the impact of lower service levels on customer satisfaction. Ideally when looking at the data, one should find situations where the cost is low and the quality and satisfaction are high. This will likely reveal a best practice.

Once the metrics and definitions have been agreed upon, then it is time to gather the data. When the data are returned, one should take the time to scrub the results for abnormalities or input errors. Data abnormalities are identified when the data deviate significantly from that of other companies participating in the benchmarking. When this occurs, it is best to talk with the company submitting the data and ask that they examine their input. If one is working in an effort sponsored by a third party, then one of the services the third party will provide is the review and scrub of the data prior to the participants viewing the data. In one benchmarking, a utility's cost per bill mailed was less than $0.10. It is likely that this utility did not include the cost of postage in the cost per bill calculation. Scrubbing the data is best completed with a group of representatives from the participating companies. This supports quick analysis and understanding of what may have been included or not included in the data provided.

With the data scrubbed, it can be sorted, and the subsequent findings can be acted upon. Cutting and slicing the data into multiple views can be very revealing. Too many times, companies just look at the top quartile. It is just as important to understand the range within the quartiles. In some cases, the difference between the top and second quartile may be very small.

Metrics in a benchmarking effort typically will be reviewed by the median, mean, and best and worst quartiles. How a company wants to perform with regard to a particular metric will depend on the company's strategic objectives.

With the benchmarking data sorted into various quartiles, it is time to identify significant gaps in a utility's performance as compared to others. To do so requires that a utility focus on the other companies and process areas where the cost is low, quality is high, and customer satisfaction is high as compared to the utility's own performance. Those are clearly areas for improvement.

Benchmarking studies

There are several firms that offer robust, formal benchmarking efforts. These comprehensive benchmarking studies generally include a participation fee, with potential additional fees for enhanced participation or consultation. For example, the fee structure may start with a base fee to participate in the study, but for an increased fee, it may offer the opportunity to design the actual survey and diagnostic tools.

One word of caution on using benchmarking consultants is that sometimes these engagements can take several months to complete. This time lag can create issues when a company has implemented process changes. One call center manager lamented to me recently that her company's management had insisted on the call center's participation in a benchmarking study. The goal for the engagement was to understand the gap in performance of her call center as compared to the top quartile. At the point of decision to participate in the benchmarking, the call center was performing poorly, but had many initiatives identified for improvement. Eight months later, the benchmarking was complete, and as predicted, it clearly indicated the call center's performance was in the bottom quartile. The problem was that the call center's current performance now matched the top quartile. The initiatives identified had worked as planned. The benefit of the benchmarking engagement in the eyes of this call center manager was marginal, due to the significant delay in learning the results.

To gather more timely benchmarking information, companies are turning to Web-enabled benchmarking. These online systems included automated processes to deliver immediate results. The Web-based benchmarking uses an online data template and includes validations in the template. Purdue University's BenchmarkPortal is an example of an online benchmarking tool targeted to call centers. Additionally, definitional parameters and subsequent expert reviews are completed. The data from benchmark participants are available, virtually in real-time, in preformatted online graphs and reports. Online tools are particularly helpful when insights are needed to understand a company's performance against industry norms. This type of tool is not as helpful when in-depth understanding and analysis of the drivers of excellent performance are the desired outcomes from the benchmarking engagement.[8]

A group of utilities may decide to complete a collective benchmarking on their own. With this, it is very important that the utility remains an active participant throughout the process to ensure that the end result has information and data that will be useful.

Industry organizations also sponsor benchmarking efforts. Since 1996, member utilities of the American Gas Association (AGA) and the EEI have benefited from a common benchmarking tool called the DataSource. Bill Mayer, EEI, notes that the DataSource is currently used as a benchmarking platform by more than 70 companies, not only for customer service metrics, but also for load management, investor relations, reliability, and other areas. The DataSource, which is an online benchmarking tool, incorporates the benefits of real-time data validation and preformatted reports. It also provides the user the ability to migrate data to in-house systems for more detailed data review. AGA and EEI sponsor annually a DataSource best practice workshop, which serves as a venue for utilities to share the practices and processes that enable top performance.

Mayer notes that one example of how the DataSource has benefited utilities is in the area of voice response units. The benchmarking data show that on average in 2002, 18% of calls were handed by VRU, and that the average is increasing at 2.5% annually.[9]

Benchmarking can be an expensive proposition. Formal benchmarking studies often cost a great deal just for basic participation. The participation also includes the numerous resources that will be required to secure, scrub, and analyze the data. Success in benchmarking occurs when a utility identifies best practices that it can implement to improve effectiveness and efficiency, and to reduce costs. Too often, though, companies benchmark and never make any changes in their operations based on the findings.

For transformational ideas, a utility could consider benchmarking processes against other businesses, like banking, retail, and credit card businesses. Companies in these industries are often using leading-edge technology and practices. For example, Bruce Gay, a well-known consultant to utilities on credit, and president of Monticello Consulting Group, points out that "even progressive utilities are a decade behind the banking industry with respect to bad debt. This is because the banking industry has had more of a focus on bad debt, as this was a significant part of their business."[10]

One caution when benchmarking is to avoid the tendency to only look at the performance at the top quartile. If a utility is in the top quartile, then many times the effort on that measure stops. However, there may be wide ranges of performance in top quartile. Additionally, the reverse can also be true. There may not be a significant difference between the top and second quartile.

When benchmark data reveals poor performance, there is sometimes a tendency for managers to get defensive. They will begin to identify the many reasons for the differences in the data or will point to variations among the companies responding. This is why common definitions of what is included in the metric are so important. For an example, one could compare cost per bill mailed. If Utility A has a cost of $0.38 per bill mailed, and Utility B has a cost of $0.65, while the average cost is $0.45, then Utility B has some opportunity for improvement. It is possible that Utility B may indicate that it included costs that Utility A excluded. However, the difference is so large in this case that improvement is still possible.

Utilities that deliver excellent service to their customers do so through defined, consistently delivered processes. The best utilities are constantly measuring their performance and looking for ways to improve their service to their customers. These utilities have a plan and execute it consistently to deliver top quartile customer service.

REFERENCES

1 Camp, Robert C. PhD, PE, Principal, Best Practice Institute; Interview, Ithaca, NY, May 2005.

2 Steele, Dave. Vice chairman, IEI Financial Services LLC, former vice president, Citizens Gas and Coke; Interview, January 27, 2005.

3 Gogel, Filomena. "The ABCs of Understanding Customer Care Costs." E Source, Platts, a division of The McGraw-Hill Companies, Inc, August 2001, UCC-8.

4 Benchmark Portal at www.benchmarkportal.com/newsite/managers/ CertificationJourney.html, accessed March 5, 2005.

5 AGA/EEI DataSource responses. "Eighty Percent Start Clock When Customer Requests to Speak to a CSR." 2004.

6 The Chartwell Customer Care Center Report 2005, Chartwell Inc., December 2004, p. 18.

7 Camp, Robert. Interview, May 2005.

8 Spencer, Steve, and Rich Shadrin. "Virtual Benchmarking." *Electric Perspectives*, March/April 2002, p. 43.

9 Mayer, Bill. "The DataSource." *Electric Perspectives*, March/April 2002, p. 44.

10 Gay, Bruce. President, Monticello Consulting Group; Interview, November 29, 2004.

11 COMPLETE A HEALTH CHECK ON THE CUSTOMER INFORMATION SYSTEM

Utility leaders continue to cite CIS functionality one of their top concerns.[1] Utility leaders are justifiably concerned, because the CIS is the platform that supports delivering quality, cost-effective customer service and accurately completing the revenue cycle functions. Utility CIS units range from very old, in-house developed systems to new, robust, highly configurable systems developed by independent software vendors.

The utility CIS is defined as the computer support system that stores customer information, houses the utility billing engine and algorithms, enables customer service order creation and fulfillment, and interfaces with multiple other utility systems. Such systems may include general ledger, financial, time management, field automation, credit and collections, and other applications. Availability and reliability of a CIS are top priorities to a utility, where service level expectations of 99.9% are not uncommon. That percentage means that a CIS is allowed less than 500 minutes per year of unplanned downtime.

CIS units are expensive to maintain, enhance, and replace. Hence there is appropriate consternation by utility executives when contemplating investment in a CIS. A utility can expect to spend $110 per customer to implement a new CIS. This fully loaded cost includes the fees related to vendors and consultants, as well as costs due to hardware, software, internal labor, and licenses. For a utility serving 100,000 customers, this translates to a cost of $11 million to implement a CIS.[2]

Customer leaders struggle with how to best enhance the functionality of their CIS. The solutions available today still include the option of building a new system in-house, buying a new system, extending the life of an existing system, or subscribing to a hosted solution. This chapter reviews the utility challenges impacting the CIS platform, reviews a typical utility CIS legacy model, and offers an approach to examine the health of the CIS. It will close with a review of options to solve CIS issues.

CHALLENGES FACED BY UTILITIES

Utilities face a variety of uncertainties that ultimately have an impact on how they serve customers, including pressures to reduce costs, improve service, and comply with changing rules and regulations. Since the CIS is integral to serving customers, the challenges must be understood in order to incorporate them into the decision-making process on the CIS strategy. Proper selection of the appropriate CIS strategy can significantly reduce costs, while the wrong decision can be disastrous. Successful utilities have a CIS strategy positioned to address future uncertainties.

Cost reduction is a major driver for utilities that are considering a change in their CIS. As utilities start to share and compare operating costs more rigorously, gaps in cost performance are highlighted. Bridging the gaps usually requires some technology enhancements. Utilities with older, inflexible CIS units face the reality that making programming enhancements to support best-in-class performance is cost prohibitive. The gap analysis thus supports the business case for a CIS.

Regulatory compliance continues to be a major driver of new CIS requirements. Each year new regulatory and other mandated rules are enacted that impact either utility bills or the way transactions are processed and stored. With the programming of each enhancement, many utilities question the continued investment in their existing CIS platform and the risk that continued change might destabilize the platform.

Utility leaders looking to improve controls on the revenue cycle will need to address the CIS platform. Utility CIS platforms provide many automated controls needed for compliance with requirements due to the Sarbanes Oxley Act. Compliance with Sarbanes Oxley (SOX) requires utilities on a controlled, systematic basis to ensure the customer data and systems are working as designed. Automated and preventative controls are preferred to manual controls from a SOX standpoint. Automated controls are not prone to human error and are more likely to quickly reveal issues that should be addressed. Preventative controls minimize rework and enhance the overall control environment. The challenge is that older CIS platforms do not always fully support needed automated controls, requiring manual workarounds.

Competitive market requirements also play into enhancements that are needed in a CIS platform. The ability to quickly respond to market needs or to offer innovative products and services is not usually built into the older CIS units. New product and service offerings may bring different billing parameters and may require sales tracking capabilities. Utilities in this situation must then evaluate enhancements to the existing CIS or the purchase of a new, more robust CIS that will complete all the required billing options.

Jackson Energy Authority, a municipal utility serving more than 40,000 customers in Tennessee, offers customers not only electric, gas, water, and sanitation services, but also offers propane and telecommunications. Their legacy CIS was not up to the task of handling the multiple billing requirements associated with each of these types of bills. For example, a typical telephone bill provides a summary of each call, including call length, and applies the appropriate rate. This is much greater detail than the electric bill, which takes the usage and typically applies one rate for a residential customer. In 1999, Jackson Energy Authority converted to a new CIS that can support the billing of all of these services. The CEO notes that their "customers are very impressed that we have all the utilities under one roof. They have one place they can do business. Our customers believe in our customer service, and this has allowed us to offer our customers more products and services."[3]

Utility mergers call to question the CIS platform. Executives want to gain the efficiencies associated with consolidating and supporting a single CIS platform. The challenge often lies in the standardization of work processes with two systems and the conversion costs associated with moving to a single system. The benefits of consolidation are the efficiencies gained from system maintenance and a technical resource support perspective. Consolidation of systems also enables the utility to pool customer service resources together from two separate utilities.

The ability to scale a CIS to support increased customer demands is a strategic consideration for a CIS. Utilities with aggressive customer growth strategies need a CIS that supports the aggregation of customers rapidly onto the CIS platform. Many older CIS platforms cannot scale up to serve significant increases in customer volumes.

In the municipal arena, the advent of 311 is causing leaders to consider a change in the CIS platform. The 311 designation is a new service number, similar to 911, that consumers can call for any type of municipal issue other than an emergency. The ultimate goal is to offer citizens 311 as a one-stop shopping convenience for consumer inquiries, from concerns about a stray dog, to an electric bill, to garbage pickup days. A few innovative cities have already implemented 311, and many others are considering doing so. The utilities implementing or considering 311 are evaluating their CIS platforms and their ability to support the broad range of inquiries and the significant number of interfaces with the respective department's work management and order systems.

How does one know when there are enough challenges that one should seriously consider an overhaul of the CIS? The answer will be very specific to each unique situation. The factors and considerations noted above, among others, will be included in the thought process on whether to replace a CIS.

Whether one is experiencing some of these warning signs or not, as a leader in customer service, it is important that one have a firm grasp on the health of the CIS engine that supports the customer service and meter-to-cash processes. The next section provides a template for thoughtful review of the CIS.

CIS PLATFORM

The CIS platform or engine can be broken down into common components. This platform will have a variety of customer contact channels from which work orders and inquiries are generated, along with a variety of systems with which it must interface (fig. 11–1).

A utility's individual CIS may not fit this model exactly. A first step in evaluating the health of a CIS is to identify the components housed in the

CIS. The model in figure 11–1 describes some of the common components. To model an individual CIS, components may need to be added or deleted, or divided into subcomponents for more accurate evaluation. There are several basics to the components included in this model.

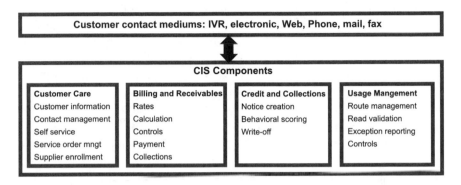

Fig. 11–1. CIS platform model

Customer care

The customer care component is a customer data repository for CSRs to access information and to complete business transactions for a customer. A dashboard provides the CSR with information needed for a large percentage of calls on one screen. Dashboards may include computer telephony integration technology and integration with other business systems that complete transactions, like outage management. Dashboards will include data edits to ensure accurate data entry and may also incorporate scripts to support quality interaction with the customer.

This component is the entry point for most customer transactions. It enables customer data search, retrieval, display, and maintenance of customer information. This component will link the customer information with other associated information on the account, service, and premise. This component supports CSRs by providing easy-to-access information to efficiently complete business transactions, and thus it facilitates first-call resolution.

Contact management is a feature of the customer care component. This provides a repository of customer interactions. This allows the CSR to know what information and actions the customers have had previously with the company and with whom.

Self-service for customers will be available within this component. Customers can access specific customer information pertinent to their account via the Web or IVR. This component may allow the customer to provide account updates, like a change in a mailing address or phone number.

This capability allows the integration of the IVR and computer telephony integration (CTI). The IVR links customers using automatic number identification data (ANI) or other data input by the customer, like account number, to attempt to identify the customer and present the customer with self-service options. CTI provides the capability of call routing and of presenting to the CSR the customer call simultaneously with the customer dashboard information.

The benefits of strong telephony components are reduced calls, since more are handled via automation, and reduced CSR handle time on the remaining calls. The CTI minimizes the search time a CSR normally requires to identify the customer. Customer satisfaction is impacted with this technology, as the customer does not have to repeat information entered into the IVR, like account number.

This component supports the transactions needed to initiate and provide customer updates on service orders. Most often, the actual work or service order management is completed on a separate provisioning system that is designed to maximize field efficiency, like mobile fieldwork management systems. These work management systems support the actual scheduling and assignment of work. These systems provide data updates to the CIS on the order status. Common orders initiated and updated in the CIS include service connections, service disconnections, transfers, and field investigations, among others.

Order status is provided on this component. This is dependent on the timeliness of the interface with various field order management systems to which the order may have been routed. For example, an outage ticket will route to an outage management system. Most outage management systems have frequent, if not real-time, updates to the order status. Other systems may not have real-time updates. If the fieldwork is still paper based, then the CSR is blind to the order status from the time the order is printed in the field until it is completed and updated in a batch process. This could take several days.

Enrollment with suppliers is a feature for utilities operating in a deregulated environment. This feature captures the customer's desire to switch service providers, while ensuring that appropriate switching procedures are followed. A supplier enrollment feature often includes self-service and electronic enrollment capabilities.

This component benefits the CSR by providing easily accessed information and order entry. A healthy service order processing component will allow easy completion of business transactions by the CSR or the customer directly. The order entry is supported with real-time edit checks to ensure accurate and complete orders. A good service order processing system will minimize rework due to entry error. Customer self-service is enabled from the service order processing component.

A well-designed customer care component is vital to providing customers with consistent quality service and first-call resolution. CSR training time will be reduced significantly with a robust customer care component. Repeat customer calls due to entry error or incorrect information are greatly reduced with a good customer care component. Utilities with robust customer care components are also achieving high rates of customer self-service.

Billing and receivables

The billing and receivables component is the true engine of a CIS, and it is what the original CIS units were designed to do. It is responsible for taking usage data, calculating usage, applying rates and determinants, and calculating accurate bills. The billing component will handle the mass marketing billing, which typically includes the high-volume, less-complicated bills. The billing engine may also handle the complex bills associated with large commercial and industrial accounts and unique contracts. The billing system may bill for assets like lights and other flat-rate arrangements. The complex billing capability needs to be robust and flexible to deal with frequently changing complex rates and customers.

The billing and receivables component will contain the rate tables and associated algorithms to complete the calculations of the bills. The rate tables need the flexibility to easily create, delete, and manage rates and appropriately apply rates to the applicable bills. Rate modeling is sometimes included as a feature of this component. Rate modeling is particularly helpful when evaluating proposed rate changes. The calculation algorithms will include those associated with applying rates to usage, but also offer estimation routines for each rate. The algorithms support associated billing offerings like flat bill or budget billing.

This component needs robust, automated controls and associated reporting. This is a fundamental requirement of the revenue cycle controls. Automated controls within the CIS provide more robust, accurate assurance that the systems are operating as designed. Augmented with manual and compensating controls, a robust CIS can provide assurance from a SOX perspective that the revenue cycle is billing accurately.

Nonenergy billing is sometimes included in the billing and receivables component. This is billing for items like contribution in aid of construction, fixtures, and claims, among others.

The billing and receivables component will support a variety of bill delivery methods, such as paper, XML, and e-mail. It also supports a variety of payment options, including electronic, over-the-counter, and automatic draft options. Payments can be received from multiple providers.

Exception identification and processing are key elements to a receivables management component. Timely exception identification and disposition assist in enhancing the financial reporting.

A healthy billing and receivables component provides timely recording of payments and prompt resolution of disputes. This improves the financial reporting for the utility and improves customer satisfaction, since payments are recorded promptly and accurately. The ability of the receivables component to handle both usage or energy and nonenergy types of billing is a plus, but it is not always incorporated into legacy CIS units.

A robust billing and receivables component is critical to key financial metrics of a utility. An engine that operates well will provide the issuance of timely, accurate bills, ultimately supporting low DRO. Billing exceptions are minimized in such a CIS billing component. Controls are in place to quickly identify and correct any billing problems.

Usage management

This component captures meter reading and usage data, which is used by the billing component to generate customer bills. This component captures usage, meter reading information, and route status. This component may also store the premises data.

Route management is a key function of this component. Information is used to optimize routes and maximize meter reading efficiency. Route management also supports accurate and timely bill generation.

Meter reading validation is especially important on complex accounts where multiple data are secured by the reading systems. This data must be matched against previous data and customer information to validate that accuracy.

Prompt identification of exceptions and robust controls are a feature of this component. Identifying exceptions quickly allows for accurate intervention to correct problems. The intervention may require a field visit to validate the information. Controls will provide assurance that all meters and usage readings by various field mechanisms were captured in the component. Controls also ensure that usage and meter information accurately flow to the billing component for the application of rates. These features are important in assuring accurate financial reporting and compliance with SOX requirements.

Premise data includes the physical attributes and is separate from the customer data. The customer may change, but the premise data are more constant. Premise data include the meter number, physical address, and service points. Newer systems will connect or move the premise information to a separate GIS database to be used not only by the CIS but also by other utility systems, like outage management and maintenance.

A healthy usage management component benefits a utility by providing accurate, timely usage information so that rates and determinants can be applied to generate a bill and maintain accurate premise data. Improved quality of usage records improves the revenue stream and supports more accurate sales forecasting. Route management ensures that field resources and equipment are maximized.

Credit and collections

The credit and collections component tracks arrears and initiates appropriate interventions to encourage payment. The module will include the capability to create a variety of notices, escalate the account appropriately as payment patterns dictate, and provide a user interface to support CSRs. The user interface will support easy creation of a variety of payment plans, along with a contact history. Contact history is particularly important in credit and collections to document customer payment requirements.

The credit and collections systems create a variety of data outputs and files for third-party use or internal use. Write-off algorithms are included based on the specifics of the utility.

More sophisticated modules include a behavioral-based scoring element, which may include both internal and external data on payment behaviors of the customer. Predictive models are created using this data to identify the most appropriate intervention. Utilities with robust behavioral-based scoring modules have been successful in lowering write-offs, with reduced field disconnects.

Financial reporting capabilities can serve as a feeder to a credit and collections module. These reports support improved financial records and receivables recovery.

The benefit to a robust credit and collections module is the ability to lower write-offs by appropriately targeting the lowest cost intervention. Additionally, easy linkage to third-party vendors is a plus in a credit and collections module.

CIS HEALTH CHECK

To evaluate each component, a customer service leader should assess the health of technology support, usability, functionality, and architecture. The health of the various CIS components may range from critical care to a clean bill of health. It may be acceptable to have some components not as healthy, depending on the criticality of the component to one's business model.

This section describes the symptoms to monitor when evaluating the CIS with respect to technology support, usability, functionality, and architecture. There are identifiable differences in components that have a clean bill of health as compared to those that are in critical care.

Please note this caution on completing self-evaluations. They are just that, the equivalent to visiting a general practitioner for one's annual physical. If there are some concerns that arise from the health check, or if one's utility is facing some significant challenges, as described earlier in the chapter, then it is advisable to bring in a specialist to assist in completing a more thorough examination of the CIS.

There are many firms and consultants that bring a great deal of experience and knowledge to bear when evaluating a CIS. These specialists can also provide realistic advice on the cost, resource requirements, and change management impacts a CIS change will have on one's operation. They provide an understanding of the opportunities to improve business processes associated with new applications. My dad was fond of saying, "You don't miss what you have never had." This is true for CIS users. They do not miss functionality or capabilities they have never had. Third-party consultants can introduce users to the new capabilities, and in some cases can reveal a business need that had not been previously identified.

What one wants to avoid is not taking the time to complete an honest health check of the utility's CIS. Greg Galluzzi, president of TMG Consulting, which provides utilities guidance on CIS installations, points out that "too many times, people have a sense something is not going right, but wait to address it, then end up in a crisis. When you are in a crisis, you take shortcuts and do not complete adequate planning. The result is a higher cost solution."[4]

A cross-functional team of business and IT professionals is in the best position to discuss, debate, and determine the health of each component. For each component, this team should evaluate the healthiness of the component with respect to technology support, usability, functionality, and architecture. The following section provides self-assessment continuums, along with descriptions to aid in the health check of the CIS.

Technology support

Unsupported technology can move a component from critical care to dead on arrival. Unsupported technology includes old technology that is no longer supported by the original creator of the application. In a custom legacy CIS, unsupported technology includes the impending loss of the technical support staff through retirement or lack of depth in the technical support staff (fig. 11–2).

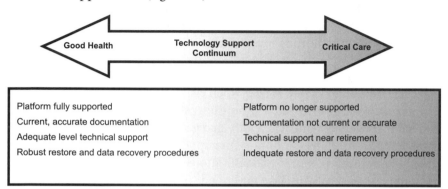

Fig. 11–2. Technology support continuum

CIS units in good health have platforms that are fully supported by in-house technical support or third-party support. This includes current documentation and subject matter experts. Systems in critical care are not fully supported. The documentation on the system is not current or accurate. The technical support staff may be nearing retirement. Versions of the application may not be supported by the vendor.

A utility takes risks with unsupported technology. By continuing to use this technology, they assume that if something breaks, they will be able to figure out how to fix it, or the vendor will provide assistance for a fee on unsupported versions. In talking to customer service leaders, I have found that there are a few of them operating with very old and often unsupported bill print systems. The applications continue to work, but the vendor would no longer provide support if the systems broke down.

The criticality of unsupported technology may be specific to a component or a subcomponent. For example, with the bill print functionality, utilities may have disaster recovery backup plans with a third-party bill print operation that allows them to continue to use the unsupported technology.

Utilities may also have arrangements or understandings with a vendor of unsupported technology so that in the case of failure, support would be provided, but at a premium fee. Completing the health check of CIS components will encourage thoughtful discussion and analysis on the options available in the case of failure. These are very good discussions to have and to document, so that in the case of a failure, a planned approach is in place to respond to it.

Utilities with a custom system or with very specialized needs, and with technical experts who may be considering retirement, need to seriously evaluate options for continuing support plans. There are several options, including cross-training existing talent, hiring in new talent to be trained to support the system, and using offshore resources. If a utility has a solid CIS support team, but just does not have the cross training in place to allow various members of the team to back each other up, then improving the health of this attribute can be achieved. Cross training is not always popular, as knowledge is perceived as power. However, it is possible to design and implement a thorough cross-training plan so that a CIS resource person who is an expert on the billing component can also support the customer care component.

Utilities do have success in hiring talent to build depth on the team. The existing specialists can train new talent. Offshore support is yet another option, but it does bring some unique challenges. Offshore resources are available to program in a variety of languages, including ones that are not so commonly available domestically, like COBOL. Offshore sourcing can bring language barriers, operating differences, and time-zone considerations. The feasibility of these options will depend on the utility and its unique CIS considerations.

The health check of technology support should include a review of the quality and robustness of documentation on the CIS and the ability to change code. Programmers require accurate documentation of the programming in place today in a CIS in order to assess whether changes to the code can be made and to determine the best way to make the changes.

Unfortunately, documentation on code and code changes is not always kept current. Documenting code changes is often viewed as a low priority when completing enhancements to existing programs. The focus is on getting the programming working, not documenting the final changes that were put in place to address application defects. At times the documentation on hand is the *as designed* documentation versus the *as built* documentation. The health check may well result in an initiative to enhance the documentation of the existing CIS and to require more robust documentation in the future to mitigate the issue of technical support problems.

Healthy CIS platforms have data backup, restore, and recovery procedures put in place and tested. If a database becomes corrupted, a data backup and restore procedure must be implemented. Robust CIS platforms can recover data in no more than 4–6 hours using the backup copy of the database and processing all transactions since that time using a replay queue function, which automatically makes the updates. Contrast that with systems that take up to 24 hours or longer as the transactions entered from the point of the last database copy must be manually processed on the system.

Usability

Usability refers to how easy the system is to use. Gaining feedback from CSRs, and reviewing operating statistics like average handle time and order errors, can provide insight on the health of the component from a usability perspective. Evaluating the training time and on-the-job time required to bring new CSRs to expected levels of performance is another way to evaluate usability (fig. 11–3).

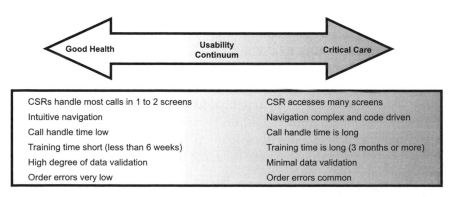

Fig. 11–3. Usability continuum

Observing and asking CSRs can be very enlightening on the usability of the system. CSRs know the so-called pain points of the system they use daily. Focus groups with CSRs can quickly identify the most critical pain points. Other usability issues, though, may not be so evident to the CSRs. Experienced CSRs are used to the system and can navigate very quickly. They may not even realize that to answer a simple customer inquiry, they accessed 13 screens of information or that it took a screen two seconds to populate, versus microseconds.

Healthy CISs have intuitive navigation and data entry validation. The intuitive navigation supports reduced CSR training time. Validation at the point of data entry minimizes entry errors and reduces rework.

BG&E evaluated its legacy CIS. From a usability perspective, it documented that "on average, the call center representative had to memorize 400 screens and navigate through three or four legacy CIS screens individually for each business process."[5] BG&E also noted that more than 150 four-letter codes had to be memorized. The result was that "training new hires was costly and difficult."[6]

Training time plus the on-the-job time to meet performance expectations with a user-friendly CIS is dramatically less. In researching utility best practices for an industry presentation, one utility noted that training and on-the-job time to meet performance expectations went from three years to three weeks with the implementation of a new user-friendly CIS.[7]

There are some key statistics one can review and even compare with other utilities to gain an insight on the usability of a CIS. Average call handle time by type of call can identify certain components of the CIS that may be more cumbersome than others. Reviewing order entry errors where rework is required can highlight usability issues. For example, one utility found that its employees were correcting a large number of service connection orders from a rate perspective. A closer review identified that to save time, the CSRs were pulling forward the rate information from the previous customer, and then not updating the information.

Functionality

Healthy CIS units support the business needs. As such, the controls needed to ensure the integrity of the revenue cycle are automated, and

CSRs use few, if any, workarounds to complete customer requests. CIS trouble tickets remain at low levels, and the backlog of enhancements is manageable (fig. 11–4).

One of the best ways to gain a handle on the functionality of a component is to inventory the workarounds and homegrown applications that employees are using when the system does not support what they need to do. Workarounds might look like manual controls because automated controls are not in place to ensure the validity of the data.

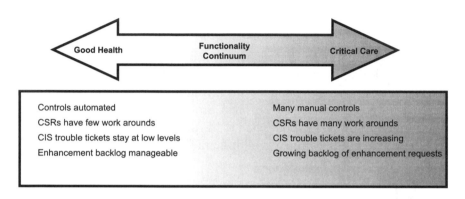

Fig. 11–4. Functionality continuum

A good way to jump-start inventorying workarounds is with employee focus groups. One should ask employees the following:

• When do you have to "trick" the CIS in order to complete a customer request?

• When do you manually track orders in order to support the customer?

• What spreadsheets or other software applications have you developed because the CIS does not support what you need to accomplish?

In the wake of SOX requirements, utilities have a thorough inventory of controls, including an understanding of which controls are manual versus automated. Automated controls are preferred as they are less prone to human error. Healthy CIS units have more automated controls to ensure the integrity of the revenue cycle.

One utility customer service manager noted after implementing a new CIS that the billing staff was reduced by 50%. This was due to the enhanced functionality of the new CIS that minimized billing exceptions, among other benefits. The billing exceptions, which require manual handling by a CSR, were reduced from 200 a day to 200 a month.[8]

Another way to evaluate functionality is to inventory and analyze the trouble tickets generated for the CIS. Trouble tickets are generally created when a business user experiences a problem or has an issue with the CIS. Increasing numbers of trouble tickets or a concentration of tickets in one CIS component may indicate some instability in the system. This instability could be due to enhancement changes where the impacts were not well understood or due to true system degradation. Many times, however, the trouble ticket refers to a situation where the system is operating as designed, but this design no longer meets the current business need. This then becomes an enhancement request. A growing trend of these enhancement requests or trouble tickets may indicate that core functionality is not available to meet the current business model, which can lead to more workarounds.

A utility should inventory the list of its CIS enhancements. Each utility has a wish list of needed enhancements to its CIS. The most adept utilities in managing their CISs have solid processes in place to evaluate and prioritize the numerous enhancements. A review of this list and the backlog provides one with a quick understanding of the most prevalent functionalities that are needed but are not available. Healthy CISs have a manageable list of enhancements that can be achieved in a cost-effective manner based upon the value to be gained.

Architecture

The architecture of a system is "loosely defined as the organizational structure of a software system including components, connections, constraints, and rationale. Components can be small pieces of code, such as modules, or larger chunks, such as stand-alone programs like database management systems."[9] This architecture is the underlying design of the code that supports data models and applications. A healthy architecture is easy to modify and integrate with other systems. Other components or functionality may be easily added (fig. 11–5).

What constitutes a good architecture evolves over time. In the old green screen days, the architectures supported logic for data access and data presentation. Architectures that separated the data access logic from the data presentation logic are more compatible to bolting on new components or functionality. Architecture where the logic for data access and presentation was intermingled is more difficult to build upon.

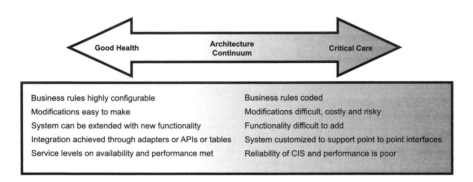

Fig. 11–5. Architecture continuum

The underlying architecture of a legacy CIS differs from utility to utility. Some of these architectures were built very well and continue to support the core CIS functions, in some cases for 20 to 30 years. Others were not as well designed and are declining in health more rapidly with each enhancement.

As utilities continue to enhance business operations and comply with changing regulations, modifications to the CIS are ongoing. With each modification, the complexity of the system increases. It is important to consider the ease with which a utility can make modifications to its CIS.

I can recall for example one enhancement that we had considered at Duke Power on the 1970s vintage CIS we were operating at the time. When the analysis on the CIS work required to make the enhancement was complete, it was evident that adding this functionality was not cost-effective. The hours of programming were cost prohibitive. This can be contrasted to a review of the same enhancement at Tampa Electric. I expected the IT folks to come back with a similar analysis, i.e., to implement this enhancement, we were looking at thousands of hours. But at Tampa Electric, the answer was, "No problem." The programming required fewer than 400 hours, and it was in place in under three weeks. This example highlighted to me that the architecture of the Tampa Electric Company CIS, while a 1980s vintage, was in reasonably good shape.

New CIS units feature configurable business rules and parameters such as town name, valid employees, and job codes. An example of business rules are the parameters by which a utility accepts a credit arrangement from a customer. Configurable CIS units allow the business to change those parameters based on business need simply by updating the business rules or parameter table. Older systems had business rules hard coded, so any changes must be completed by a programmer and could affect other areas of the CIS program.

Questions the team completing the health check should consider from an architecture standpoint include:

- How easy is it to Web-enable the CIS?

- Is it easy to integrate other technologies like geographical information systems (GIS) and AMR?

- Does the business or data model architecture reflect today's business, and can it be easily enhanced or expanded, as today's business model requires?

- Is the CIS customer focused, meter focused, or premise focused?

- How robust is the underlying architecture?

As utilities add new functionality to the CIS, the underpinning architecture can become unstable. One utility IT director told of her experience in dealing with an unstable infrastructure. The utility had rapidly added functionality but did not identify all the touch points that functionality impacted. The result manifested itself in poor system reliability and even system failure at times. This situation reinforced to this IT director the criticality of thorough regression testing and not just that of the new feature before moving into production. The compounded impact of a lack of thorough regression testing placed this utility in a difficult situation that required extraordinary effort by IT resources to correct.

A CIS must link and integrate with many systems. As such, the integration effort alone when adding functionality to a CIS or replacing a CIS requires significant time and resources. Newer systems achieve integration by updating configurable tables for business rules or parameters, using message adapters or with standardized application program interfaces (API). Adapters and APIs make it easier to develop a program by providing all the building blocks. Integrating with older systems is much more labor intensive and typically involves hard coding by a programmer.

The CIS system needs to be available 24/7 and thus must be reliable. Often the standard for a CIS is 99.9% availability during critical business hours. During noncritical hours, an impact to the CIS will not impact customers immediately, but since CIS units generally have batch processes that must be run daily, a long outage during nonbusiness hours can ultimately impact the customers if extended.

OPTIONS

Customer service leaders have a lot more options today when facing a CIS that is not performing at levels desired or needed. In the late 1980s and early 1990s, the best option was to replace the system. This is a costly, labor-intensive option.

Utilities are cautious about CIS replacement. There are too many stories about replacements that have not gone well. In a recent survey by the American Water Works Association, 30% of the utilities that had recently implemented a new CIS said that they had a "smooth" installation. Another 45% said that they had a "tough but ok" installation, and 10% stated that they had a "very difficult or failed" installation.[10] Greg Galluzzi, president of TMG Consulting, notes that only 27% of CIS projects are implemented on time and on budget.[11]

New CIS platforms today come with the benefit of best practice business logic built into the system. Utilities that can implement a new

CIS out of the box, with little customization, will gain the benefit of the best-in-class practices. Galluzzi notes that with configurable systems, customization of 10% or less is achievable.[12] A key driver in achieving the maximum synergy is determining up front the proper project team for implementation. This project team is tasked with balancing the need for customization with the cost benefit.

Today in addition to CIS replacement, there are viable options to extend the life of a CIS through targeted enhancements and/or systematic replacement of key components. This section will discuss the pros and cons of two common approaches, which are legacy extension and CIS replacements. The strategy that is right for a utility will be predicated on the health of its CIS, its business environment, and its corporate strategy.

Legacy extension

The term legacy system refers to the incumbent CIS platform. Many utilities with older legacy systems designed and programmed these systems with in-house resources. As the legacy systems age, their general health declines. Charles Vincent, a consultant with IBM's National Center for Excellence for Utilities and Energy Services, sees the root cause of this as code entropy. He notes,

> *As code gets older, code entropy begins to play a role. As each change is made to a system, it moves the system a bit further away from what the original architects envisioned and generally adds to the complexity of the system. This complexity continues to grow as more and more changes are made to the system, making the effort required for each change increase as well. This complexity can lead to changes having unexpected consequences that in turn must be fixed. Eventually you can reach a point where the effort required making a change overwhelms the benefits of the change itself. This is code entropy.*[13]

These older systems do not incorporate the latest architectural advancements or offer flexibility for a rapidly changing business model. Often the systems are written in an older programming language like COBOL. The systems were designed to support the various business practices that were in place at the time. Research by UtiliPoint indicates that more than 51% of CIS units date prior to 1996, with 17% dating prior to 1985.[14]

Utilities with legacy systems generally have staff on board who know the system architecture very well and are able to navigate with the older style technology. Sometimes the business and the technology folks gain a level of comfort with the legacy system, as its performance is predictable and its flaws are known.

One utility executive with a 30-year-old CIS likened the legacy CIS to a dependable old Chevy. The old CIS, like an old Chevy car, was getting the job done. It allowed timely and accurate billing of customers. It was well designed and supported targeted refurbishing and added functionality.

With this being the case, a legacy extension strategy was appropriate to consider. With a legacy extension strategy, components of the CIS that are ailing are targeted for replacement or enhancements. If the user interface on a CIS, for example, is not user-friendly and is in the old green screen format, then a bolt-on GUI may meet the business needs.

BG&E highlighted its legacy extension project called GUIdance at an industry conference. The goal for this project was to create a more effective user interface for call center representatives while leveraging investment in the existing billing system. Specifically the team targeted reducing training time for CSRs, improving phone service levels, and lowering agent turnover. The results were tremendous. Call taking positions were reduced from 209 to 135. This success was largely due to the 25% reduction in average call handle time. Training time reduced from 15 weeks to 8 weeks.[15]

New CIS system

A review of the health of a utility's CIS, its business environment, and its strategic plans may lead to the decision to implement a new CIS. Today's CIS units are robust and are designed in a style that supports real-time, rapid business change. These systems separate core hard coding from business rules, enabling the business to dynamically adjust business rules, in a timely, low-cost fashion.

These systems come out of the box with utility best practices like support for Web-enabled customer self-service and IVR interfaces. Controls to support enhanced financial reporting and alignment with SOX are standard. Conversion from the old system to the new CIS is documented and is relatively easy to follow. Each of the companies providing a new CIS has staff or can suggest consultants who can map a solid, robust conversion plan that minimizes any negative business impact.

Rose Minton, vice president of TMG Consulting, states, "A primary driver for replacing a CIS system is unsupported technology."[16] Companies choosing this path will build into the business case not only the technology support, but also the business gains from a customer, CSR, billing, controls, and strategy standpoint. Utilities competing in deregulated markets realize the criticality of the CIS. An executive for ConEdison Solutions notes that CISs "are the life blood of a retail organization. If you can't bill it, you can't collect it, enough said."[17]

If the decision is to replace the CIS, utilities have more options available to them today than in the past. They can build the new CIS in-house, buy a new system, or use a hosted CIS. Each of these options has unique benefits. The choice for each utility will depend a great deal on the input from its information technology team. This team has to assess whether the talent exists in-house to design, build, and maintain a new system, or if a variation of that is more appropriate.

Hosted solution. There are a variety of companies offering hosted CIS solutions to utilities. These solutions include single applications via an application service provider (ASP) or entire business process outsourcing (BPO).

An ASP "manages and delivers end-user computer applications living in a data center, to end users based on a 'per click' charge."[18] BPO occurs "when an organization turns over the management and optimization of a business function or process, such a billing or customer service, to a third party that conducts the activity based on a set of predetermined performance metrics."[19] A key benefit to a hosted solution is that the utility does not face the huge capital outlay needed to initiate a project. Instead, the utility pays as it goes. This also provides the utility with the benefit of application upgrades and ongoing support.

Puget Sound Energy is an example of a BPO implementation. Puget Sound Energy found that the best practice methodology employed by its BPO partner increased transaction productivity by an estimated 25%–50%. The time frame for work completing reporting was cut by

50%, high volume transaction handling time was reduced by 10 to 60 seconds per transaction, and trouble ticket backlog was reduced by 76%.[20]

In-house CIS development. It is possible for a utility to design, build, and maintain its own CIS. However, this option is not as popular. Greg Gallauzzi notes that utilities do not often choose this option, as "they are concerned about product upkeep and how to maintain it in a cost-effective manner."[21] Duke Power did choose an in-house development project to replace its antiquated CIS, vintage 1976. Duke Power executives at a CIS conference noted that "the Phoenix Project was building the next generation in customer systems."[22] They undertook this project, noting, "We had a technologically old and unhealthy system."[23] Duke's legacy CIS over two decades "had expanded to six times the original CIS, but with code that was brittle and patched."[24] This project took an incremental approach involving six phases over a span of six years. The new system built by Duke Power is a real-time system. The benefits include earlier billing and improved cash flow.[25]

CIS replacement. Many utilities have chosen the route of buying and installing a new CIS. There are a variety of firms providing CIS units. While they all offer the core functionality of supporting the meter-to-cash cycle and customer service, each company's products have unique features that may appeal to different utilities.

Hamilton Hydro Inc. is an example of a utility that replaced its CIS. The drivers for replacement included forced amalgamation of five utilities into one and Ontario's deregulation. Hamilton Hydro evaluated upgrading its existing CIS. Its leaders realized that it was not feasible to incorporate all the requirements into the existing CIS. They identified a CIS solution provider that was proven in the marketplace and provided a system that was configurable. They focused on a quick implementation and limited modification or customization of the package. The scope included hardware upgrades, data cleansing and conversion, modifications and interfaces, acceptance testing, and end-user training. After some ups and downs and long project hours, the new CIS was implemented five months from the start date. The benefits were realized quickly. The new system created an annual savings to the city of Hamilton of more than $375,000.[26]

The CIS is fundamental to the meter-to-cash cycle. It is important as a utility leader to have a handle on the capabilities and limitations of a CIS in order to prepare appropriate strategies for the future. Customer service leaders should have at least a five-year plan for their CIS. This plan may be to continue with ongoing application enhancements or to prepare for a wholesale replacement of the system.

In order to create the strategy, one must evaluate the health of each component of the CIS and integrate the company's business plans and go-forward strategies. This analysis will reveal the direction for the next efforts for the utility's CIS. Once the five-year plan is developed, the utility must adhere to its plan.

REFERENCES

1   Chartwell CIS & Customer Care Systems Report, 2004.

2   Burkhart, Lori A. "CIS: The New Profit Machine." *Public Utilities Fortnightly*. May 2004, p. 33.

3   Turner, Sam. Manager of customer service, Jackson Energy Authority; Interview, August 2004.

4   Galluzzi, Greg. President, TMG Consulting Inc.; Interview, March 16, 2005.

5   "Extending the Life of Our CIS Legacy System." BG&E presentation, CIS Conference, Miami, FL, May 6, 2004.

6   Ibid.

7   Research for presentation. "Customer Service Best Practices." CIS Conference, May 2004.

8   Ibid.

9   Clements 94-2 Carnegie Mellon Software Engineering Institute. www.sei.cmu.edu/architecture/definitions.html.

10   Weseloh, Gary. Manager and senior consultant, TMG Consulting, Inc. "CIS Implementation Timeframes." May 2004.

11   Galluzzi, Greg. President, TMG Consulting, Inc. "CIS Industry Update." CIS Conference. June 2002.

12   Galluzzi, Greg. Interview, March 16, 2005.

13   Vincent, Charles. Consultant, IBM's National Center for Excellence for Utilities and Energy Services; Interview, April 25, 2005.

14   "Effective Project Management Ensures a Positive Return." UtiliPoint International, Inc. March 23, 2004, p. 3.

15   "Extending the Life of Our CIS Legacy System." BG&E presentation,
      May 6, 2004.

16   Minton, Rose. Vice president, TMG Consulting Inc.; Interview, March
      21, 2005.

17   Buck, Louis E. "ConEdison Solution." CIS Conference, Miami, FL,
      May 2005.

18   Brock, Jon T. Chief operating officer, UtiliPoint International, Inc.
      "White Paper: Business Process Outsourcing: Is It for the Utility
      Market?" August 11, 2003.

19   Ibid.

20   Ibid.

21   Galluzzi, Greg. Interview, March 16, 2005.

22   McCutcheon, Hugh T. "Paint My System Red Hot, Completing the
      Phoenix Project." Duke Power Co., CIS Conference, June 2002.

23   McCutcheon, Hugh. "Duke Power Makes CIS Implementation Voyage
      Along, Received Regional and National Recognition for Its Efforts."
      Case Studies in CIS Implementations series, Chartwell Inc., October
      2003.

24   Ibid.

25   Ibid.

26   Burdick, Gordon. "Municipal CIS Implementation Case Study."
      Hamilton Hydro, Inc., CIS 2002 Conference, Baltimore, MD, June 2002.

12 APPLY TECHNOLOGY TO ENHANCE CUSTOMER SERVICE

Utility customer service is delivered superbly when the people, process, and technology elements are tightly integrated. Technology enhancements over the past decade have transformed many of the ways in which utilities deliver service to customers. In the book *Good to Great*, author Jim Collins observes, "Good-to-great organizations think differently about technology and technological change than mediocre ones." He goes on to note that "Good-to-great companies used technology as an accelerator of momentum, not a creator of it."[1]

Savvy utilities understand how to use technology as an accelerator of change by clearly linking it to business needs. Business needs should drive and dictate technology applications. There are many technologies available in the marketplace today. The technology vendors can be very tempting. To achieve success in implementing a technology, the technology must address a business need. The business, in this case the customer service organization, drives the business case for a technology implementation.

When the business drives the technology application, there is ownership by the business to make the other changes needed to ensure a successful implementation. Most technology applications require process and people changes in order to be fully successful. Process change and the employee change management efforts are owned by the business. Technology that is implemented where the user or business does not have ownership usually is underutilized.

Over the years, I have heard many utility customer service leaders lament the fact that they have implemented a new graphical interface front end, only to find that employees were reverting to the old CIS green screens to process customer calls. While the seemingly simple answer is to just turn off the old CIS, that may not be practical depending on the utility's situation. The old CIS interface may be the preferred interface for employees working in metering or billing, for example.

It is situations like this where the business must own the results expected from the technology. Utilities can and have been successful implementing a user-friendly front end while maintaining traditional CIS access. This success, though, did not come without a thoughtful, planned effort to migrate employees to the new interface. Successfully implementing new technology requires the business to develop a thorough change management plan that includes communications, metrics, incentives, and ongoing coaching to fully take advantage of the new system. It is not enough to hope that new users will adopt the new technology. Rather, it takes business leadership implementing a comprehensive change management plan to achieve desired results.

Utility customer service organizations are faced with many technology choices. New technologies seem to emerge daily. This brings a challenge for customer service leaders on what to implement and when to implement it.

Today there are a wide array of technologies available that can aid in customer contact, resource management, and productivity. Many of the technologies not only improve efficiency but also result in improved customer service delivery and satisfaction. This chapter will review key customer service technologies that support customer contact, productivity, and resource management. Beyond providing a primer on what the technology is, this chapter will identify the business benefits that have been realized when applying the technology.

CUSTOMER CONTACT TECHNOLOGY

Customer contact technology options are numerous. This technology area continues to grow and enhance in capabilities. Common customer contact technologies that utilities are implementing are interactive voice response systems (IVRs), automated speech recognition (ASR), computer telephony integration (CTI), and quality monitoring systems.

Interactive voice response systems

IVR systems are telephony-based systems in which someone uses a touch-tone telephone to interact with the CIS or other computer system to acquire information from or enter data into the system. The interactivity is the element that differentiates IVRs from voice mail or similar types of systems. Customers using an IVR must either enter touchtone digits on their phone or use ASR to complete their transactions. In essence, voice is converted to data entry into a computer system.

IVRs have evolved rapidly over the past decade as companies have been striving to provide cost-effective 24-hour service. This advancement combined with the significantly increased consumer acceptance of self-service has allowed utilities to significantly reduce their cost to service customers while also increasing satisfaction.

The business case for utilities is to increase the number of calls handled via automation. The IVR provides customers with 24/7 service for many basic inquiries and requests. Utilities are averaging 23.5% of calls handled by the IVR. Some utilities have achieved between 30% and 50% of all calls handled through IVRs, while achieving high customer satisfaction marks.[2] IVRs offer the utility the opportunity to move a call from expensive live-voice handling to automation at a fraction of the cost. Costs for calls handled by live voice can range from $3.00 to $10.00 and up per call, as opposed to an IVR-handled call, which costs far less than $1.00 per call.[3]

The business opportunity with IVR is to handle more transactions through this channel. It is important to identify which transactions are the best candidates for self-service. Simple transactions that are high volume are the most effective applications. Account balance, payment plans, and outage reporting are common utility applications.

A fallout of implementing an IVR is that CSR average handle time may increase. This phenomenon is caused by the removal of the simple calls now handled with automation in the IVR. These simple calls previously were handled by CSRs with very short average handle times.

When these calls are removed from the mix of calls handled by live voice, the average handling time per call increases. It is important that this fact be understood and built into staffing models by the business to ensure that after implementation, appropriate staffing is in place for the remaining calls.

Utilities can achieve quick gains with an investment in IVR technology. Aquila Networks, a utility serving customers in the Midwest, completed a project that integrated IVR and CTI technology. Aquila completed research that indicated its IVR utilization was well below the utility industry average. Hence Aquila launched a project to enhance the IVR and CTI capabilities and used customer research as a foundation. Their customer research indicated that customers wanted simple, concise menus, a reduction in the number of key strokes needed to secure information, and the ability to enter meter readings, make payments, and make payment arrangements. Aquila noted that within four months, IVR utilization almost doubled, rising to utility industry norms. They expect this percentage to continue to increase as the system is tuned and refined.[4] The innovation of speech recognition is transforming IVR technology and its consumer appeal. Research from Chartwell indicates that 17% of utilities now offer ASR technology.[5]

Automatic speech recognition

ASR is the ability of a computer to recognize and act on information spoken by the customer. It enables the customer to speak requests to the system to enable or complete transactions and recognizes phrases and speech from a wide variety of users.

ASR takes the IVR to a new level in customer service and automates more complex calls. Dr. Jon Anton, author and leading call center expert, notes, "Speech saves customers the time and hassle of waiting on hold or navigating through complex touchtone menu trees. Speech allows customers to get information, conduct transactions and even place phone calls, all with voice commands."[6] Anton's research reveals that "consumers are becoming more accustomed to and accepting of automated speech recognition as a method for doing business with companies." He continues by saying that "consumers recognize that speech systems are faster, easier and more accessible than a live customer service representative or Web/online access."[7]

ASR providers bring systems that support hundreds of accents and recognize multiple synonyms for common words. They also bring both hardware and software that is specific to speech capabilities. ASR models include both directed dialog and natural language. Directed dialog offers customers command prompts, such as, "Would you like to make a payment or report an outage?" Directed dialog applications expect one of those two responses and will act based on the response. Natural language ASR offers customers the ability to use freestyle speech, or naturally flowing utterances. Directed dialog offers a higher level of accuracy and transaction completion rate over natural language. Natural language is useful at the beginning of a call to determine the intent of the caller. Offering the customer the opportunity to simply state what he wants to do can eliminate the need for a lot of prompts.

Companies are blending natural language and directed dialog models. A natural language interface is used up front to determine what the customer wants to do and is followed by a directed dialog application to complete the specific transaction. These systems allow power users, or frequent users, to accelerate their transactions with barge in capabilities that allow the user to bypass prompts.

Speech recognition calls are 40% faster on average than touch-tone calls, according to the Kelsey Group, because customers do not have to listen to lists of menu options.[8] Total spending on speech recognition technology in 2002 was $680 million, a 60% increase over the previous year.[9]

The accuracy of an ASR system is impaired if many of the applications require alphanumeric codes. Alphanumeric codes, like account numbers, are difficult for an ASR system. Many letters sound alike, which is why people will say, "M as in Mary," to ensure accurate communication. Callers in a noisy environment can also impact the accuracy of an ASR system.

Utilities that implement ASR do so to not only increase the percentage of calls handled by self-service, but also as a strategy to increase customer satisfaction. Pepco, serving the Washington, D.C. area, implemented natural language ASR to create a competitive advantage and enhance its brand, along with serving customers at a reduced cost. Their business case for ASR indicated a payback of 25 months. Pepco has found that "a speech system creates additional savings beyond just a traditional IVR system because through customer selection, speech increased the number of successful automated calls."[10]

An ASR interface transforms the customer's experience by flattening menus and reducing the number of steps for customers to get what they need. Additionally, ASR enhances the customer experience. Gartner research indicates that 47% of customers are much more satisfied with a voice recognition application versus touchtone. ASR provides the capability to automate more calls than traditional touchtone.

Computer telephony integration

CTI is most often associated with *screen pops*, where the connection to the customer on the phone and the customer's account information arrive simultaneously to the CSR. In fact a strong business case driver for implementing CTI is the reduced average handle time for a call due to screen pops. This is a core function of CTI, but a fully leveraged CTI application also enables other productivity and reporting capabilities.

CTI is the integration of the telephone system with the data environment.[11] CTI uses the ANI data gained from the telephony exchange, along with other customer input, to route calls. It can be used for both inbound and outbound capabilities. CTI will integrate with the IVR, CRM, and telephony to route and direct calls.

The business benefits of CTI result from productivity and quality. From a productivity standpoint, the soft phone, call routing, and screen pops support more efficient call handling. CTI reduces talk times with an average of 15 seconds per call.[12] This benefit alone is often enough to support a business case to implement the technology. From a quality standpoint, customer satisfaction is often increased as well, because the customer can input information while waiting. Advanced systems use this information to route calls.

However, utilities implementing CTI should not stop with the screen pop capability. Many have found the implementation of a soft phone, which is a system whereby the phone set is integrated in the PC with a

GUI, also enhances productivity. The soft phone replaces the hard phone set on the desk and allows the agent to focus all of his attention on the workstation screen. With a traditional phone set, the agents are dividing attention between needed information that is displayed on the phone set and the workstation. This can add time to a call and increase the opportunity for error.

An underutilized benefit of CTI is the information it can provide on the customer interaction. With CTI, utilities have the capability to track a customer's behavior throughout the call, from the interface with the IVR to the CSR. Data can be captured that accurately matches call handle time by type of call in a more granular level than that provided by traditional queuing system statistics. The customer behavior can be analyzed to identify where IVR transactions are cumbersome for the customer or frequently fail and result in the caller being routed to a CSR.

A robust use of CTI enables intelligent call routing. Logic can be built within the CTI application that identifies unique parameters to route the call based on that data. For example, if a utility is having issues with repeat high-bill callers, CTI could identify that the caller was a repeat high-bill caller and route the call to a more experienced agent for handling. This is a great tool to use dynamically when an event occurs that requires more targeted call routing. This capability could be very beneficial, for example, to customers impacted by a planned outage. The customers could be routed to a select group of CSRs with intimate knowledge of the situation.

One utility found that CTI-enabled intelligent call routing was a great solution to a problem they were experiencing with customers calling to make a payment on their bill. Many of these customers were credit customers. The utility used a third party to process credit calls, but since the customer indicated in the IVR that they wanted to make a payment, the call was connected to the utility's call center. Intelligent routing solved this dilemma. Now when the customer requests to make a payment via phone, the system checks to see if the customer is in a credit situation. If so, the customer is routed to the third party; if not, then the customer is routed to the utility's call center.

Outbound calling is also supported by CTI. The same screen pop functionality that helps on an inbound call is also helpful on an outbound call, allowing the CSR to preview the account being contacted.

CTI is an enabling technology that provides direct business benefits, but it also enables many other productivity and call management opportunities. For utilities, the good news is that most CTI applications can be justified on the screen pop functionality alone. In order to gain the full value of a CTI investment, utilities are wise to fully understand the other capabilities enabled by CTI.

Quality monitoring systems

There are tools available to record customer interactions via phone for quality monitoring purposes. These include both call logging and quality monitoring technologies. These systems record an event so that it can be played back later for quality purposes.

Many utilities use the call logging to record all calls. Utilities record calls for safety and liability reasons. Gas companies have long recorded emergency calls to ensure they had a well-documented record of any customer situation. Call recordings are used to verify transactions. The call logging tools are excellent in customer complaint situations to both reassure the customer that the utility takes the issue seriously and to more objectively assess what really happened on a call. When recordings are not available, determining what really occurred during a particular conversation is difficult and becomes a *he said, she said* situation.

One unexpected benefit we see is that CSRs will request that we pull call recordings to follow up on situations in which a customer has been threatening. This provides an added level of comfort for CSRs that appropriate follow-up and security can be put into place in the case of a highly irate and threatening customer.

Quality monitoring technology is used in evaluating a sampling of contacts for quality assurance and CSR feedback. These systems randomly record calls. More robust systems record the call and capture how the CSR interacted with the computer system. For example, when playing back the call, a supervisor hears the interaction and views the data entry used by the CSR.

The benefit to having software randomly record calls versus asking supervisors to record calls is that the technology reduces an administrative burden and ensures a random sample of calls of all CSRs throughout the hours of operation. Supervisors are often predictable concerning the times at which they monitor calls. The randomness of an automated quality monitoring system provides a more fair assessment of how a CSR is performing.

Systems that record both the call and the CIS interaction are more robust applications. The benefit to these systems is the potential to reduce CSR average handle time by reviewing the flow in which a CSR processes the call. Observing this flow will reveal steps a CSR completes that are unnecessary. It also identifies common mistakes that CSRs make, which can be incorporated into training.

Quality monitoring equipment business cases are not generally built on efficiency improvements. Rather, the business case focus is on providing a level of insurance and documentation of what is occurring in the contact center along with an improvement in the customer's experience. There are some efficiency gains if one compares technology-enabled quality monitoring versus manual monitoring. Metrics that will be impacted by a quality focus include first-call resolution, repeat calls, and transactional customer satisfaction.

PRODUCTIVITY TECHNOLOGY

Improving productivity is expected in business and industry. Technology applications can increase productivity if successfully implemented. Major productivity improvements in the utility customer service area result from AMR, predictive dialers, GUI, CRM applications, and virtual call centers.

Automated meter reading

Growth in AMR continues to be strong. More than 60 million North American meters are automated. The expected growth rate is predicted to be strong, approaching 20% annually.[13] Most utilities have deployed AMR in a surgical manner, or in other words, they have strategically identified high-cost-to-read meters and targeted AMR for those locations. Research indicates that most utilities use AMR on only 20% of the meter population.[14] LeRoy Nosbaum, CEO of Itron, notes that "there is no question the pure cost of AMR has gone down. Volumes have gone up, hardware costs have reduced, and installations costs have reduced."[15]

AMR deployments can be defined as traditional or advanced. Traditional AMR is characterized by one-way communication from the meter on a set periodic basis. Advanced AMR is characterized by two-way communication supporting frequent or real-time data transfer back and forth from the meter and utility. Advanced AMR offers interval data metering, which is more robust than a traditional deployment that most often just provides the monthly dial read.

Traditional AMR is by far the most common deployment, accounting for 75% of AMR modules in North America.[16] Traditional AMR has a lower implementation cost, typically 60% to 70% of the cost of advanced metering installations.[17] Traditional AMR requires deployment of field personnel to collect meter reads via mobile technology or hand-held devices.

Wireless mobile technology is the most common method to capture meter readings from the basic AMR installation. Vehicles are equipped to poll the AMR meter, capture the usage, and denote date and time.

Handheld devices can also be equipped to poll the meter and capture key meter reading information. Such devices are used to secure reads where a vehicle does not have access or cannot get close enough to capture the signal from the device. An example of this is in high-rise buildings. At NSTAR, we have found there are limitations to securing the signal from the AMR unit on higher floors. To read higher level floors, we deploy a meter reader equipped with a handheld unit. Even though a person is being deployed, access issues associated with manual reading are avoided. Typically the meter reader will just have to be near the meter closet, and not actually in the closet, to secure the meter readings. Another solution that is now available to address this particular situation is an external antenna or micro-network to propagate the signal down to the mobile unit.

Advanced AMR provides two-way communication with each meter. This technology virtually eliminates the need to dispatch field personnel, as much of the work can be done remotely. A fixed network can be arranged to support one-way or two-way communication. Fixed networks supporting two-way communication use surgically positioned collectors. The collectors are two-way communication devices. Each collector then uses one-way communication to gather information from assigned meters. Fixed network meter reading systems are deployed through a variety of mechanics, including phone, power line carrier, fiber, cable TV, radio, satellite, and cellular.

Both traditional and advanced AMR systems greatly reduce the number of field resources required to read meters and complete meter service requests. With traditional AMR, utilities dispatch field personnel to read meters via mobile or handheld units, but far fewer personnel are need than required when walking a meter route. Advanced AMR is now being combined with other hardware applications, like remote connect and disconnect devices, to further reduce the field workforce by eliminating the need to dispatch personnel for a variety of field work.

Advanced AMR systems offer the potential for transformational enterprise-wide benefits. Advanced systems support on-demand reads, remote modification of meter functionality, complex rate capability, and revenue protection capabilities.

From an enterprise perspective, the availability of real-time, robust usage data offers new capabilities in corporate organizations for load forecasting, rate design, and support of new products and services. With advanced AMR, detailed customer usage behaviors can be secured, analyzed, and fed into an energy forecasting application, providing much higher levels of accuracy in forward projections. In a deregulated market, these meters support robust meter data collection that has value not only to the incumbent utility, but also to suppliers. These meters support operations organizations by providing data that when analyzed can identify areas of load loss or equipment overloading. Advanced metering can also identify outage events in real time. Revenue protection teams have more robust tamper flags and usage information to quickly identify areas where revenue may be leaking.

From a customer service perspective, advanced metering opens a new vista of services by providing access to the meter usage data in real time. Consider, for example, a high-bill call. With advanced AMR, the CSR can complete an off-cycle read validating whether billed usage was in line with current consumption, all while the customer remains on the phone. Final reads for move-outs are a few clicks away instead of hours, days, and dollars away as required by sending out a truck. A final bill amount can be communicated to the customer by the CSR during the disconnect call. The CSR can generate a bill transaction and have the accurate bill in the mail the next day. This is a very powerful way to satisfy the customer. Advanced AMR supports more complex tariffs and billing options.

Advanced AMR also supports a more tightly controlled meter-to-cash cycle. Companies that employ a soft disconnect strategy, where the service remains energized between customers, can minimize exposure to losses due to unaccounted for energy with advanced AMR. Usage on a meter that is greater than established thresholds can be identified promptly and acted upon. With a traditional AMR installation, the only data points on consumption are monthly. Furthermore, with advanced AMR, the CSR is in a better position to work with a new customer establishing service to ensure that the appropriate date of service initiation is recorded. The CSR is empowered with actual, accurate meter usage data. Finally, utilities can precisely quantify the cost and revenue loss associated with vacant premises.

Advanced metering has several communications platforms that are important to understand. Radio-based communications are common and can be on private or public platforms. The benefits to radio include availability and low cost, particularly in situations where the utility has an existing investment in a private radio system. The downside to radio involves its coverage, necessary licensing, speed, and battery life.

Power line carrier or telephony systems are also options. A power line carrier has the benefit of ownership by the utility. Both provide the benefit of surgically implementing AMR. With telephony, concerns occur when the lines is shared for other purposes. Dedicated telephony has a higher communications cost.

Broadband systems, which can be carried over fiber on power lines or cable, provide high-speed communications with robust bandwidth. Utilities are strategically deploying this technology as part of an expanded offering of new products and services. Broadband systems support rich data transfer. Broadband over power line is a relatively new opportunity that leverages the existing utility plant.

The business case for AMR is framed around reduced costs, improved customer service, and in the case of advanced AMR, strategic enterprise value. Dominion, a large utility headquartered in Richmond, Virginia, has implemented AMR using a surgical deployment strategy. The savings have been significant from a labor, safety, and productivity standpoint. From the customer's perspective, AMR has enhanced the timeliness and accuracy of billing.[18]

The business case for one's utility will depend on its strategy of AMR installation. Does the utility want traditional or advanced AMR, or a combination of both? Is the goal to implement AMR with the entire meter population, or to surgically target AMR installations? The utility's ROI will be predicated on the labor costs and service territory characteristics. Utilities are achieving typical ROIs of 14% to 20% with traditional AMR deployment.[19] A utility with a low labor cost and predominately outside meters has a more difficult time making a business case as compared to a utility with high labor costs and a high percentage of inside meters.

Predictive dialer technology

Predictive dialers automatically place outbound calls, classify calls, and deliver calls to agents. The technology uses call classification to detect busy signals, answering machines, and ring/no answer situations. The dialing software tracks and acts on the outcome based on the defined campaign.[20] Sophisticated algorithms are built into the dialer software that incorporate connect rates and average call handle time. These algorithms are also used to identify situations where contact cannot be made with the customer, like busy signals. Predictive dialers increase agent productivity by eliminating the agent time to dial and screen out calls that cannot be completed due to situations like busy signals.

To use the dialer, a utility will create a call campaign. The campaign will identify the target customer segments and define the script for the CSR or automated messaging. Other parameters that are needed for the campaign include hours to call, amount of time after a busy signal or no answer before trying again, and the number of attempts.

Utilities use predictive dialers often in their credit and collections activities. The dialer can queue up customers to be contacted to encourage payment. The predictive dialer technology can also be used for a variety of other applications, like contacting customers about upcoming service interruptions or confirming field appointments. Utilities that are promoting products and services may use the dialer technology in a more traditional manner with outbound marketing campaigns. When I was at

Duke Power, we launched a very successful campaign to sign up customers for outdoor lighting using the outbound dialer.

The dialer can be connected with a live voice or automated messages by linking to other systems. Utilities also use the fully automated outbound dialing in applications like providing a customer with an estimated time of restoration (ETR). In this case, there is linkage from the outage management system to the dialer technology to identify the customers, phone numbers, and specific ETR. Automated messaging with the predicative dialer is a great way to notify customers of impending fieldwork. Utilities might use this technology to call ahead to notify customers of a meter change out.

Utilities also use outbound calling to contact crews. In situations where additional crews are needed, the system automatically places outbound calls to appropriate personnel. Often these systems are connected to a self-service IVR, where the employee receiving the notification to report to work can confirm the receipt of the call and provided a response. The benefit of call tracking is really valued in this situation, as it is easy to confirm whether or not an employee received a call, what number was called, and the exact time of the call.

Utilities may find that the best way to leverage predictive dialing technology is with a third-party partner. This eliminates a large capital expenditure by the utility on predictive dialing technology and telephony infrastructure. Outbound dialing requires a robust telephony trunking infrastructure. If the dialing is concurrent with high inbound call patterns, then additional phone trunks may be necessary to support both inbound and outbound calls. Additionally, predictive dialing technology, as with other technology, requires technical support staff to maintain the technology.

An outsourced partner will typically have a setup fee and then a cost per transaction fee. The transaction fees are generally very low. Credit outsourcing companies have robust predictive dialing systems that provide for automated and live-voice outbound calling. Since this capability is core to the credit world, the technology remains current and effective. There are also many companies that can complete outbound messaging for a very low cost per transaction.

The business case for predictive dialers generally centers on productivity improvements and enhanced customer satisfaction. Automated predictive dialer campaigns, such as those used to notify customers of a meter change or of planned maintenance, can be up to 40% cheaper per contact than mail. Predictive dialer technology can increase customer satisfaction when used to provide order updates or proactively communicate to a customer.

Graphical user interface and customer relationship management applications

GUI applications are user-friendly front ends designed to provide point-and-click control for normal operations. CRM applications include a user-friendly front end and support reliable processes and procedures for interacting with customers. Utilities are using these applications to improve productivity, customer service, and CSR training.

GUI applications provide utilities with quick benefits from a productivity and training perspective. Utilities operating with legacy green screen applications that are code driven find a GUI interface an excellent way to reduce call handle time by placing key information that a CSR needs to process a call on one or two screens. Training is simplified as a GUI will have drop-down menus for quick referencing, real-time data edit, and call scripting. BG&E noted that its training time was reduced by close to 50% and call handle time by 25%.[21]

CRM tools are also being deployed by utilities either as part of a CIS strategy or for support in other areas, like the sales or marketing departments. CRM is most successful when deployed as a part of a holistic business strategy of serving customers with defined business processes. The CRM applications provide operations, analytical, and contact management tools.

The operations tools support the basic business processes of sales and/or customer service. For example, a CRM can keep track of a customer's preferences. One utility kept customer language preference in its CRM. The utility incorporated business rules to ensure that customer calls were routed to a CSR with those language skills, if available. From a sales perspective, a CRM can offer lead tracking.

The analytical tools support the analysis of customer behavior. A CRM application will include a database of customer transactions that can be reviewed and analyzed for trends. At NSTAR, we are using our CRM database to understand why customers call repeatedly. From a sales perspective, analysis on the sales pipeline can be completed.

Contact management tools with CRM support can provide customers information in the format they prefer. It supports phone, fax, and e-mail. This is helpful, for example, when contacting large customers about planned outages. With a CRM, the utility can customize how its contacts the customers. Company A may want a phone call to its plant manager. Company B may want its plant manager called and its facilities manager paged.

CRM is a more expensive application as compared to GUI, but it also brings more benefits. It too will support the productivity and training benefits noted for GUI. Additionally it provides the ability to enhance customer service delivery by customer segments, with the incorporation of additional customer preference data and business process rules for each segment.

Virtual call center

A virtual call center is the virtual consolidation of physically distant call centers, leveraging the telephony network. The multiple call centers operate as a single logical system, even though they are geographically dispersed.

The business case for physical call center consolidation is based on employee productivity and facility utilization. Utility leaders understand the employee productivity gains achieved in pooling together call center resources.

Telephony advances have redefined call center consolidation and permit the concept of virtual consolidation. Virtually consolidating call centers provides the same benefit from a resource utilization standpoint as physical consolidation. There are added benefits of minimizing the need to relocate or disrupt personnel and providing inherent disaster recovery flexibility.

There are challenges associated with virtually consolidating call centers. The scheduling, forecasting, and reporting functions are best centralized. Communications and training for remote call centers are more difficult and require extra planning. Recruitment and hiring may be more challenged in a dispersed call center environment. Ensuring that the employee and customer experience is similar in each of the dispersed call centers can be a challenge.

When I was at TECO Energy, we implemented the virtual call center model to leverage CSRs displaced when we closed offices. These CSRs were redeployed to satellite call centers to augment call center staffing. From an employee and customer perspective, this was a great move, as it allowed us to retain very experienced CSRs, people that the local customers knew and cared about. The downside from my perspective was that a couple of the remote call centers were almost too small. We had one with only four employees and a supervisor. The call center was also the most remote from the main office. It seemed the amount of effort and resources that went into ensuring that this small employee group was happy and providing good service met with diminishing returns.

Many utility customer service leaders are considering virtual call centers as a way to gain productivity and enhance customer service via phone. The question is how many call centers are needed, as well as how many CSRs per call center makes sense. The answer to those questions is going to be unique to the company, the employee situation, community relations, and other considerations. It may be that a phased transition over time will provide insight and guidance to utility leaders as they learn from their experiences.

There are companies, like Office Depot, that are taking the virtual call center to a new level with home-based agents. Office Depot saves 30%–40% on the cost of each call because it is not providing work space or benefits for its home-based agents. Early attempts at home-based agents were challenged when telephony or IT problems developed.[22] In a call center, CSRs can be relocated to another workstation, but a home agent is not available if the tools of the computer and telephony are not working. Today's capabilities of remote computer diagnostics and repair, along with more robust telephony networks, make home-based virtual agents more appealing This is a trend to watch as the technology continues to be enhanced.

The business case for virtual consolidation is compelling. It creates employee efficiency gains from pooling resources, but the disruption associated with relocating employees is eliminated.

RESOURCE MANAGEMENT TECHNOLOGY

Utility customer service organizations are labor intensive. Utility customer service budgets commonly consist of 70% or more in labor costs. As such, it is critical to ensure the effective management of the workforce. There are technology tools available that enhance the ability to manage both the field and office workforce. These technologies include call center scheduling tools, field workforce management, and geographic positioning systems (GPS).

Call center scheduling

The Incoming Calls Management Institute (ICMI) defines call center management as "the art of having the right number of properly skilled people and supporting resources in place at the right times to handle an accurately forecasted workload, at service level and with quality."[23] A critical tool to achieve effective call center management is a robust scheduling and forecasting application.

For industrial engineers like me, call center scheduling is a tempting, challenging queuing equation to be solved. One of my industrial engineering courses focused entirely on designing queuing systems to minimize wait time. The test questions and examples were always physical queues, like in the fast food and banking industries. The test would provide some historical information on the fast-food operator performance, the number of customers, and the average time to fill an order. Then the test question would be to determine how many fast food order stations were needed to reduce the customer wait time from five minutes to three minutes.

When I started at Duke's call center, it was like taking an advanced course in queuing systems. Instead of 5 bank tellers, the number of customer queues was 300 or more. Added to this was the potential for different types of queues for simple to more complex calls. Obviously solving this equation was going to require more power than was in my calculator. Fortunately, Duke Power had invested in a call center scheduling application that supported a more sophisticated analysis of call center queues.

There are many providers of call center forecasting technology. These technologies use a telecommunications model that was developed by A. K. Erlang. Erlang's model, which incorporates the statistical concept of random call arrival, is built into computer applications available on the market to enable a call center manager to estimate staffing and trunking requirements. These computer applications will need historical call volume and duration data to develop accurate staffing models.

These scheduling and forecasting tools provide abilities to dynamically manage staff and forecast staffing needs for the future. Call center managers often complete two types of forecasts. One is a long-range forecast, which is helpful in a budgeting situation. A mid-range forecast may only forecast over the next couple of weeks. This is used to make minor adjustments in the staffing to adjust to recent call developments. The scheduling tool is also used dynamically to view and manage the real-time experience of callers by adjusting agent staffing to address developing call queues.

If a utility does not have call center scheduling and forecasting tools, it should consider making this investment. There are huge benefits in more effectively staffing a call center that will reduce a utility's operating costs and improve the customer's experience.

Field workforce management

Field workforce management tools are productivity tools that provide data in real time to field employees. Field workforce management tools improve workforce productivity and customer satisfaction by connecting the call center to the field workforce and improving the efficiency of field work management. There are a variety of portable devices available today to support two-way communication of data from the field to host applications, like CIS and work management. Cellular and radio communications are the platforms upon which two-way voice and data communications are completed. Improvements are realized in resource utilization in the office and in the field, as well as with customer service.

Work management tools are continuing to evolve, creating more user-friendly tools for field personnel. The potential users of field workforce management tools include engineers, sales executives, and field technicians. While there is a change management effort needed, utilities often find that field personnel welcome this technology as it empowers them with knowledge to work more effectively and confidently with a customer.

Field collectors and field service technicians are excellent candidates for mobile data because they process a high volume of orders, and their workload is subject to dynamic change due to customer behavior. For the field collectors and technicians, having real-time customer information is helpful when responding to a customer's claims or questions. In the situation of a disconnection for nonpayment in which the customer claims to have paid, the field technician can verify this by reviewing the account to check the current payment status. Field technicians will often check the account before entering the property, so they are fully up to date on the current status of the customer's account.

From a call center perspective, having real-time information on the status of work orders is tremendously satisfying to customers. Field workforce management technology connects the CSR with the field resource, supporting real-time transfer of information and data. For example, if a credit customer scheduled for disconnection completes a payment, the CSR deletes the disconnect order, and the field technician is notified immediately. When an order is completed, the field technician can update the system. For the CSR handling a customer call, knowing this information is powerful.

From a work management perspective, field workforce management systems aid in efficiency gains by allowing easy review, prioritization, and routing of work both by management and in real time by the field employee. For management, these systems provide volumes of information on employee productivity and route optimization. Information on the average number of orders completed and the average order handle time are some of the basics provided by the system. These systems support management of the workload to ensure orders are completed in a timely basis and do not get lost in the process. Unlike paper orders, which can literally get blown away in the wind, these computer-based field workforce management systems track order status to ensure all orders are dispositioned. The ability to review work and define the most efficient route is a great benefit of field workforce management systems. A dispatcher can review upcoming work and sort it to various field employees, enabling optimization of the routes for that day.

For the field employee, these systems provide the ability for the performer to sort the orders and to reprioritize them based on new information. Field credit employees may choose to sort orders by dollar amount in arrears, by location, or by both. As new orders or canceled orders are recorded, the field employee can adjust the route to maximize efficiency. The availability of real-time customer information supports the employee's ability to respond to customer questions in a professional, accurate manner.

The business case for field workforce management generally is based on field productivity, improved customer service, improved safety, and field management. Productivity improvements in the range of 10%–20% come from the more effective management of work and elimination of back office tasks, such as data entry.[24] Additionally, individual field performer productivity increases from having real-time, accurate information. Customer service is greatly enhanced as customers can receive current information about their order status. CSR productivity is improved as CSRs are more often able to answer a customer's questions on orders with the first call.

Global positioning system

Global positioning system (GPS) is a technology that enables real-time capture of data and information from mobile vehicles and equipment. Data from a GPS can be used to respond in real-time to events like long stops. Data can also be used to support real-time dispatch and to provide management with robust information on field resource movements and productivity.

A major business benefit to GPS is the reporting in real time of significant events. From a safety standpoint, the ability to be notified when a vehicle has been stopped for a prolonged period of time is a positive attribute to communicate with employees. GPS can capture other events like speeding, late arrival and departure, and locational status. Detailed reports can include such information as the exact times a vehicle left the office, returned to the office, and stopped for lunch.

One utility was able to use the event-based reporting to identify that an employee stopped every morning to fill up the vehicle with gas. The size of the gas tank did not require daily refueling, so productive time was being lost daily at the gas pump. Another utility had set up work zones and was able to quickly identify when an employee left the authorized work zone.

The real-time availability of fleet location and individual vehicle location is a benefit when dispatching orders. The GPS allows the dispatcher to quickly determine which field resource is in the best position based on location and status of the job to respond to a critical order. GPS provides the dispatcher with a view of the fleet as whole and detailed information on the status of a particular field unit.

The advanced data analytics and reporting provide the business with the capability to improve field resource routing. Review of field movements can be used to fine-tune routing of future work. The summary reports, which show average daily miles driven, average speed, average number of stops, and average stop time by employee, provide insight into productivity. These systems can be integrated with multiple systems to enhance efficiencies and customer service. Linkage to payroll and billing systems, where applicable, can expedite and simplify these processes. Connection to a CIS provides the CSR with real-time order status. From a risk management perspective, GPS provides a higher visibility into incidents and offers the ability to lower insurance costs.

Utilities implementing GPS build a business case based on productivity improvements, improved fleet utilization, and improved risk management. There are additional benefits in customer service from the more accurate and prompt dispatch of customer work.

Technology has the potential to accelerate change and offer transformational business opportunities. Transformational business operations occur when service delivery after the implementation of a new technology and associated re-engineered processes is dramatically different that the previous way of delivering the service. With transformation, the technology actually changes the nature of the work.

Not all companies are able to capitalize on the transformative nature of technology, nor are all technology investments necessarily transformational in nature. Well-executed technology installations combine process re-engineering and robust change management plans to achieve business results. For a utility to fully capitalize on a technology investment requires leadership commitment, clear objectives and goals, a strong business case, and a commitment by the business to capture the identified benefits.

REFERENCES

1   Collins, Jim. *Good to Great.* HarperCollins Publishers, Inc; New York, NY, 2001, p. 162.

2   Duke Power received Electric Light and Power and Chartwell's Projects of the Year Award in 2004.

3   Bengtson, Dave, and Lori Boklund. *Call Center Technology Demystified.* Vanguard Communications Company, 2002.

4   "How to Integrate an IVR/CTI Application with Your CIS System That Customers Want to Use." Aquila Inc., CIS Conference 2002, Baltimore, MD, June 2002.

5   "Speech-Enabled Customer Service Applications in the Utility Industry." part of The Chartwell CIS and Customer Service Research Series, Chartwell, Inc., February 2004.

6   Anton, Dr. Jon. "Enabling IVR Self Service with Speech Recognition." Customer Interface, *The ICCM Journal.* Web site: www.c-interface.com; © 2002–2005 Advanstar Communications.

7   Ibid.

8   Spencer, Jane. "EasyIVR Tech Library." Web site: www.easyivr.com/tech-ivr-speech; Kelsey Group, April 2005.

9   Ibid.

10   Kuberski, Michael, and Alberto Osterling. "New Solutions for Customer Self Service." CIS Conference, Miami, FL, May 2004.

11   Bengtson and Boklund. *Call Center Technology Demystified.*

12   Prosci Benchmarking Report, 2001. Referenced in Cap Gemini Ernst & Young Analysis Report for NSTAR, May 8, 2002.

13 "Data Summary and Report 2004." 9th ed. Chartwell Metering Research Series, Chartwell Publishing, September 2004.

14 Kozolosky, Christine. "Meter Reading Benchmarking—Achieving Best-In-Class Performance." *Metering International.* Issue 3, 2004, p. 16.

15 Nosbaum, LeRoy. CEO, Itron; Interview, December 13, 2004.

16 Iuliano, Giro. Itron; Interview, May 2005.

17 Ibid.

18 Armstrong, Bill. "Automated Meter Reading: An Investment in Customer Service and Productivity." Dominion, 2003.

19 Iuliano, Giro; Interview, May 2005.

20 Bengtson and Boklund. *Call Center Technology Demystified.* 2002.

21 "Extending the Life of Our CIS Legacy System." BG&E presentation, CIS Conference, Miami, FL, May 6, 2004.

22 Incoming Call Center Management Institute. "Call Center Glossary." http://www.incoming.com/Glossary/s2glossary4asnx?selectednote=glossary (accessed August 2005)

23 "Just Don't Ask If They're in PJs." Global Business-MSNBC.com; msnbc.msn.com

24 Iuliano, Giro. Itron; Interview, May 2005.

13 SUCCESSFULLY IMPLEMENT THESE AND OTHER BEST PRACTICES

Information on customer service best practices and innovations is readily available through various consultants, publications, industry meetings, and networking. The opportunity utility customer service organizations face is implementing the best practices.

At various meetings with utility leaders, I hear comments like:

- "Oh, we are great planners, but we just can't seem to implement."

- "We started an implementation of 'new technology,' but had a budget crisis and had to stop the project."

- "We had a great process mapped out but could not gain approval from management to make the change."

- "The new technology is great, but we can't get our employees to use it right."

- "We implemented a new CIS, but our CSRs still use the green screens."

- "We were told the new system would bring us benefits, but we have been very disappointed."

- "We planned for the new system to be implemented in 6 months, but now we are 12 months into the project, and it is still not completed."

Do these sound familiar? Situations like these can be mitigated with a solid project planning and implementation approach. This chapter explores the basics of successfully implementing the best practices shared in this book. It will review key elements needed, including project identification, leadership support, project management, change management, and the use of consultants.

PROJECT IDENTIFICATION

Which projects should a utility attempt? This is a question that customer service leaders face, and there are many best practices and improvements an organization can make to improve service to customers. One of the most important steps for a utility customer service organization is to clearly identify the few, but significant, initiatives that bring the most value and then ensure these are delivered. Darryl Conner notes, "Most organizations jeopardize their ability to sustain imperative changes because they embark on too many good ideas—changes that they want to do, are justified in doing, ones that will produce benefits and may be popular with employees, but are not imperatives."[1]

The reality is that implementing best practices is not easy. Rather, successfully implementing best practices requires leaders to clearly identify a few key initiatives, set clear goals and objectives around those initiatives, and provide resources to implement them. Authors Larry Bossidy and Ram Charan comment on the need to set clear goals and priorities. They note that in business, "There's competition for resources, and ambiguity over decision rights and working relationships. Without carefully thought-out and clear priorities, people can get bogged down in warfare of who gets what and why."[2]

A robust business planning process that includes discussion on strategic goals, performance, and improvement opportunities is the best way to identify the few most significant initiatives. A good business planning process includes a thoughtful discussion on current operational performance and desired performance, based on the company's strategy. Performance gaps and ideas to bridge those gaps are discussed, analyzed, and prioritized. The business planning process is finalized with resource allocation provided for the key projects.

Successful projects clearly link to key business priorities. If the projects do not have clear linkage, it is likely that they will not be successful. Projects without clear linkage will not gain the support from management for resources when competing against other projects that clearly have benefits. NSTAR's CIO, Gene Zimon, notes that he has found successful IT projects are ones where "the business needs drive where enhancement and project dollars are deployed."[3]

LEADERSHIP SUPPORT

Leadership support for key initiatives is imperative for successful implementation. LeRoy Nosbaum, CEO of Itron, comments on the many metering and associated projects his organization has been involved with at utilities. He states, "By far the most successful projects have top down and bottom up support for the activity. If you don't, you will get minimal or no benefit for the investment."[4] Authors Bossidy and Charan note, "Execution requires a comprehensive understanding of a business, its people, and its environment. The leader is the only person in a position to achieve that understanding. And only the leader can make execution happen, through his or her deep personal involvement in the substance and even the details of execution."[5]

Leadership has several key responsibilities in ensuring successful implementation of best practices. They must link the project to key business priorities, clearly set project goals and objectives, allocate resources to implement them, provide ongoing guidance as the project progresses, and achieve business benefits.

The leader's role is first identifying projects that are clearly linked to business objectives. Successful companies have clear business planning processes where leaders can identify key initiatives that will achieve business objectives. Leaders play a very key role in communicating the linkage of the project to various stakeholders. Reinforcing the reasons behind the project is critical to engaging employees and successfully changing the process. Leaders face a challenge to ensure key communication messages are filtering all the way down to project team members and to business management that will own the new process or technology.

Leaders need to set clear goals and objectives for the project and ensure accountability for achieving those goals. Setting a specific, measurable goal allows a leader to monitor progress toward that goal and supports celebrating the final achievement. In order to be measurable, accurate data must be available. For example, a project may have a goal to reduce repeat calls but then have no way of measuring how many calls are repetitive in an objective, sustainable manner. The goals need to be achievable. In the example of IVR utilization, a goal for a utility of 80% of all calls handled by the IVR would not be appropriate, since no one in the industry has yet achieved that level. There are only a handful of utilities that are achieving 50%. In the banking world, on the other hand, 80% may be a more reasonable goal.

Leaders need to ensure accountability and ownership by linking the project goals into individual performance management goals. This creates the line of sight for employees working on the project or initiative.

Leaders are responsible for securing resources needed to successfully implement the goals. The resources may be people or equipment. Depending on the size of the project, budgeting for the resources may also be required. Securing people to work on the project is not insignificant. For some projects, a full-time commitment from an employee is needed. A leader in this situation must identify how the employee's normal work will be accomplished during the project. Depending on the project, the labor needed may ramp up and down during the lifetime of the project. Consultants and support from other areas of the organization may be necessary for successful implementation. In large CIS projects, it is not uncommon to bring in a consultant for systems integration and project management support. Equipment will be needed for the project. This could include work space, computers, phone access, project management tools, and software.

One common mistake leaders make, particularly with technology projects, is not budgeting and staffing appropriately to support implementation. Rose Minton, a former utility executive who now consults on CIS projects, notes that "utilities underestimate how much a CIS implementation will cost, how many resources they will have to provide, and how long it will take to get the system working as planned."[6] Employee productivity will decline as employees take extra time to get familiar with the new tools and processes. Adequate time and resources must be built into the plan to account for these hurdles.

Once a project is initiated, leaders need to be involved to steer the project. Many questions will arise as the project progresses, and decisions will need to be made. Leaders must ensure the project scope is managed and adhered to, which will be further explored later in this chapter. One of the best projects I worked on was the implementation of the new payroll system at TECO Energy. The steering team was made up of a diverse group of leaders, representing all areas of the company, including human resources, IT, electric operations, and transportation. This project was a model for successful implementation. The scope was clearly defined and detailed through well-documented business requirements.

The steering team focused on managing and adhering to the project scope. We met weekly at 7:30 AM to review progress from the past week and discuss issues. During the six-month project, we regularly faced decisions that had scope implications. Because the project was very tightly linked to business objectives and had clear business goals, it was relatively easy as a steering team to review and make decisions. Our mantra was, "No Scope Creep." And in this project, there was very little variance from the designated scope of the project.

This is a project where the steering team and leadership had to add resources near the end of the project to bring the project in on time. I was so impressed at the dedication of the leaders on this steering team to offer additional resources, including themselves, to make the final push to production. It was truly a team effort, with many long days and weekends. The end result was a tremendously successful project, completed on time and within budget, and it achieved the defined business benefits.

PROJECT MANAGEMENT

Project management combines people, processes, and tools to complete a project within established time frames, budget, and quality. It is both an art and a science. The Project Management Institute (PMI) identifies five activities involved in effective project management: project initiation, project planning, project execution, project control, and project close.

Project initiation

Project initiation involves defining the specific goals of the project. Gaining an understanding of the expectations of the key stakeholders of the process is a part of this activity. Management is a key stakeholder. Other stakeholders include employees and customers. This understanding can be gained through interviews or other employee and customer data. Identifying who will work on the project team and their expected time commitment is part of the initiation.

Once the goals of the project have been defined, it is important to ensure there is agreement and signoff by the project sponsors. As the project unfolds, project managers will reference and monitor progress based on this initial set of goals. If the goals are not clearly defined and agreed upon by all the sponsors, then a project manager will have a difficult time achieving success.

During project initiation, the project governance and communication channels will be defined. The magnitude of the project will dictate the robustness of the governance structure. A simple project may just have a project manager who reports to one or two leaders for decisions. A large project may have project teams, steering teams, and executive steering teams.

The statement of work along with vendor contracts, if needed, will be finalized during this process. A statement of work is a document that details the deliverables expected by the team, along with risk factors and contingencies for dealing with known risks. The vendor contracts will also include statements of work of deliverables by the vendor. In the example of an IT project, the contract and associated statement of work will detail exactly what the company is purchasing from an equipment, software, and schedule perspective, among other items.

Project planning

Project planning process involves identifying the many tasks and activities that must be completed in order to implement the project. An outcome of this process is the creation of a project plan. The project plan will include high-level tasks and milestones. High-level tasks will be further detailed in the plan, with specific activities required to complete the tasks. Understanding the relationship and sequence of these tasks and activities is important. Some tasks must be completed before others can begin, while others can be run concurrently. The project plan will identify the overall project flow and how tasks interrelate.

Typically the project planning is supported by project management software, in which tasks, supporting activities, and dependencies can be recorded along with a centralized repository of project information. The software provides a variety of management reports for monitoring the progress of the project. The repository of project documents provides an auditable trail on the project by retaining in an organized manner such project documents as meeting agendas, notes, decision points, and options evaluated.

The project planning will identify resources needed for the project. The resource loading will clearly identify people and equipment that will be needed throughout the phases of a project.

Project execution

Project execution involves implementing the project plan. At this point, the team members are working on various assignments outlined in the plan. A project manager is vital at this stage to oversee the progress on the project plan, provide updates to various stakeholder groups, and identify issues impacting the plan progress.

A project manager will use a project management methodology, which is a documented approach to managing a project. Project methodology includes a standard set of procedures, templates, workflows, and guides for documenting the entire process. There are a variety of project management methodologies. On projects managed in-house, this methodology will be the standard project management approach. If a utility is using a third party to manage the project, they will provide a project methodology that best fits the particular project.

Project management software that provides clear and timely project information is critical. The software not only enables the project manager to monitor progress, but it supports financial reporting and provides an audit trail for future review and projects.

Project control

Project control involves monitoring the project progress and is a fundamental responsibility of the project manager. Effective project control includes project governance, escalation procedures, risk management, scope management, training, and change management.

A governance structure for the project and defined roles and responsibilities of each of the parties in the governance are fundamental to success. A well-prepared governance structure provides a project manager with a clear understanding of decision rights and owners and linkages between various decision makers in the project. On small projects, the governance may be a single department head. Large projects may have executive steering teams, business area steering teams, working teams, and vendor teams.

On large and small projects, issues surface. To resolve them effectively, a good project manager needs interpersonal communication and conflict management skills in order to identify the issues. The project manager also needs a defined procedure on how and with whom to address the issues. Strong project governance and a clear escalation process can expedite decision making and minimize rework. When there is not a clear escalation process, then the project manager is left to decide where to take issues.

In one project I worked on, the escalation process was not clear. This lack of clarity became a problem when dealing with issues that were unclear on who owned the issue, i.e., the business, the vendor, or IT. The good news is that we realized this lack of clarity early on in the project. To address this, we outlined a decision-rights matrix, which detailed types of issues and identified who owned the decisions on those issues. This proved valuable as the project progressed to ensure the right people were involved in making decisions on issues.

Risk management is an important project control function. The project plan will identify key risks and mitigation strategies. The project manager will monitor the risks and ensure that as risk events occur, a thoughtful approach is used to determine the most appropriate mitigation plan.

A project manager is constantly reviewing progress on project milestones. A variety of reports, along with stakeholder feedback, can ensure the project continues to remain on course, or that issues are quickly resolved. Project metrics derived from the project goals are monitored.

Addressing project scope changes is another project control function. A method for identifying, resolving, and documenting scope changes must be defined and used. For large projects, scope changes must be defined from a requirements and resource perspective. A scope change document that outlines the proposed change and requires sponsor sign-off is a good tool for scope management. These documents provide an auditable trail for the project.

To successfully implement a project, defined training and change management plans must be in place. An important aspect of project control is to ensure that training and change management plans are documented, resourced, and delivered so that the project can successfully achieve its goals.

Project close

Project closing involves both celebrating success and also identifying next steps and acquired knowledge that can be incorporated into future projects. Closing a project is as important as launching a project. The team and organization needs closure so that they can clearly move on to the next challenge. It is important to debrief on projects that go well as well as those that were challenging. Both have lessons to offer. This information can be used for future projects.

The project closing identifies the operational owners of the newly implemented technology or process. The objective is to operationalize the new system. The project closing will often include a final analysis on the total costs, business impact, and outcomes. Project closing also involves dismantling the team and moving them back into their normal organizational responsibilities.

CHANGE MANAGEMENT

Change management is often overlooked in major projects. Time and resources built into a schedule for change management are easy targets when looking to shrink costs and time on a project. Unfortunately, when this happens, the actual time and cost impact to the organization may increase, due to longer implementation time. Successful change management involves a series of activities that range from understanding the scope of change to institutionalizing the change. Successful projects will build time and resources into the plan for change management

Understand the scope of the change

To understand the scope of change, one should consider the basic questions of who, what, when, where, and how. The answers to these questions provide the scope of the change.

The project team needs to document who is affected by the change and how they are affected. The team needs to identify what is changing and how this will impact an employee's role. It also needs to highlight the benefits of the changes. A timeline of when changes will occur and at what locations they will occur is fundamental in this stage. Documenting how the change will occur is also important.

Engage the team

To be successful, change management efforts will expand participation in the project beyond core project team members. The engagement of employees who will be impacted by the change helps them become navigators and change champions rather than victims, critics, and bystanders. In addition to involving the people most impacted by the change, one should consider involving key sponsors and stakeholders.

When I was leading the re-engineering effort of a new customer connection process, the team came up with a very innovative way of engaging the sponsors in the process redesign. The team created and played out various customer scenarios using the new process models. The sponsors were able to view these scenarios and ask questions about the various components of the process. While all the process owners had reviewed process charts of the re-engineered process, experiencing typical customer scenarios and watching how they played out was powerful. There were two important outcomes to this exercise. The first was increased support and understanding by the sponsors of the work to date by the team. The second was the identification of some process gaps that were overlooked when re-engineering via process charts. What looked good on paper did not necessarily play out well in simulated customer situations.

Build a business case for change

To create momentum for change, there must be a compelling business case. The strongest business cases for change are tightly linked to a company's goals and objectives. Author Darryl Conner describes this business case as a business imperative, or a *burning platform*. Conner notes that "an organizational burning platform exists when maintaining the status quo becomes prohibitively expensive. Major change is always costly, but when the present course of action is even more expensive, a burning platform situation erupts." He adds, "When an organization is on a burning platform, the decision to make a major change is not just a good idea—it is a business imperative."[7]

At TECO Energy, the burning platform for change in customer service was cost and customer satisfaction. Our cost to serve customers was high as compared to other utilities, while our customer satisfaction rates were not correspondingly as high. Best practices in other utilities demonstrated that the cost to serve customers could be reduced by migrating customers to phone-based service. Benchmark data on our cost and customer satisfaction performance along with utility best practice research were key elements in our business case for change. The result was a project that involved closing business offices, redeploying experienced resources to provide phone-based service, and offering expanded payment options.

Communicate the vision and strategy

Communicating the vision and strategy involves designing a plan of specific messages, audiences, timelines, and ownership. This communications strategy will involve not only employees impacted by the change, but also support groups, like human resources. The communications plan will identify key messages, metrics, and milestones of the project. It will also identify audience and communication channels to deliver the key messages to those audiences. Ownership of action items in the plan is clearly identified. This phase of the change management process offers a great opportunity to engage employees impacted by the change. These employees have the best understanding of the issues they will personally face with this change.

At TECO Energy, the entire customer care leadership team was involved in designing the communications plan for closing offices. The basic structure of the plan was developed in a full-day workshop. The communications plan identified key audiences and messages. The basic messages were:

- We must improve our phone service levels for our customers.

- We must improve the quality of our service via the phone by augmenting our call center team with experienced CSRs.

- We must expand payment options and hours of availability for customers.

The team then identified how our office plan would address the key reasons for change. We explained that adding experienced CSRs from the business offices would improve both quality and phone service levels. Tripling pay agent locations and offering payment via credit card and check over the phone would offer customers a variety of ways to pay, available 24/7.

Empower others to act

Success with change management involves empowering employees impacted by the change, rather than having employees resist or ignore the change. To empower employees, they must perceive personal value in adopting the proposed change and understand the linkage of their individual roles in the changed process.

Keys to aid empowerment include encouraging employee input at each stage of the project. It is important that the project team communicate often with employees concerning the proposed changes and updates on progress of the project. It is important to understand that feedback, even negative feedback, is positive in the sense that it means employees care about their jobs and want to explain their perception of the impacts of the change. The opportunity for leadership is to not throw out negative feedback because it is negative, but rather to listen for nuggets of insight.

To empower the customer service team at TECO, the customer service leadership asked employees for feedback on the office-closing implementation plan. This provided the opportunity for individual employees to take ownership of the plan. This was a success in a couple of respects. First, the employees valued being asked about the plan from a customer perspective. Each of these employees had a passion for serving the customers and wanted to ensure service would be as good with the new plan. They wanted to make sure there were no issues missed. Second, this employee involvement empowered them to take ownership in implementing the plan. This engagement was important to the ultimate success of this initiative from a customer and employee perspective.

Celebrate success along the way

Significant change takes time and often involves several iterations. It can at times become overwhelming and seemingly impossible to achieve the needed changes. To keep the project team motivated, one should celebrate milestones along the way. The celebration can range from simple recognition to an elaborate event.

Institutionalize the change

It takes time for change to become habit. When the change becomes "just the way things are done around here," then the project is successful. To institutionalize the change, one should *inspect* rather than *expect*. It takes inspection to see that the process is working as designed and to identify gaps and areas where old behaviors have come into play. It is not enough to merely expect the change.

One utility re-engineered its new customer connect process. After the new process was implemented, a small team audited work orders completed in the new customer connect process to evaluate adherence to the new process. As expected, the audit revealed that some customers and employees were reverting to old habits and calling engineers directly. The inspection allowed the team to identify how to mitigate this issue. A part of this mitigation plan included further communication and training with the engineers in how to successfully migrate customers to the new process. A few months later, the engineers noted that they were indeed receiving fewer customer calls.

USING CONSULTANTS

Consultants can speed up a project. Third-party consultants provide project management experience, methodology, and tools necessary to properly manage large projects. They can also provide an understanding of projects risks and proven mitigation approaches, as well as offer norms with respect to project resource and timing requirements. The support from a consultant will depend on the project. It may include assistance in crafting and evaluating an RFP, systems integration, and/or project management. There are large consulting firms that provide a wide range of expertise, and smaller boutique firms that specialize in a particular aspect or type of project.

I often share a story when a group is considering bringing on a consultant, as it clearly and concisely highlights why a consultant may be the right choice. In the story, a man falls into a deep hole and cannot get out. A person walks by the hole and responds to the man's pleas for help. This person leaves for a ladder and does not return. A second person walks by and also offers to help. The second person says, "I will go get a rope." But the second person does not return. A third person walks by and responds to the man's plea for help by jumping into the hole. The man exclaims, "Why did you jump in here? Now you are trapped!" The man replies, "I have been here before, and I know the way out."

Consultants assist clients in achieving their business goals. They can offer a utility experience they have gained in working with other clients. This experience can help a utility avoid pitfalls that others have encountered while engaged in similar projects.

Consultants can provide guidance in identifying and prioritizing work initiatives. They can provide proven experience in implementing major software packages. They can provide project management expertise and support. Consultants bring knowledge of other companies concerning what has worked and what has not worked.

Let me close with a look at a project at NSTAR that met all of these requirements. This was an AMR project, and the compelling business case for change included a payback in five years or less, depending on the service area. NSTAR provides both electric and gas service, and the gas meters had been equipped with AMR devices years before. This fact, combined with the high percentage of electric meters that were inside and the reduction in cost of the devices, made the business case very compelling. This combination made AMR a strong project.

Leadership support could not have been stronger. Joe Nolan, the senior vice president of customer care and community relations, was the vocal champion. His compelling arguments during the company's strategic planning sessions resulted in overwhelming support by the CEO and other members of the senior team for implementation. Joe's support did not stop at securing the funds. Joe has been a visible champion for AMR. He personally met with the team of installers and the project managers to check on status and provide encouragement. He personally addressed issues where schedule, scope, or resources could be potentially impacted.

Joe also made sure there was good project management. A key success factor in the project was the assignment of a very talented project manager using NSTAR's project management methodology. This project manager monitored the progress and updated Joe, me, and other key stakeholders on the project status.

Change management was a joint effort of management and union. Together a small team identified the key communication messages and jointly delivered these messages to employees.

Under Joe's passionate leadership over the past three years, more than 75% of the NSTAR system has been converted to AMR. Each year, the project team has come in under budget and ahead of schedule. To date, joint management and union communications with employees have been effective in retooling employees. Many have moved to opportunities in operations, the call center, or billing. Employees realize that the change is coming and have had time and resources provided to prepare for this change.

Identifying the right projects to implement that have a compelling business case for change is the first step toward successfully implementing best practices in one's utility. Supporting the project with sound project management and change management will allow these best practices to be implemented quickly and effectively.

REFERENCES

1   Conner, Darryl R. *Managing at the Speed of Change.* O.D. Resources, Inc., Villard Books, 1992.

2   Bossidy, Larry, and Ram Charan. *Execution: The Discipline of Getting Things Done.* Crown Business, New York, NY, 2002, p. 69.

3   Zimon, Gene. CIO, NSTAR; Interview, May 2005.

4   Nosbaum, LeRoy. CEO of Itron; Interview, December 13, 2004.

5   Bossidy and Charan. *Execution: The Discipline of Getting Things Done.* 2002, p. 24.

6   Minton, Rose. Vice president, TMG Consulting, Interview, March 16, 2005.

7   Conner, Darryl R. *Managing at the Speed of Change.* 1992.

APPENDIX A:
Acronyms and Abbreviations

ACD	automatic call distribution
AGA	American Gas Association
AMR	automated meter reading
ANI	automatic number identification
API	application program interfaces
ASP	application service provider
ASR	automated speech recognition
ATM	automated teller machine
BG&E	Baltimore Gas & Electric
BPO	business process outsourcing
CAP	community action program
CEO	chief executive officer
CIS	customer information system
CRM	customer relationship management
CSR	customer service representative

CT	current transformer
CTI	computer telephony integration
DRO	days revenue outstanding
EEI	Edison Electric Institute
ERT	encoder receiver transmitter
ETR	estimated time of restoration
FSR	field service representative
GIS	geographical information system
GPS	geographical position system
GUI	graphical user interface
HVAC	heating, ventilation, and air conditioning
ICMI	Incoming Calls Management Institute
IOU	investor-owned utility
IVR	interactive voice response
OMS	outage management systems
OPEIU	Office and Professional Employees International Union
Pepco	Potomac Electric Power Company
PSNH	Public Service of New Hampshire
PT	potential transformer
RFI	request for information
RFP	request for proposals

ROI	return on investment
SLA	service level agreements
SOX	Sarbanes-Oxley Act
SRP	Salt River Project
UWUA	United Workers Union of America

INDEX